Constructing Disability after the Great War

DISABILITY HISTORIES

Series editors: Stephanie Hunt-Kennedy, Kim E. Nielsen, and Michael Rembis

Disability Histories seeks scholarship that explores the lived experiences of individuals and groups from a broad range of societies, cultures, time periods, and geographic locations, who either identified as disabled or were considered by the dominant culture to be disabled.

We conceive of disability and disabled experiences broadly and seek to include scholarship that spans a range of embodiments, including the emerging field of mad studies. We are especially interested in scholarship that not only employs innovative approaches to using disability—in constant interaction with systems of race, class, gender, and sexuality—as an analytical tool to deepen our understanding of larger power relations, ideologies, and institutions, but also engages in meaningful dialogue with other subdisciplines within history, such as legal and political histories, social histories, histories of technology, science, and medicine, histories of the body and sexuality, and histories of the development of capitalism and imperialism. We welcome submissions from a variety of geopolitical locations, especially those that situate disability history outside European and North American contexts, including regions or nations that would become identified as the "global South." We are interested in scholarship that moves beyond traditional disability frameworks and offers methodologies and approaches to disability history that are rooted in decolonial, transnational, and transimperial perspectives.

For a list of books in the series, please see our website at www.press.uillinois.edu.

Constructing Disability after the Great War

Blind Veterans in the Progressive Era

EVAN P. SULLIVAN

UNIVERSITY OF ILLINOIS PRESS
Urbana, Chicago, and Springfield

Manufactured in the United States of America
1 2 3 4 5 C P 5 4 3 2 1
♾ This book is printed on acid-free paper.

Library of Congress Cataloging-in-Publication Data
Names: Sullivan, Evan P., 1989– author.
Title: Constructing disability after the Great War : blind Veterans in the Progressive era / Evan P. Sullivan.
Other titles: Blind Veterans in the Progressive era
Description: Urbana : University of Illinois Press, [2024] | Series: Disability histories | Includes index.
Identifiers: LCCN 2024006021 (print) | LCCN 2024006022 (ebook) | ISBN 9780252046162 (cloth) | ISBN 9780252088247 (paperback) | ISBN 9780252047428 (ebook)
Subjects: LCSH: Disabled veterans—United States—Social conditions—20th century. | Blind—United States—Medical care—History—20th century. | Disabled veterans—Rehabilitation—United States—History—20th century. | People with disabilities—Rehabilitation—United States—History—20th century. | World War, 1914–1918—Veterans—United States. | World War, 1914–1918—Medical care—United States. | Red Cross Institute for the Blind (Baltimore, Md.)—History.
Classification: LCC UB363 .S85 2024 (print) | LCC UB363 (ebook) | DDC 362.4086/970973—dc23/eng/20240315
LC record available at https://lccn.loc.gov/2024006021
LC ebook record available at https://lccn.loc.gov/2024006022

For Alex

Contents

Acknowledgments

I have benefited from the generous assistance of numerous individuals and organizations from the moment I began researching blind veterans. This book first started, unbeknownst to me, at the New York State Archives in Albany, New York, in June 2015 when I thought I would be researching education policies during World War I. My advisor, Rick Fogarty, convinced me to consult the New York State Education Commissioner John Finley's wartime diaries. Tucked into one of the pages of that diary I found a pamphlet for a rehabilitation school for blind French soldiers along with Finley's own experiences visiting there. I knew nothing about blind veterans, veterans' history, or disability history, but this one piece of primary source evidence changed the trajectory of my career in the most fulfilling way.

That single page in the wartime diary of a New York State official sent me on an archival journey for which I am truly grateful. I thank Jennifer Arnott and Jennifer Hale at the Samuel P. Hayes Research Library at the Perkins School for the Blind in Watertown, Massachusetts, for helping me explore the War Blind collection and other pertinent records. Patricia Anderson and Damon Talbot were helpful during an early visit to the Maryland Historical Society to view images of Evergreen. The archival staff at the National Archives in College Park, Maryland, were most helpful on my numerous visits there to explore the records of the surgeon general. Trenton Streck-Havill and Laura Cutter were kind and accommodating during my visit to the National Museum of Health and Medicine in Silver Spring, Maryland. Thomas Zampieri of the Blinded Veterans Association was also generous with his conversations and research leads. I also cannot thank enough the families of blind World War I veterans who graciously sent information about, and photographs of, their ancestors, especially Erin DiManno, Ciaran McDonnell, Andy Banks, Betty Ellis, and Chris Keefrider.

I was fortunate to have received numerous and invaluable sources of help during my archival visits. Thanks first to my cousin Karen Ogden for providing a place to stay, good food, snuggles with her sweet dog, Molly, and, as always, great conversations during my numerous visits to Boston and Cambridge while researching at Perkins School for the Blind. Thanks also to my Aunt Marianne and Uncle Brian for opening their home on more than one occasion. Numerous sources of financial support made research trips possible. The State University of New York at Albany History Department, the University at Albany Benevolent Association, the University at Albany Office of the Dean for Graduate Education, and the University at Albany Graduate Student Association provided fellowship and grant funding to offset the cost of research trips. Thanks also to the SUNY Albany Libraries and SUNY Adirondack Library for making source texts available through interlibrary loan.

Academic conferences enabled me to workshop ideas and gain insights from scholars and friends. Most recently, I want to thank John Kinder, Sarah Handley-Cousins, and David Gerber for organizing our panel "Disabled Veterans, New Histories" at the Organization of American Historians conference in 2021. That experience, your support, and the comments I received were all so valuable. Thanks also to the "No End to War" conference at the University of Manchester in the United Kingdom in January 2019. Alexia Moncrieff, Jessica Meyer, Michael Robinson, Helena de Silva, Hilary Buxton, Adam Luptak, Tammy Proctor, Ana Carden-Coyne, Justin Fantauzzo, and Marjorie Gehrhardt all provided stimulating discussions and First World War solidarity, while John Horne offered insightful comments that helped me think about war-related sensory disabilities in new ways. The James A. Barnes Conference at Temple University and the Researching New York Conference at the University at Albany offered invaluable experiences for me to present, as a nervous grad student, early versions of this book.

I have benefitted immensely from professional connections that I have made along the way and that helped me consider my project in new ways. At the State University of New York at Albany I received guidance from my dissertation committee, Richard Hamm, Kori Graves, John Kinder, and Rick Fogarty. Thanks especially to Rick for serving as my dissertation adviser, and continuing to mentor me beyond graduate school when I have needed professional guidance. John graciously agreed to serve on my dissertation committee as an outside reader, and has been an important part of my intellectual journey thus far. I would also like to thank former professors Carl Bon Tempo, Susan Gauss, Lauren Kozakiewicz, and Dan White for playing a role in this project in some way, as well as my many former classmates in the graduate program at the University of Albany who created a productive and welcoming atmosphere. I have received guidance and had impactful conversations with numerous scholars who have made their mark on this project in different ways both big and small, including Beth Linker, Chris Capozzola, Catherine Kudlick, Stephen Ortiz, and Jennifer Keene. My colleagues at Nursing Clio helped me hone my writing and explore my interests in a scholarly setting. Thanks especially to Jacqueline Antonovich, Sarah Handley-Cousins, Laura Ansley, Cassia Roth, R. E. Fulton, Lauren MacIvor Thompson, Averill Earls, Bridget Keown, and Emily Contois. I am ever grateful for your encouragement and solidarity.

This book would not have been possible without the support of the University of Illinois Press and its Disability Histories series editors. Thanks to Alison Syring for reading many drafts and numerous emails to get this book where it needed to be. Thanks to Mike Rembis, Kim Nielsen, and Stefanie Hunt-Kennedy for guiding this project and helping it become a better book than I could have created on my own. Your feedback and steadfast support have been so very appreciated. Thank you to everyone else at the University of Illinois Press who made the production of this book possible, especially Megan Donnan, Marilyn Campbell, and Jennie Fisher.

I finished this book while beginning my new journey as a history professor at SUNY Adirondack, and the connections I have made there enabled me to confidently proceed with this project while also educating my students. Thanks to my colleagues in the Social Science Division for creating an atmosphere of collegiality and support: John Pennachio, Drew Costa, Joanne Malkani, Anna Hill, Jon McCarthy, Keith Pomakoy, Valerie Haskins, Wendy Johnston, Phil Naftaly, Carol Hopper, Catherine Basila, Lydia Treadway, Alan Wishart, Mark Dragoni, and Tom Bobal. Thanks also to colleagues in other academic divisions and administration and staff that have, in ways large and small, made my experience at Adirondack a positive one during the process of writing this book, including John Jablonski, Kris Duffy, Diane Wildey, Mindy Wilson, John Delate, Cornelius Gilbert, Kelly Hammond, Jeevan Gurung, Khristeena Lute, Kathleen McCoy, Krista Rivera, Naftali Rottenstreich, Stephanie Drotos, John Arpey, Kelli Hatin, Bert Rawert, Carrie Menard, Roger Eagan, Amy Macaluso, Charlie D'Souza, Holly Irion, Beth Braxton, Luke Musto, Emily Goodspeed, Danielle Walkup, Jessica Wieprzowski, Adriana Umana, Nancy White, Rhonda Triller, and many others.

Friends and family have eagerly supported my work and provided numerous opportunities to enjoy life beyond academia. Thanks especially to the following friends for enriching my life beyond measure: Rob and Carissa O'Rourke; Ben and Lauren Nelson; Heather, Andy, Gemma, and Sage Unser; Tom, Kathy, Colleen, and Brian Callaghan; Ellie Burhans and David Breault; Eric and Dara Morgenson; Eric and Charity Martell; Mark Gagnon; and former high school teachers Erin Wever, Kurt Conduzio, Elizabeth Strader, Michael Shaver, and Andrea Winter-Barclay for fostering a love of learning and growth in my years preceding college. I appreciate the additional support and encouragement that I received from family, including my brother Brenden; Chris Chagnon; Aunt Dianne; Aunt Marianne and Uncle Brian; my grandparents; Uncle Ken; Uncle Chip and Aunt Sheree; cousins Ben, Sarah, Lauren, Jonathan, and Lacey; in-laws Dan and Ellie McNutt; Olivia; Erica, Wes, and John; Shana and Bryan; Adam, Katie, Keanu, and Camille; and Rick and Sharon Butto; and my sweet cat Molly, who has purred, meowed, and nuzzled her way through my completion of this book. No list of supporters would be complete without my mom and dad. You have fostered my interests in history since day one. From our earliest trips to museums to my time in grad school, your excitement about my historical studies has helped propel me forward.

This book has been the product of many years of hard work, uncertainty, and physical and emotional highs and lows, all of which would have been impossible without the support of my wife, Alex, and our son, Grayson. I could not imagine doing life without you both. Grayson, you remind me to slow down and find joy in the outdoors, trucks, and dinosaurs. Alex, you remind me that gratitude can be found in any moment, and your presence fills me with love and ease. You supported my dreams when my dreams were filled with uncertainty, and before a book or a career in academia was even within reach. I am so happy to dedicate this book to you, Alex.

Constructing Disability after the Great War

Introduction

Beginning with Carl Bronner

By the mid-1920s, Charles or "Carl" Bronner had become one of the most widely written about blind American veterans of World War I. Completely blind, partially deaf, and missing both hands from an explosive, Bronner's cheerful attitude, his determination, and his ability to use his hand and hearing prosthetics as well as special prosthetic attachments for his typewriter enabled him to earn a law degree at the University of Maryland and then practice law until his untimely death in 1934 that resulted from lingering service-related health problems. Bronner assumed a leadership role at the United States Blind Veterans of the World War organization, which advocated on behalf of blind veterans who sought better benefits from the state and less stigmatizing discussions about their disability from the public. Despite Carl Bronner's steadfast determination to pursue a life of service on his own terms, he instead became a model for emotionally charged, inspirational stories about postwar rehabilitation and overcoming disability.

Some commenters found Carl Bronner's multiple disabilities tragic, others found him inspiring, but all found him worthy of public attention. Writer Francis T. Kimball published a poem titled "To Carl Bronner" in the *Red Cross Courier* in 1922. Kimball praised Bronner's ingenuity, but tempered the praise with, "I brood your blasted youth," suggesting that Bronner's life was all but over despite his best efforts to adapt to his new bodily realities. How could nondisabled individuals carry on with their lives pursuing all their material and physical desires, the writer asked, while Bronner must "bear these grim rewards" of his service that have so thoroughly disabled him. "Dwelling upon your sightless eyes," Kimball concluded in a manner that suggested Bronner's saintly sacrifice in service of the nation, "I see / Behind them visions brighter, lovelier far / Than selfish rounds of triviality / And in that smile transfiguring your scar / The healing touch of hands nailed to a tree."[1]

President Warren Harding was less religious in his praise of Carl Bronner, but was no less inspired by his apparent ability to overcome the obstacles imposed by his disabled body. Harding wrote to Bronner that he admired Bronner's "undaunted resolution and . . . cheerful hopefulness."[2] The first introduction between Bronner and Harding that led to their correspondence took place at a White House garden party for disabled veterans in June 1921—a soon-to-be tradition that would feature Bronner on more than one occasion. Bronner was part of a contingent of blind veterans that had arrived at the White House from the Red Cross Institute for the Blind, also called Evergreen—the rehabilitation center in Baltimore for blind American veterans of World War I—to meet the president and First Lady Florence Harding. The Hardings greeted close to two thousand disabled ex-soldiers from hospitals in the Washington, DC, area one by one in single file before the couple mingled with groups of veterans on the lawn in a more informal fashion. When President Harding came to the group of Evergreen vets, he paid particular attention to Carl. "I wish I could restore your sight," Harding said to the young veteran. After also noticing that Bronner had lost both of his hands, he continued, "I wish I could restore your hands, too." Bronner replied "cheerfully" that he was "getting along very well."[3]

Carl Bronner also attracted the gratitude of the US Congress when he sat with his mother in the gallery of the House of Representatives in June 1926, around the same time that he earned his law degree from the University of Maryland. The House had been in the midst of a heated filibuster about monetary provisions for rivers and harbors when Massachusetts Republican congresswoman Edith Nourse Rogers, a tireless advocate on behalf of veterans in the interwar years, delivered a speech "in eulogy" of Bronner's military record to set her colleagues straight about how trivial their concerns were compared to his.[4] "Doomed to a lifetime of darkness," she stated emphatically, "it would have been so easy . . . for Charles Bronner to have abandoned himself to an all-consuming despair, or, from the cushioned depths of a rocking chair by the fire to have ended his life in whining self-pity," suggesting that the easy—and logical—remedy to Bronner's situation as a multiply-disabled blind man might be suicide. Instead, she told her congressional colleagues, his courage and perseverance possessed "a magic talisman before which difficulties disappear and obstacles vanish into thin air"—arguing that his success came at least in part from supernatural or unexplainable sources rather than from his own body and mind.

To Edith Nourse Rogers, Carl Bronner was "placed on earth as a guide post." Men like Bronner, Rogers concluded, reminded nondisabled people to "square our shoulders, [to] take a new grip on things and [to] forge

US Representative Edith Nourse Rogers standing next to Carl Bronner—blind, partially deaf, and double hand amputee—at a White House garden party in June 1926 hosted by President Calvin Coolidge and the First Lady. (Library of Congress, Prints & Photographs Division, LC-DIG-ppmsca-40801)

ahead." After the passionate speech, the *Cincinnati Enquirer* and about a dozen other American newspapers reported that the whole of the House of Representatives stood and cheered "this hero" who had become "in the face of monumental obstacles . . . an honor to the citizenship of this nation," and who "[had] accomplished more for [the country]" than anyone as a result of his service. By serving the nation and succeeding in life, he stood as a "guide post," "as an illustrious example for the shaming of many pitiable specimens of American young manhood" who have eyes and hands but "still cravenly shrink before what they are pleased to term obstacles in the way of successful life development."[5] Ultimately, newspapers hoped the scene would display Bronner's heroism in "overcoming" his disability and demonstrate the fact that "Congress Has a Heart."[6]

Earlier captivated by the young veteran's story, in 1921 the *Washington Times* published a tribute to the great and inspiring Carl Bronner. According to the article, Bronner was wounded in the final days of the Great War when a German soldier threw a hand grenade at him as he was "in a front line trench waiting for the signal to go over the top." The explosion rendered Bronner blind, handless, and hearing impaired. "In spite of the obvious and almost insurmountable handicaps," the article concluded, "Bronner is today one of the happiest, most loved and respected students at . . . Evergreen, and is in a fair way of becoming a useful citizen of this country."[7]

The sentimental renderings of Carl Bronner's military service and postwar life that appeared in the preceding sources are only partly true. Bronner was indeed blinded in the trenches of World War I, though not in the manner suggested by newspapers or by political leaders. Bronner had left Detroit, Michigan, to enlist in the US Navy in March 1917, a few weeks before the United States entered the war. He was first assigned to the battleship USS *New Hampshire* before serving as an armed guard on merchant ships in the dangerous submarine-infested Atlantic Ocean, and then he was finally stationed on the USS *J. Fred Talbot* off the coast of Italy. On August 19, 1919, nine months after World War I ended and two months after the signing of the Treaty of Versailles, Bronner toured the trenches of Monfalcone in northern Italy looking for souvenirs to bring home. He and several of his shipmen "found two grenades lying in a field." They picked them up because they did not know that the battlefield "souvenirs" were explosives—they looked unfamiliar compared to American grenades. One of the grenades exploded, killing one sailor and wounding Bronner, rendering him blind, partially deaf, and without hands.[8]

Carl Bronner spent several months in Italian and American hospitals. He underwent numerous operations at Fort McHenry in Baltimore, Maryland. Before his operation on August 23, 1920, the *Baltimore Sun* reported that Bronner was "cheerful and hopeful" that he would have better use of his arms after they were surgically shortened by one inch on the right and half an inch on the left.[9] Bronner was fitted with artificial hands and attachments that enabled him to use a typewriter and to shave his face. He laughed to

Carl Bronner sits in a chair at a desk in a small room at Evergreen and uses specially fitted hand prosthetics to enable him to type letters on a typewriter, ca. 1920. (Library of Congress, Prints & Photographs Division, American National Red Cross Collection, LC-DIG-anrc-14603)

reporters of his hometown newspaper the *Detroit Free Press* that "I have got to get the folks to tell me when I miss the high spots" of his facial hair.[10] Bronner also received a pension of $225 per month for double total disability, as his wound was judged "not in line of duty" but "not the result of his own misconduct."[11] He trained at Evergreen, and then obtained a law degree from the University of Maryland. Revered by many of his blind comrades, Bronner was elected to the position of national commander of the United States Blind Veterans of the World War organization, and continuously argued to the sighted American public that "We blind men feel that we have come back from the war bigger and better men. . . . We are not unfortunates, for we have gained."[12]

Public reactions to Carl Bronner from Congresswoman Edith Nourse Rogers, US President Warren Harding, and the numerous journals and newspapers that wrote about him were not just misrepresentations, but were also shaped by the contours of turn-of-the-century conversations about class and social welfare, gender, disability, citizenship, and race. Rogers's "eulogy" to Bronner's life-that-could-have-been had he not been disabled stood out precisely because of how potentially economically limiting his war wound was. Nondisabled people regularly assumed that disabled people were unproductive. The United States' transition to industrial capitalism and mechanized labor made work more dangerous and produced more urbanized cities. To meet the changing face of modern life and its social and economic uncertainties, public policies such as workers' compensation laws, municipal begging ordnances, and restrictive immigration laws identified disabled bodies as potential liabilities and dangers to public health and the social body politic.[13] For the *Cincinnati Enquirer*, Bronner's success despite all of these barriers served as a way to shame unproductive nondisabled people, both veteran and nonveteran alike, who "still cravenly shrink" from their social responsibilities such as work and family.

The *Enquirer*'s focus on Bronner as a rebuke to men who shirked economic responsibilities to their families also had much to do with the gendered politics of social welfare around the turn of the century.[14] The Anglo-American white women reformers who framed US social welfare policy during the Progressive Era imagined women and mothers as economically dependent on men's wages and focusing their energies on child rearing.[15] Maternalist reformers concentrated on providing welfare services for primarily poor white European immigrant women, which formulated one side to gendered US social welfare policy. The other side of the proverbial social welfare coin targeted men. Reformers contributed to a heightened public concern about "slacker" husbands who failed to support their families through gainful employment, and precipitated social regulations such as family courts and criminal sanctions to compel potentially delinquent husbands to provide for their families or else face strict penalties.[16] Bronner, therefore, served as a model for those nondisabled workers who supposedly shirked their familial and economic responsibilities because, according to the *Enquirer*'s logic, Bronner's disability could have precluded him from seeking status as a breadwinner husband.

The *Washington Times*'s emphasis on Bronner's usefulness as a model American citizen contrasted with contemporary mainstream assumptions about disabled peoples' *lack* of qualities of citizenship. Disability, as the historian Douglas Baynton argues, played a central role in the formation of US immigration and social policy and was shaped in turn by eugenics and limiting conceptions of Americanness that restricted disabled peoples' access to citizenship. Nondisabled policymakers and writers, for example, assumed that disabled people were socially and economically "inefficient" drags on the evolutionary and economic progress of the nation, which led to new screening procedures to prevent disabled immigrants from entry to the United States.[17] Ultimately, citizenship has historically assumed able-bodiedness, and the concept of citizenship has been a force that has marginalized some people and created second-class status on groups such as women, African Americans, and disabled people.[18] That Bronner was held up as a model citizen implied that he deviated from stereotypically disabled people who could not conform to idealized versions of American citizenship that were contingent on socioeconomic status, race, ability, and gender.

The fact that Carl Bronner was white may have made his claims to citizenship as a disabled man more appealing to the nondisabled readers of the *Washington Times* and other newspapers. World War I was a transformative moment for race relations as the war mobilized African Americans at home and abroad and presented opportunities for Black Americans to challenge racism, provoking a violent racist backlash from white Americans.[19] Racist exclusions extended to rehabilitation, as vocational rehabilitation officials routinely "devalued, deskilled, and institutionalized" disabled African American vets and "dismissed their claims to rehabilitation as spurious attempts to unjustly profit from their 'natural inferiority,'" so as not to undermine white supremacy.[20] Administrators denied claims and undercut Black disabled veterans' efforts to succeed after the war, and the images in rehabilitation propaganda overwhelmingly depicted white men.[21] Bronner, a white disabled veteran who succeeded in life after the war, seemed to have cemented his status as a model American citizen in ways that may not have been as accessible to Black disabled veterans.

Public reactions to Carl Bronner called up sighted observers' imaginations, fears, and anxieties about blindness. In blind writer, academic, and actor M. Leona Godin's discussion of the centuries of blind characters in literature, she writes that blindness is often used for sighted audiences as a form of punishment, prophecy, or spiritual overcoming. Cultural tropes about blind people such as this "say very little about the sentiments of actual blind people and much more about the fears and hyperbolic claims of sighted people that they'd rather be dead than blind," and form part of what disability studies scholar David Bolt refers to as the "metanarrative of blindness."[22] For journalists covering blind veterans, Carl Bronner's blindness, as well as the fact that he was a double hand amputee and partially deaf, illustrated the worst excesses of modern industrial warfare that condemned individual American soldiers like himself to a fate worse than death. Prevented from fulfilling his role as productive citizen and breadwinner of a family, as the manufactured stories about Bronner suggested, he saved himself only through courageous grit and determination.

Carl Bronner's media reception fits within what disability scholars call "inspiration porn," which is typically "an uplifting story that tends to leave nondisabled people feeling grateful for what they have and confident in the powers of the plucky individual to overcome obstacles."[23] As will be discussed, sighted Americans with little or no understanding about blind people or their lives were nonetheless convinced that blindness was a fate worse than death, and that the select few blind people who succeeded in life did so because of individual grit and determination rather than other factors such as privileged status as a war veteran, socioeconomic class status, or whiteness. Such stories of redemption ultimately served as inspiration for nondisabled people rather than highlighting the inadequate support systems and stigmatizing views that, if changed to become more inclusive and accepting, could have helped more blind people succeed as well. In Carl Bronner's case, as well as many other blind veterans of World War I, American audiences preferred inspiration.

The inspirational stories that defined blind veterans' public reception depended in part on the fact that the veterans themselves lived in an ocularcentric society. Ocularcentrism, according to Godin, "dictates that blindness . . . translates into not just a different but a lesser way of perceiving the world."[24] American reporters and the American public were less interested in the complex intricacies of blind veterans' individual lives, their ideas, their feelings, their hopes, and their fears. They were more interested in what meanings blind veterans' lives could convey to sighted observers, which was certainly the case with Carl Bronner, who served as a "guide post" for the desires of American public officials to make sighted Americans feel guilty about not doing enough or happy about spending their tax money on rehabilitation programs. "We blind people," Godin writes of her own experiences and the experiences of blind people throughout history, "parade through the theater of sighted people's lives as representations. Blindness must mean something. We are regarded as signs and symbols, not people."[25]

Blind veterans also lived in an ableist world that defined blindness and disability more broadly as medical problems to be solved rather than lived realities of biological diversity that would benefit from accessibility and therefore enrich society. Today many scholars consider disability through the social model that argues that disabled people are more marginalized by nondisabled people's limiting beliefs and society's inaccessibility in the built environment rather than their biological differences.[26] In Carl Bronner's time, disabled and nondisabled Americans understood disability as nothing short of a problem that required a cure through what modern scholars call the "medical model"—in this case, specifically through medical interventions and newly developed rehabilitation programs.[27] Disability was accordingly classified by nondisabled populations as inherently bad or "defective," and Progressive Era reformers, eugenicists, and physicians took myriad steps to address and "fix" the "problems" posed by disabled people, including incarcerating disabled people in institutions and forcibly sterilizing them, passing laws that barred disabled people from public places and from the workforce, and pursuing medical solutions to "cure" disabled people or enable them to "overcome" their disabilities.[28]

For blind people in particular, paternalism and ocularcentric ableism meant that they were reliant on the good will of sighted people to provide opportunities for their success, which initially took the form of the nineteenth-century sheltered workshops paid for by philanthropic or tax funds.[29] First established by Samuel Gridley Howe in the 1840s, workshops provided wage labor in supervised settings where blind people manufactured chairs, brooms, baskets, and other items included in the "blind trades."[30] Workshops seemed a logical alternative to begging in the streets, which was not an uncommon experience for disabled people in the nineteenth century due to the structures of society including industrialization, poverty, ableist public policies, and disability stigma. That is, until Progressive Era reformers looked to vocational training, and institutions such as the New York Association for the Blind lobbied to increase blind workers' presence in fields such as sales.[31] Yet even these avenues for economic stability were limited by ableist attitudes and bureaucratic wrangling.[32]

It was in this context that wounded and sick World War I soldiers like Carl Bronner returned to the United States and encountered Progressive Era reforms that aimed to replace vast and expensive Civil War-era military pensions with vocational training services to rehabilitate veterans into economically self-sufficient citizens. Through rehabilitation, Progressives argued, the American government could "rebuild" disabled veterans into masculine wage earners, and therefore save money on what would have been the war's human "waste."[33] While scholars have persuasively charted the state's rehabilitation programs for veterans of World War I, cultural perceptions of the disabled veteran as a "problem," and the development of modern veteran health care, blind veterans have thus far received little attention despite the relatively prominent position they occupied in the social imaginary during the interwar years.[34] To Progressive Era observers, blind veterans suffered the most intrusive wound and the most difficult to "overcome." In the minds of sighted audiences, for Carl Bronner, a veteran who had multiple disabilities including blindness, to transcend his physical limitations seemed truly inspiring.

The ocularcentric ableism that defined blind veterans' public reception by sighted people tended to collapse blindness—both the medical realities of blindness and the lived experiences of visual impairment—into a singular identity that belied the complexities of living as a person with a visual impairment. "Not simply reduced to the facts of blindness," writes David Bolt, "the complex person is lumbered with what may be called the 'old vestments' of blindness [and] are frequently keyed to an extensive metanarrative of blindness that is shaped by cultural representations" that displaces agency.[35] Despite what American observers may have believed about blind veterans, visual impairment was not a static, unchanging experience, but varied in the levels of light, darkness, and color that the veterans experienced based on their wounds or illnesses.[36] Metaphorically speaking, blind veterans were not ignorant, in the dark, depressed, or purposeless, despite the fact that Americans interested in blind veterans regularly ascribed such conditions to blindness.[37] The sentimentality that accompanied American efforts to define blindness came not necessarily as a result of qualities that elucidated visually-impaired people's lived experiences, but were necessarily shaped by emotional wartime considerations of patriotic self-sacrifice and the needs of state-sponsored rehabilitation.

Blind veterans' own lived experiences at times contested or challenged contemporaneous cultural constructions of their identities. They recognized that, in terms of their lived realities, being visually impaired was just one part of their identity that intersected with gender, sexuality, socioeconomic status, race, and ethnicity, despite the fact that stories about blind veterans almost always focused exclusively on their blindness, unless other aspects of their identity said something important about their blindness, physical ability, and moral qualities of citizenship.[38] Therefore, *Constructing Disability after the Great War* argues that as Americans—both civilians and veterans—sought to determine the meanings of blind veteran identity in the context of World War I, the process of culturally constructing blindness was bound to all the emotions and contingencies of mobilizing, fighting, and healing from war's traumas. Through their lived experiences blind veterans often challenged American society's assumptions about blindness, but, ultimately, such wartime contestations about blindness accentuated ableism and ocularcentrism that already existed in American society rather than creating a new public acceptance of disability and new avenues of accessibility.[39]

By understanding the complexities of blind veterans' lives, *Constructing Disability after the Great War* seeks to unpack the inspirational narratives that existed about blind veterans of World War I in the American press that suggested the men were either downcast wrecks of their former selves or were morally superior and relatively flawless as they triumphantly journeyed toward successful citizenship. In reality, there was no singular "blinded veteran" or "blinded soldier," terms that suggest homogenous experiences and grand assertions about visual impairment.[40] This book will not use the term "blinded" unless discussing a soldier, sailor, or veteran who was blinded in combat, because in the context of World War I "blinded" came to imply the act of having been blinded by artillery shrapnel, a flying bullet, or poison gas in the heat of battle, and the proportion of American soldiers blinded in this way was by no means representative of the whole. Just as numerous were the soldiers or sailors who became blind through illness, the veterans who were partially blind in one or both eyes but who eventually lost their vision years after the war ended, when the trappings of war fever—its parades, its patriotic and emotionally charged rhetoric—had long receded. In this sense, and because the veterans themselves more often used "blind" rather than "blinded" in their correspondences, books, articles, and speeches, it is more accurate to use the terms "blind soldier" and "blind veteran."

Constructing Disability after the Great War proceeds with the nomenclature of blindness cautiously, taking into consideration disability studies scholar David Bolt's terminological arguments while also remaining true to the historical context of the time. The term "blind," Bolt argues, can be problematic "because it denotes much that bears no intrinsic relation to visual impairment," and it contains moral and ethical assumptions derived through culture such as punishment for sin, lack of awareness, lack of knowledge, darkness (despite the fact that visual impairment does not always include the absence of light), and irrationality. Bolt ultimately refers to the myriad negative cultural constructions of visual impairment cued by the term "blind" as part of a "metanarrative of blindness." For this reason and others, Bolt primarily uses "visually impaired," which alludes to the social model, reduces the implications of homogeneous experiences of visual impairment, and accommodates the continuum of visual limitations that are "complex, temporary, and variable." Bolt reserves the application of "blind" for "references to literary characters, tropes, motifs, stereotypes, and the mythos of blindness in general."[41]

If this study uses the term "blind" more liberally than scholars such as Bolt, it is primarily because visually impaired World War I veterans repeatedly used the term "blind" and did not use "visually impaired." Either through written attestations about their experiences or through the creation of organizations such as the United States Blind Veterans of the World War or the Blind Veterans' Chapter of the Disabled American Veterans of the World War, the term "blind" was meaningful for blind veterans. It signified their status as a privileged category of disabled veterans that warranted, in the view of rehabilitationists, unique provisions. For this and other reasons people, organizations, and cultural messages consciously invoked the term "blind" in service of their own needs and identities.

Constructing Disability after the Great War also uses the terms "soldier" and "veteran" selectively.[42] In his landmark edited volume *Disabled Veterans in History,* the historian David Gerber sensibly used the term "veteran" to denote a wounded soldier "from the moment it is clear that he cannot return to active duty, and is headed for civilian life."[43] Historian Beth Linker, though, demonstrates the practicality of calling disabled soldiers "soldier-patients" in the context of World War I, as the US Army did not demobilize the wounded or sick until they reached the highest possible level of physical and vocational rehabilitation.[44] It will be clear through some of the case studies outlined in this book that blind soldiers were cognizant of the benefits they lost out on by being classified by the state as soldier-patients rather than as veterans, and the status of their title had very real material consequences for them and their families. This book uses the term "soldier" until the point of discharge from the US Army. Whether they were soldiers or veterans, though, the men continuously felt the friction that existed between the idealized "blinded" veteran and the complexities of the "blind" veteran, as many of them inhabited the complex space in between.

Constructing Disability after the Great War highlights the continuous metaphorical tug-of-war in American society between the idealized "blinded veteran" and the more complex "blind veteran," and what that tug-of-war over the meanings of blindness, citizenship, and martial manhood says about understandings of worthiness, disability stigma, and ultimately sighted Americans themselves. American culture sometimes preferred to use the term "blinded soldier," as it evoked the emotional appeal and passion of a battle wound, and stimulated advocacy on behalf of organizations that were built to service such soldiers with the help of public money. Alongside public depictions of "the blinded soldier" were also the lesser understood realities of "blind soldiers" who may not have been battle blinded; who did their best to make something of themselves after the war while also confronting ocularcentric ableism that pigeonholed their lives into a singular experience; who worked against barriers that existed for all blind people; who gained an education and employment, but also struggled financially; who balanced the public reception of their successes or failures while trying to manage their own self-image as blind men; and who confronted injustices while in the public spotlight. This book, therefore, aims to cut through the cultural tropes about "blinded" soldiers to elucidate the lives of blind soldiers, sailors, and veterans and their families, while also exploring the cultural narratives that they had no choice but to accept or confront and contest.

The many histories of blind veterans of World War I explored in this book address some important questions not only about blindness and disability, but also about American society more broadly. Who, for example, constituted a "blind veteran," and who among blind veterans were considered by the American public or the American state as "worthy" of public praise, remembrance, and material support? Did public praise of blind veterans automatically signify heroic war service, regardless of the cause of their disability? How did blind veterans themselves feel about public praise? What do these stories tell us about American cultures of performative patriotism and the honoring of wartime sacrifice? What implications does the language we use for wartime sacrifice have on disability and disabled people in general?

Constructing Disability after the Great War will aim to answer these questions by exploring the many histories of blind soldiers/veterans and American society during and after World War I. Americans' first sustained exposure to blindness during the war years happened almost from the earliest moments the guns started firing. After the German army invaded Belgium and northern France in August and September 1914, American newspapers reported on the prevalence of young, healthy soldiers blinded in combat, scattered throughout the war zone, and only "discovered" by American aid workers. Chapter 1 examines Americans' public philanthropic efforts to aid blind French soldiers in the opening months of World War I through the activities of the Committee for Men Blinded in Battle and the British, French, and Belgian Blind Relief War Fund. The two aid organizations harnessed modern advertising and philanthropy to make blindness a public issue between August 1914 and April 1917, and in so doing they constructed cultural messaging that equated blind soldiers with dependency, helplessness, and depression.

It was not long after the United States entered the war in April 1917 that word of American soldiers blinded in battle began trickling back to eager audiences, but the stories they consumed were markedly different from the tragic tales they had heard about blind poilus being benevolently aided by saintly American women. Chapter 2 explores the ways that American media tried to reimagine the cultural image of "the blinded soldier" as the first blind American soldiers returned from Europe and entered vocational rehabilitation. Images and rhetoric from rehabilitation magazines such as *Carry On* and the *Evergreen Review* as well as popular journals, newspapers, and magazines suggested that blind American soldiers, unlike their French counterparts, were full of happiness, independence, and determination to make good in their postwar lives as disabled men performing productive labor. While the messages Americans published about blind US soldiers were different from those used about French soldiers, American rehabilitationists working with and covering US soldiers nonetheless rested their arguments on the ableist notion of blindness as an almost insurmountable impairment in order to emphasize the successes of their subjects.

Blind American soldiers had rich lives, as is evidenced through the social activities that happened within the halls of Evergreen—the colloquial term for the rehabilitation center for blind American soldiers of World War I in Baltimore, Maryland—where the men learned how to navigate blindness, how to manage public perceptions of their disabled bodies, how to live up to public expectations of them to become breadwinner husbands, and how to fit in with each other. Chapter 3 explores the lived experiences of blind soldiers and sailors, and then veterans, including how they either conformed to or challenged notions of gender, racial, and disability identity, especially after Evergreen demobilized as a US Army hospital and came under the direction of the Red Cross Institute for the Blind in 1919. Ultimately, blind veterans' lives were far more complex than the headlines suggested.

Chapter 4 follows the story into the 1920s to explore the lived experiences of blind veterans as they formed advocacy organizations, and examines the issues that drove them to form such organizations in the first place. By examining the activities of the United States Blind Veterans of the World War as well as the Blind Veterans' Chapter of the Disabled American Veterans of the World War, the chapter explores how blind veterans' politics diverged in the 1920s, and that the source of argumentation between the two organizations was partially due to ideas about ableism, one's privileged status as a war-wounded veteran, and access to benefits. Blind veterans' disagreements manifested as they sought to shape public opinion in their own often conflicting ways, while also trying to confront public misconceptions about life as a blind person.

By examining the four case studies, *Constructing Disability after the Great War* seeks to investigate the popular conceptions of blindness that drove discussions about blind veterans in ways that constrained their lives, collapsed their complexities, and ultimately further stigmatized disability. There existed no singular "blind soldier" or "blind veteran." Each blind veteran had unique circumstances, opportunities, and challenges based on their gender, race, socioeconomic class status, and disability, as well as where they lived. They confronted and contested age-old stigmatizing representations of blindness that many blind civilians experienced, but had the privilege of their veteran status to challenge those representations or to lean into them. Understanding these complexities challenges our own existing historiography and more contemporary conversations about blindness and/or veterans, and confronts the accuracy, or lack thereof, of our own discussions about war and disability.

1

Blindness Comes Home

How American Charities Made Blind French Soldiers a Public Issue

On Sunday evening, April 23, 1916—one year before the United States entered World War I—crowds flocked to the Hippodrome Theatre in New York City for what promised to be the event of the year. The British, French, and Belgian Permanent Blind Relief War Fund held a massive extravaganza on behalf of European blind soldiers of World War I that ultimately raised $25,000. Audiences enjoyed talks and performances by English actor Cyril Maude, vaudeville actor Sam Bernard, and film actress Kitty Gordon, among others.[1] The *New York Herald* proclaimed that more celebrities appeared at the Hippodrome that evening "than on any recent similar occasion."[2] One exhibit that visitors viewed was a tableau depicting "the plight of a shell-blinded" French soldier: "alone, helpless, and downcast" and sitting in an attic "groping hungrily" toward the sunlight that "he feels but cannot see." Also in the tableau was a representation of shell-strewn Verdun. Then a depiction of Belgium in a "field of desolation." Toward the end of the long tableau, a rabbi "stepped to the stage and pleaded for generosity . . . toward the sightless war victims."[3]

New York celebrities took center stage in the evening's events. The act that most captivated audiences was a performance by Ziegfeld Follies star Billie Burke. Burke—who was later known for her role as Glinda the Good Witch in *The Wizard of Oz*—appeared on stage "before the glaring floodlights . . . gowned in white, a vision of loveliness." She addressed the crowd, asking her viewers to cover their eyes. Then "every light in the house went out. . . . It was as if the whole audience had suddenly become blind." When the lights turned on again, and the audience was no longer made to "feel blindness," Burke appealed to them for donations in support of the Blind Relief War Fund, while "the prettiest society . . . matrons" walked through the theater collecting thousands of dollars.[4]

Events such as the Hippodrome fundraiser, which raised public awareness about aid organizations for blind soldiers including the Blind Relief War Fund, were part of a broader culture that created paternalistic and ableist representations of blind soldiers to raise money.[5] To create a sense of urgency for the fundraising campaigns, news outlets regularly reported about poor, destitute, and blind soldiers and civilians in the war zone in Europe alongside the more widely recognized German atrocities against Belgian and French civilians in the first months of the war. Men and women who were engaged in relief and charity work during the war described blindness as akin to the worst suffering of civilian casualties in Belgium and France. These victims were in dire need of American monetary aid to save them from a purgatory of anguish. Early reports shaped subsequent conversations about the war's blind soldiers, even if their actual lived experiences did not always align.

Two American relief organizations transferred resources and expertise to Europe for allied soldiers blind from World War I. The first was the Committee for Men Blinded in Battle. Created in the early weeks of the war by the social reformer Winifred Holt's New York Association for the Blind, the committee brought emotional stories of blind soldiers to American audiences. The Committee for Men Blinded in Battle operated institutions called Lighthouses in France to train French soldiers who were blind due to their war service. Committee publicity portrayed blind soldiers as the most helpless, depressed, and tragic figures of the war. The second organization, the British, French, and Belgian Blind Relief War Fund (which eventually added "American" to its name) exploited similar damaging public assumptions about the blind men in an even more exploitative way with its extensive, nationwide fundraising campaigns through 1916 and 1917.

This chapter demonstrates that, given the actual occurrence of war blindness, blind soldiers made up a disproportionately significant subsection of philanthropic organizations' wartime relief efforts before 1917. Additionally, this chapter illustrates how American media consumption before 1917 relied on paternalistic, ableist depictions of helpless, white, and masculine blinded soldiers—organizations emphasized that they were blinded rather than blind for sympathetic appeal—being benevolently aided by the American public through events that simultaneously decentered the actual disabled soldiers' experiences and exploited their disabilities. American relief organizations used exploitative representations for monetary gain, and blind soldiers' actual experiences are far more complex than what events such as the Hippodrome fundraiser suggested. Ultimately, American philanthropic organizations significantly shaped public perceptions of blindness and blind people beyond 1917 and the US entry into the war, when American soldiers required rehabilitation.

Creating the "Blinded Soldier" amid the Tragedy of War

Americans' first sustained contact with blind soldiers during World War I came through the New York Association for the Blind (NYAB). Winifred Holt and her sister Edith—daughters of the New York publisher Henry Holt—had founded the NYAB just eight years before the start of the war. The NYAB organized vocational training programs for blind civilians through an institution called the Lighthouse. The metaphorical lighthouse was meant to help blind individuals whom the Holts considered lost in darkness to find light through work. The NYAB created a subsidiary organization, the Committee for Men Blinded in Battle (CMBB), in the wake of the German invasion of Belgium and France in August and September 1914. The CMBB joined other major humanitarian organizations such as the American Red Cross and the Committee for Relief in Belgium that provided much-needed relief to France and Belgium in the form of food, sanitary aid, and medical supplies while also helping to shape early romanticized rhetoric about the war.[6] The CMBB's work ultimately played a large part in shaping public conversations about blindness and blind soldiers in the context of war and violence, as its founder Winifred Holt surveyed the war zone providing humanitarian aid to blind soldiers and civilians while writing about her experiences for American audiences.

The CMBB's campaign to aid blind French soldiers, however, was not the first public crusade to confront blindness in the twentieth-century United States. "One of the most dramatic crusades against blindness," the historian Frances Koestler has argued, "was already well along the road to successful completion" by World War I. Motivated by the Progressive Era optimism in the ability of professional expertise and modern science to cure social and medical "ills," the twenty-year crusade against ophthalmia neonatorum, or colloquially called "babies' sore eyes," mobilized social reformers, physicians, lawmakers, and many others concerned with the exorbitant numbers of cases of infant blindness.[7] The inflammation in newborns' eyes was typically a result of a gonorrheal infection in the mother's birth canal. Until the widespread use of prophylactic eye drops, the condition was responsible for up to 30 percent of all blindness in children. Ultimately, the ophthalmic reform efforts led to the creation of new state laws mandating the use of eyedrops for newborns, and the formation in 1908 of the National Society for the Prevention of Blindness.[8]

Blindness prevention literature before World War I in some ways foreshadowed the emotionally charged public discussions about apparently helpless blind people that defined events such as the April 1916 Hippodrome Theatre fundraiser. "Save Baby's Eyes! Save It from Life of Darkness!" exclaimed the *Wilkes-Barre Times-Leader* in Pennsylvania in April 1910. All it took to prevent blindness from "babies' sore eyes," the article assured its readers, was a simple two-cent medication.[9] Media coverage of the NYAB's activities in 1910 likewise reassured readers of how preventable blindness was in many children if it was caught and remedied in time. Those children whose cases went unnoticed were instead "doomed to lifelong darkness."[10] News coverage that appeared in the papers of the New York Association for the Blind and the *Wilkes-Barre Times-Leader* usually emphasized the "unnecessary" and "preventable" nature of most cases of infant and adolescent blindness, suggesting the tragedy of vibrant youth lost to disability. Significant as it was, the nationwide attention given to ophthalmia neonatorum would pale in comparison to American humanitarian responses to blindness during World War I.

Ableist rhetoric that suggested the supposed helplessness of blind people did not necessarily represent the actual lived experiences of many blind civilians around the turn of the century, which is evident through public advocacy efforts of blind people themselves. Blind people experienced poverty and job insecurities, though they successfully channeled advocacy efforts to push for increased public funding for pensions and industrial workshops, and to address various educational and social inadequacies.[11] By 1919, at least thirteen US states had passed some form of blind aid thanks to the efforts of blind activists and their allies.[12] The most robust public advocacy effort took place in Colorado, where blind activists created the Society of United Workers for the Blind. The organization lobbied for blind pensions and highlighted issues such as lack of accessibility services and outreach programs, education and literacy, poverty, inadequate funding, lack of affordable housing, and societal stigma, which prevented them from earning a living wage and were lived realities that disabled blind people more than their physical impairment.[13]

In addition to lobbying for favorable legislative changes to counter the deleterious effects ableism, blind people also created cultural forums to promote social solidarity and economic advancement. The American Blind People's Higher Education and General Improvement Association, founded in the 1890s by a group of blind intellectuals, created an influential yet short-lived publication titled *The Problem*. The philosophy of *The Problem*'s editors and writers was, until it ceased publication in 1903, to portray blindness realistically and to allow blind people to address each other, conveying a sense of optimism and inclusiveness for blind Americans by highlighting their own perspectives on life.[14]

Blind citizens advocating on behalf of themselves, however, could not overcome the ableism of sighted society that positioned them as inherently dependent. Organizations such as the NYAB perpetuated age-old stereotypes of blind people as dependent and in need of professional support, while also borrowing rhetorical strategies of one of the foremost magazines that published stories about blind people: *The Outlook.* Inaugurated in 1907 four years after *The Problem* ceased production, *The Outlook* was a magazine associated with the American Association of Workers for the Blind that featured stories about blind people that catered primarily, though not exclusively, to a reading public that could see.[15] As historian Catherine Kudlick argues, early twentieth-century publications such as *The Outlook* "simultaneously promoted images of blindness that suggested dependence before independence and weakness over strength," and ultimately suggested blind people had to rely on philanthropic organizations. Specialist publications and popular periodicals that chronicled people involved in work *for* the blind had ableist assumptions about blind people as inherently dependent.[16]

When World War I began, then, blind Americans had experienced self-advocacy limited by ableism and the growing influence of sighted specialists and philanthropists who increasingly shaped conversations about blindness. Blind people had advocated on behalf of themselves, shaping public policies and highlighting the marginalizing power of ableism, and they created cultural avenues to speak to one another about blindness. But the shifts in conversations about blindness, evidenced through the changing tone of *The Outlook,* accelerated with World War I and reached Americans who may not have had any form of sustained contact with blind organizations such as the American Association of Workers for the Blind. The NYAB's work in the early months of World War I depended on existing frameworks of supposed blind dependency on sighted organizations, and harnessed emotionally charged rhetoric of wartime catastrophe to present blindness in a way meant to shock audiences into donating money for a worthy cause.

The broader culture of violence in the initial months of World War I significantly shaped the early rhetoric of American relief organizations such as the CMBB and influenced the stories they told to American audiences to raise money. Germany's invasion of Belgium and France according to the Schlieffen Plan—the German military strategy that depended on quickly defeating France by going through neutral Belgium before turning the full weight of the German army against Russia in the East—sowed violence, fear, and confusion.[17] American newspapers published numerous stories about German atrocities perpetrated against Belgian and French civilians in the summer of 1914 alongside stories about vulnerable blind Belgian civilian refugees and atrocities that centered on the physical act of blinding soldiers. What emerged was a subtle correlation of blindness as a tragic war crime akin to German military conduct in Belgium, which was a narrative that played on the sympathies of American philanthropic organizations and the general public, urging them to step in as humanitarian saviors.[18]

When she first arrived in Europe on behalf of the CMBB, Winifred Holt focused almost exclusively on the dire situation of blind civilians rather than on blind soldiers in her dispatches home. Playing on the sympathies of her American readers who were eager to understand the fate of the Belgians, Holt wrote, "I cannot tell where the blind of Belgium are—because I do not know—nobody knows." Holt thought that the "helpless ones" were somewhere "starving." "When the besieged cities fell," she continued, "not only were the institutions for the blind opened, but the prisons and insane asylums as well poured forth . . . among the refugees." Holt wrote that there were institutions for blind people in Antwerp, Bruges, Brussels, and Liège, all of which fell within the German-occupied zone. She worried in particular about the Royal Institution for the Dumb, Deaf, and Blind in Liège, where, as she told her readers, there was no telling what had become of that institution or the people in it during the German onslaught.[19]

It is not surprising that Holt referenced the Belgian city of Liège in her speaking engagements. That city was the site of particularly troubling atrocities against Belgian civilians during a period of the war that predated the lengthy trench stalemate of the Western Front. Beginning on August 5, Liège took the brunt of the German assault before the main invasion of Belgium. After German soldiers mistakenly shot at each other during the battle and then blamed Belgian civilians for it, they executed around 850 civilians and burned down 1,500 buildings. If public reprisals over false resistance was not enough, German soldiers used a number of civilians as human shields as they entered the city.[20] No information exists about the fate of the Royal Institution for the Dumb, Deaf, and Blind, or the Belgian civilians who lived there. Curiously enough, Holt did not mention it more than a couple of times in appeals for monetary support, and when she did she spoke only of blind civilians, neglecting the existence of deaf or deafblind civilians at the Royal Institution. Ultimately, her focus shifted almost exclusively to blind soldiers, which generated significantly more public attention.

Winifred Holt's public appeals for monetary aid after witnessing the state of war refugees were carefully calculated and relied on an uncontested and misrepresented concept of war-related blindness that combined with pressure tactics meant to arouse guilt in primarily able-bodied observers. Blind children at the Lighthouse in New York made monetary contributions of their own, and publicity surrounding their donations suggested to sighted Americans that they should donate what they could, too.[21] The Committee of American Physicians for the Aid of Belgian Professionals used Holt's inflated estimates without question about the number of vulnerable Belgian blind civilians to raise money for their European colleagues. Dr. F. F. Simpson of that organization asked physicians to aid "8,000 homeless blind" in Belgium, which was based on Holt's own testimonies.[22] Holt's estimates of the number of blind Belgian civilians in need were based on the total number of blind Belgians at the outbreak of war in the late summer of 1914, rather than post-invasion sources. She, therefore, assumed that the German invasion wrecked all the institutions, and that blind Belgian civilians were inevitably helpless as a result.

Holt emphasized this point in a lecture she gave to the New York City Board of Education about her early wartime philanthropic work, in which she linked the experiences of "helpless" blind civilians in Belgium to soldiers blinded in battle. In one hospital in France "there are a hundred young men who were blinded in battle," Holt claimed. She credited modern war as the primary cause for elevated levels of eye injuries, with artillery explosions and shrapnel that "reap a large harvest of blindness" on eyes left vulnerable and exposed. In an effort to further link blind civilians and soldiers in the European war zone, Holt held a fundraiser on April 6, 1915, at New York's Hotel Astor, the proceeds of which benefited men blinded in battle *and* blind civilian refugees.[23] Holt's careful rhetorical strategies clearly linked the atrocities perpetrated against Belgian and French civilians by the German army with blind civilians and soldiers blinded in battle, constructing a common tale of tragedy. This is significant because it blurred the lines between wartime combat-related blindness among soldiers and the lived experiences of blind civilians.

Holt was not alone in her efforts to appeal to the public on behalf of blind people in the war zone, nor in her reliance on ableist rhetoric about them. Kathleen Burke, a British nurse in the Scottish Women's Hospitals and a descendant of eighteenth-century English philosopher Edmund Burke, told American audiences in the *New York Telegram* that she had gone to Europe to aid Belgian refugees in Antwerp, but then came across more "pitiful" blind soldiers, suggesting that Burke conceived of a hierarchy of worthy blind people in which blind soldiers occupied the top.[24] The American novelist Dorothy Canfield Fisher, who was a leading figure in blind war relief efforts in Paris during the war and who wrote about her experiences while working with blind soldiers there, also told American audiences similar tales about the sufferings of war refugees.[25]

At times the stories that individuals and organizations related to American audiences about wartime blinding seemed almost unbelievable in their scale and intensity. Caroline Gardner Bartlett, "Sister Beatrice," was a relief worker from the United States who relayed to the American public some of the jarring stories of German atrocities. By October 1915, she had made over fifty trips from England to Belgium with supplies and told Americans in the *Providence Bulletin* that she had witnessed "many pitiful scenes" of mutilation. Bartlett told an audience in Providence, Rhode Island, that she saw babies with their hands cut off, men with severed noses, and women with their breasts mutilated.[26] Bartlett may have been influenced by stories about German atrocities that had already made their rounds through the Allied press. Historians John Horne and Alan Kramer have demonstrated that while German atrocities did happen there was no medical evidence to prove some of the more barbaric stories leveled against invading German armies, which suggests that press reports sometimes published unsubstantiated stories because of the emotional appeal editors knew they would generate among Americans.[27]

Lack of medical evidence for some atrocities aside, German conduct in Belgium nonetheless gave plenty of evidence to support the notion of its "rape" of the country's citizens.[28] In the first weeks of the war, there were large-scale massacres in numerous cities and towns, including Andenne, Seilles, Tamines, and Dinant, where victims numbered in the hundreds and included men, women, and children. In Tamines, the hostages were gunned down in the town square and the survivors bayonetted. "Our advance in Belgium is certainly brutal," wrote the German Chief of the General Staff Helmuth von Moltke on August 5, "but we are fighting for our lives and all who get in the way must take the consequences."[29] Such experiences provided plenty of reference points for Allied propaganda, such as the 1915 British "Remember Belgium" recruitment poster that depicts a stoic British soldier coming to the aid of Belgian civilians as a city burns in the background, or the 1918 American Liberty Loan poster of the same title that illustrated a German soldier marauding through a Belgian city on fire and kidnapping a young Belgian girl.[30]

Stories about eye mutilation abounded in early wartime propaganda, purportedly used as evidence of the extremes of either German or Belgian barbarity. French government officials claimed that Germans committed various atrocities against French soldiers, such as amputations, castration, and gouging eyes out.[31] Germans soldiers' fear of being blinded was one reason for their massacre of Belgians in Warsage on August 6, 1914, after accusations that Belgian *francs-tireurs*—irregular civilian partisans—had gouged out the eyes and cut off the ears of a number of German soldiers.[32] The Belgian city of Namur narrowly escaped the fate of Warsage. After the surrender of Namur to the German army, German soldiers were convinced that the city was filled with francs-tireurs. On August 25, Germans rounded up civilians and one German officer stated to his captives, "You too . . . are going to be shot because you've fired on our soldiers. . . . You Belgians have also cut off our soldiers' noses, ears, eyes and fingers. For that, you will be shot." But the hostages were ultimately released.[33]

German and French fears about eye mutilation—and the prevalence of such stories in American newspapers—speaks to an enduring symbolism attributed to the act of blinding in Western literature. Writer M. Leona Godin traces this symbolism back to Ancient Greece in the figure of Oedipus who, after his search for truth that led him to the knowledge that he killed his father and married his mother, gouges out his own eyes as a form of tragic punishment worse than death. "The Oedipus trope of eye-gouging" as a fate reserved for someone who committed an unspeakable offense, Godin concludes, "has been ingrained in our culture ever since."[34] The story of Oedipus is instructive because, compared with his crime of killing his own father and marrying his mother, eye gouging in World War I seemed to have been used by both sides to accentuate the tragedy of otherwise innocent soldiers who were allegedly mercilessly mutilated at the hands of barbaric adversaries (for example, the French officials who claimed that German soldiers blinded French soldiers, and the German soldiers who claimed that Belgian irregular francs-tireurs partisans committed war crimes by mutilating German soldiers).

Whether the stories about eye mutilation were true or not, Caroline Gardner Bartlett made subtle connections between the tragedy of civilian suffering under enemy occupation and the existence of blindness as a tragic and atrocious consequence of modern war on the bodies of primarily young, able-bodied men. Among the examples of atrocities she noted was the ample evidence of blindness throughout war hospitals, including "5000 cases in one of several hospitals" in late 1915, for which she blamed "poisonous gases used by the Germans." Bartlett argued that the loss of sight was "a terrible fate," and worse than any other wound inflicted on Allied soldiers.[35] There were two rhetorical strategies Bartlett used in her testimony about blindness from poison gas. First, she linked the more general wartime atrocity stories from occupied zones to the very specific trauma of war-related blindness. Second, she made the case seem dire based on the sheer numbers of blind soldiers.

Bartlett could very well have encountered such high numbers of blind soldiers, the likes of which observers after 1919 might have recognized from John Singer Sargent's painting *Gassed*—a group of British soldiers with bandaged eyes, blinded by German mustard gas and leading each other back to a dressing station—though she could have also simply witnessed the immediate aftermath of a gas attack that did not present an accurate indication of the levels of permanent blindness.[36] The German army first used poison gas at Ypres on April 22, 1915.[37] Early forms of gas included tear gas, chlorine gas, and phosgene gas. While most of the early forms of gas caused excessive eye, lung, and throat irritation, permanent blindness was not typically a common result.[38] Mustard gas, which does cause blindness, was not used until 1917. Bartlett could have been either relaying her actual observations or she could have been inflating the levels of blindness for dramatization alongside the stories of the German slaughter of Belgians as two tragedies in one. Even if she did not see so many blind combatants and noncombatants herself, Belgian refugees flooded parts of France and Holland with almost unbelievable stories, which could have at least formed part of her own retelling.[39]

Nonetheless, Americans saw German violence against Belgian civilians, their use of poison gas, and the physical act of blinding as part of broader affronts to civilization alongside the 1915 sinking of the *Lusitania*. Though the United States was politically neutral, Allied merchant ships continued to supply Britain and France from across the Atlantic Ocean with necessary materials for the war effort including food, medical supplies, and munitions. German unrestricted submarine warfare targeted such shipping, and on numerous occasions after 1914 submarine attacks had almost brought the United States to war with Germany. The most well-known occasion happened on May 7, 1915, when a German submarine sank the British passenger ship *Lusitania*. The ship, which had close to 2,000 civilians on board including 128 Americans, was carrying munitions across the Atlantic when the Germans torpedoed and sank it. The tragedy quickly became a symbol of German barbarity, memorialized in prints such as Fred Spear's *Enlist* that illustrates a woman sinking into the depths of the Atlantic Ocean while clutching her infant.[40]

The famous American actress Elsie Janis, who regularly performed for the American Expeditionary Forces after the United States entered the war, wrote and published a poem titled, "Where Are You God?" as a very public protest against the sinking of the *Lusitania* and against German use of poison gas on the battlefields of Europe that led to blindness.[41] The poem reads, in part, "Where are you God? . . . I can't believe that you have seen the things they have done . . . with poisoned gas and crucifixion, battles have been won . . . Yet, after this upon your earth, there still exists the Hun. Where are you God?"[42] Though this was a condemnation of the *Lusitania* and poison gas, Janis connected those tragedies to the existence of soldiers blinded in battle when she sold the poem for $2,500 to help raise money for British and French soldiers blinded in the first months of the war.[43]

Ultimately, scholars John Horne and Alan Kramer have argued that there existed a "myth complex" that reduced emotionally charged situations such as violence against civilians on land and at sea, the use of poison gas, or—in this case—the blinding of European soldiers to "an emblematic person or action."[44] In other words, Europeans and Americans pinpointed a single event or action as symbolic of broader assumptions about an enemy's supposed barbarity. Sometimes that emblematic person or action was the wholesale destruction of Louvain and its university library's 300,000 manuscripts by the German army in late August 1914, which surely influenced Allied propaganda.[45] In other instances, the emblematic person or action was the Belgian civilian or French soldier blinded by a piece of flying steel. Stories about helpless blind soldiers and civilians existed alongside stories about German soldiers pillaging, raping, and killing helpless Belgian and French civilians. The stories retold throughout American newspapers, at least, were examples meant to prove to readers the futility and utter tragedy of war, while also solidifying broader public opinion against Germany.

This is significant because the storytellers made no effort to delineate between the very real and traumatic tragedy of a war wound that caused blindness—which would have been traumatic regardless of what specific consequences the wound wrought on the body or mind—and the existence of blindness and blind people more generally in the United States who, despite demeaning assumptions about their lives and lack of accessibility, lived fulfilling, complex, and worthy lives.[46] The stories of blind civilians in German occupation zones that philanthropic organizations used to raise money, by contrast, did not suggest that the civilians were competent individuals who could care for themselves. Instead, narratives depicted blind people as helpless dependents who required paternalistic aid from sighted people. Blind soldier narratives before 1917 were similar in this regard. Blindness in the context of war generated emotional appeal due to the heroic sense of self-sacrifice that veterans elicited, and philanthropic organizations benefited monetarily from such messaging regardless of whether the messages were harmful to modern conceptions of blind people.[47] Americans latched onto comfortable yet ableist assumptions about blindness and blind people, such as age-old myths about blindness as social liability, punishment for sin, or guarantee of uselessness, and in the context of war those myths assumed greater proportions.[48]

The Committee for Men Blinded in Battle

Winifred Holt, Elsie Janis, Dorothy Canfield Fisher, and "Sister Beatrice" Bartlett portrayed blind soldiers as tragic and helpless in the hope that it would move Americans whose government was still politically neutral to offer assistance. The Committee for Men Blinded in Battle (CMBB) was one of the first American organizations to aid blind soldiers in the war zone in the aftermath of Winifred Holt's tour of Belgium and northern France. The committee's publicity in the United States about its operations in France was a formative step in portraying blind soldiers as simultaneously tragically lost, yet also with the chance to be saved by generous benefactors, therefore constructing a narrative of dependence like that used by *The Outlook*, as this section will demonstrate.[49]

From the beginning of her observations in Europe, Holt overestimated the need for American aid. In her initial fundraising efforts to support the CMBB, Holt claimed there to have been 3,000 to 4,000 blind soldiers in Paris alone, "But the [French] Government knows of only 200."[50] It is not clear how Holt and her contemporaries arrived at such high numbers, especially considering so few soldiers of all belligerent countries were blinded through their war service.[51] We have already established that early forms of poison gas could have led to inflated numbers due to temporary blindness. This certainly could have accounted for what seemed like hundreds or thousands of blind soldiers in hospitals during the first months of the war.

It is also not clear why Winifred Holt overestimated the need for American aid. One reason could have been that the CMBB was new and surely competing with other aid organizations for the public's attention, and she was seeking as much publicity as possible through emotional appeal regardless of the negative stereotypes her language perpetuated. This fact was not lost on blind Americans. Henry Randolph Latimer, partially blind since childhood, wrote in 1920 that despite the increased attention many Americans had given to blind soldiers during the war, the quality of the attention was unwise. Sighted Americans, he argued, had plenty of ambition to "do something good" for blind civilians and soldiers, but were largely apathetic and indifferent to the outcomes of their actions, including how they characterized blind people as either "supernaturally endowed, or as creatures preordained to pitiable dependence."[52] That Latimer wrote this in 1920 in response to the trajectory of Americans' direct experiences interacting with blind American soldiers suggests that little changed after US entry into the war in 1917.

Newspapers and other philanthropic organizations nonetheless uncritically accepted Holt's testimony as the expert in the field due in part to her personal investigations in Europe during the opening months of the war. Harold Goad of the Boston-based French Wounded Fund, for example, claimed that French authorities could expect over 5,000 blind soldiers within months of his writing in December 1915.[53] And the British, French, and Belgian Permanent Blind Relief War Fund claimed, also for the purpose of fundraising, that there were at least 12,000 soldiers blinded "for life" by mid-1916.[54]

Newspaper reports also uncritically accepted the ways American aid groups discussed blind soldiers, as supremely tragic, hopeless, and depressed. One article claimed that blind soldiers were "doomed for the melancholy" of the rest of their days, and that they were "infinitely pathetic," and "pathetic discards of war."[55] A *Boston Herald* article meant to stimulate fundraising for the French Wounded Fund, for example, wrote about a French officer who was blinded, and whose mother devoted her life "to caring for him as though he were a baby."[56] The fate of such men, accordingly, was unquestionably hopeless and depressing, so much so that "life no longer tempts him . . . and the pistol seems very near at hand," therefore suggesting the erroneous notion that blind people would prefer suicide to blindness.[57] None of these descriptions took into account the actual experiences or thoughts of blind soldiers themselves, for that would be less likely to generate revenue than the theatrics that seemed to play well with American audiences.

Winifred Holt also replicated the despairing and, in some cases, infantilizing descriptions of blind soldiers for the seeing public. In a letter to the newly formed CMBB in late 1915—a letter the committee published for fundraising purposes—Holt described the "pitiful" scenes in French hospitals where she observed "human wrecks." She stopped at a hospital in Lyon, where one soldier, Nicolai, was recuperating after a grenade exploded near him taking his eyes, feet, and one arm. She also visited a military hospital in Toulon at which she saw another blind soldier where "there was very little left of him, excepting his courage." "His huge eyes," she continued, "were blind and he was carried like a child." There, she concluded, "we came to the lowest circle of Hell, where the poor blind spirits wait uncomplainingly without hope, without courage."[58] The "blind remnants," Holt argued, *had* courage, yet were left *without* courage, implying that the men were desperate enough to necessitate foreign aid, but not so hopeless as to render that aid useless.

Holt's rhetoric, which positioned blind soldiers as hopeless yet courageous for a predominantly seeing public, is strikingly similar to how *The Outlook* magazine relayed information to its readers. Much like *The Outlook*, Holt had a stake in portraying blind people as helpless but with the capacity to become self-sufficient with the aid of specialists' training and the public's money by the very fact that her organization relied on public donations to continue its rehabilitation work for blind soldiers.[59] Holt's correspondence with American audiences *was* clear in its argument that

Americans needed to do something to help the most unfortunate class of war victims.

Holt's writings also assumed that the French government was doing almost nothing for blind soldiers who, according to her reports, were scattered in under-equipped institutions. American newspapers, for example, regularly cited the French institution Quinze-Vingts as a symbol of institutional degradation. Quinze-Vingts was built in 1260 for soldiers blinded during the Crusades.[60] A 1915 *Providence Journal* article argued that the French blind soldiers should not be at an outdated asylum from the Middle Ages because it is associated "in the minds of the entire French nation . . . with all the real and imagined terrors of blindness." The same report also informed readers that the French Ministry of War was overburdened and gave only cursory support to its disabled veterans by way of a pension and with little in the way of vocational training. The blind French soldier was, therefore, left as a "groping, helpless, aimless creature . . . hemmed in with walls of utter darkness and isolated from all the world."[61]

This is not to say that there did not exist French philanthropic organizations or hospitals meant to aid blind soldiers. Wartime societies for that purpose included, for example, the Société des Amis des Soldats Aveugles, the Association Valentine Haüy, the Foyer du Soldat Aveugles, among others.[62] The Société des Amis des Soldats Aveugles, or the Society for Friends of Blind Soldiers, headed by Rene Valely-Rarot of the Pasteur Institute, organized services for blind soldiers to help "revive [their] broken spirits" and train them for postwar work. Yet these organizations also relied on tragic imagery of disabled soldiers helpless and alone, destined for a lifetime of isolation if not for immediate aid.[63]

Most media reports argued that blind soldiers were too numerous to count, were quite literally lost, alone, and in need of being saved, and those assumptions were crucial to convincing Americans to support humanitarian relief. In response to the perceived pressing need of aiding blind soldiers in Europe, a group of New Yorkers of "national reputation" formed the CMBB in summer 1915. The committee included such figures as New York lawyer Joseph H. Choate, New York State Education Commissioner John Finley, former president William Howard Taft, blind US Senator Thomas Gore of Oklahoma, and the head of the New York Association of the Blind, Winifred Holt. The committee's goal from its inception adopted many of the ableist narratives Holt had used, such as understanding blind people as by nature helpless and hopeless. Additionally, the committee aimed to aid the "sufferers," and then to "cheer them in the despondency that always grips the freshly blinded" while also teaching them trades "as the sightless

Winifred Holt teaching blind French soldiers checkers. (Library of Congress, Prints & Photographs Division, American National Red Cross photograph collection, LC-DIG-anrc-11048)

can learn."[64] But the organization made no clarifying statements to the effect that soldiers' suffering came from a violent war wound and a sudden loss of the sense they had previously relied on as well as the inaccessibility of an ocularcentric world, rather than from a perceived quality inherent to all blind people everywhere.

The CMBB simultaneously perpetuated ableist depictions of blind soldiers and provided valuable training for such soldiers. Winifred Holt and the committee did not abandon wording that assumed blind soldiers to be tragically depressed and hopeless. Such expressions, however, were accompanied by offers of hope at the benevolent hands of the committee and its Lighthouses. The committee was, if nothing else, successful in marshaling the dual messages of tragedy and triumph to American audiences and using those messages—regardless of how harmful they may have been to blind civilians—to garner public donations. Little did they know that they only charted a path that other American organizations, namely the British, French, and Belgian Permanent Blind Relief War Fund, would take to a whole new level.

The British, French, and Belgian Blind Relief War Fund

The British, French, and Belgian Blind Relief War Fund (BRWF) intensified the Committee for Men Blinded in Battle's ableist rhetoric after 1915. The new events of 1916, as suggested by the Hippodrome fundraiser described in the introduction, drew on showmanship and extravagance to the extent that public entertainment seemed to supersede war relief goals. Such events displayed blind soldiers, but in ways that stigmatized blindness far more deleteriously than anything the CMBB disseminated to its supporters. The BRWF also, and perhaps most controversially, made fundraising rather than genuine aid the ultimate goal of the organization, which resulted in scandal about the ways in which it marketed the cause and used its money.

That American war blind relief work to Europe escalated in 1916 is of no surprise because the war's brutality escalated significantly by the summer of that year. Unable to outmaneuver the opposing side on the Western Front, British, French, and German armies settled into defensive trench positions that stretched from the North Sea to the border of Switzerland covering about 1,300 miles.[65] While more conventional battles continued in Eastern Europe, the Middle East, and Africa, soldiers in Western Europe were embroiled in a war of attrition under heavy artillery and machine gun fire, and the war was therefore defined by battles that produced casualties in the hundreds of thousands on either side with little or no territorial changes. At the Battle of Verdun where the German commanders measured victory not necessarily by geographical gain but by how many French soldiers they could slaughter in defense of the fortress region, German and French casualties numbered over 300,000 on both sides in just over nine months.[66] The Battle of the Somme in turn produced a staggering one million casualties in under four months.[67] As battles like Verdun and the Somme became more destructive, the rhetoric of war injury as well as the stakes for American humanitarian organizations such as the British, French, and Belgian Blind Relief War Fund escalated.

American city planner George Kessler and his wife Cora created the BRWF in November 1915 shortly after George survived the sinking of the *Lusitania* and just three months before the Battle of Verdun began. Though their early work was linked to a school and workshop for blind Belgians in 1916, the organization began large-scale fundraising in the United States to support unaffiliated institutions such as England's St. Dunstan's Hostel for Blinded Soldiers and Sailors in London and the Committee for Men Blinded in Battle's Lighthouses in France.[68] As the name suggests, the organization intended to be a "permanent" relief organization, and even had the goal of opening permanent institutions and workshops for soldiers who were blind from their service in the war.

The fact that the BRWF insisted on being a permanent relief organization differentiated the Kessler organization from Holt's Lighthouses, where French soldiers were taught to be as independent as they could before returning home. The goal of establishing a permanent institution—a plan increasingly out of fashion among blind educators by the time World War I started—did not seem to dissuade certain leaders in blind rehabilitation from attaching their names to the BRWF. Sir Arthur Pearson, for example, was a leading member of the BRWF's British committee, and was also the founder of St. Dunstan's Hostel for Blinded Soldiers and Sailors in London. Pearson was a steadfast opponent of confining blind soldiers to permanent institutions or sheltered workshops, which made his support of the fund at least somewhat puzzling. Pearson, as will be shown, played a much larger role in later efforts to rehabilitate American soldiers blind from their service in the war.

Nonetheless, the BRWF benefitted from a number of high-ranking endorsements. Its English committee had support from the king and queen of England, Lord Kitchener, Sir Douglas Haig, Prime Minister Herbert Asquith, Prime Minister David Lloyd George, and writer Sir Arthur Conan Doyle. Its French and Belgian sections claimed membership from French President Raymond Poincare, the dramatist Eugene Brieux, the head physician of the Quinze-Vingts hospital, the king and queen of Belgium, and Princess Clementine of Belgium who was the daughter of the infamous King Leopold II and wife of Victor Napoleon (whose great uncle was none other than Napoleon Bonaparte). And the New York section, which represented the United States, included former Secretary of War Elihu Root, and members of the Du Pont and Vanderbilt families, and, later, Helen Keller.[69] Quite simply, the organization had prestige.

Aside from its prestigious membership of figureheads and leading individuals on the international scene of blind philanthropy, the fund very early on sought to shape American cultural imaginations of European soldiers blinded in battle. In April 1916, American artists contributed sketches and designs of blind soldiers to the organization that were then printed on BRWF literature and collection boxes. The fund wanted the imagery to play on the sympathies of American civilians and, therefore, the imagery pictorialized some of the themes Winifred Holt and others had only written about in 1915. For example, Emil Fuchs's design showed a blind officer "groping his way along with a stick and leaning on a child," representing an extreme form of dependence. The child, Fuchs argued, was in a greater position of authority than the blind man in the image. Thure de Thulstrup's

A section of a poster by H. A. Ogdon for the Blind Relief War Fund. (H. A. Ogden BRWF Poster. Hoover Institution Library & Archives)

drawing showed a young girl leading a blind soldier along a road, with the ruins of a house in the background—presumably a house destroyed by German atrocities. The imagery presented in philanthropy art directly linked the tragedy of civilian suffering in the war with what the fund wanted to convey as the unquestionably tragic nature of blindness that stemmed from a war wound.[70]

The BRWF used Emil Fuchs's design on its official pamphlet for the purposes of educating potential donors. The fund, according to the organization's pamphlet, aimed to show American benevolence to blind soldiers through "generosity" and "sympathy." After viewing Fuchs's drawing of a child caring for a blind soldier, viewers turned the pamphlet over and read in big, bold, bright letters: "THINK OF IT! BLINDED! Never again to see Mother, Father, Wife, Brother, Sister, Sweetheart or Friend. Never again to look upon the beauties of Nature. Never again to see to work, to read, to write. PERMANENTLY BLINDED. Does he deserve our sympathy, our help? Can there be any one who can afford to give, no matter how small, who will not?" The pamphlet explicitly asked viewers to make checks "as large as possible" to help the men "who have suffered the worst calamity that can befall a human being."[71] In its appeal to civilians, the BRWF made no distinction between the real trauma of a war injury that led to blindness, and the existence and lived experiences of blind people more generally.[72] By contrast, it used sensationally large print to evoke tragedy and suffering in blindness as a state of being.

Other artists contributed their imagery to the tapestry of tragedy. F. C. Yohn, for example, drew a blinded soldier on the battlefield, holding his hands toward the air, palms outward, "to express complete helplessness and supplicate Divine aid."[73] Yohn gave a public talk in New York City in May 1916, in which he explained his reasoning behind the drawing. "In conceiving the figure of a soldier, suddenly blinded in battle," he said, "I drew the recently discussed hand . . . because I felt that, in an overpowering human calamity of this kind, there can be only one appeal—the appeal for Divine aid." Yohn recognized that his drawing was not meant to reflect realism. Instead, he tried to depict "an entirely imaginative and idealistic conception. I sought to picture the man, not bodily mangled, but realizing his utter helplessness throughout the rest of his life, unless aid were given."[74] Yohn's explanation of his drawing mirrored Winifred Holt's descriptions of blind soldiers as helpless, dependent, and seeking aid. But what is significant about Yohn's example is that he gives testimony about why he made the decision to depict the blind soldier to evoke sympathy from the American public, and that he emphasized the contingency of the blind soldier's sense of self-worth and happiness.

Interestingly, all the drawings idealized white soldiers with no visible wound to speak of, or with nothing more than a bandage over their eyes, and it did not take long for the fictional blinded white soldier to become reality. The BRWF found their idealized blinded soldier in the figure of British Sergeant Major Robert Middlemiss. Middlemiss was blinded by a grenade explosion at the Battle of Gallipoli in April 1915.[75] He had almost completed his vocational training at St. Dunstan's in London when the BRWF invited him to campaign for them in the United States.[76] The fund made no mistake that Middlemiss was the ideal blind soldier for American audiences because he was white and had no visible signs of war trauma. One Philadelphia newspaper, for example, wrote that he was "one of the most picturesque types in all the vast war relief work. . . . He is typical of the many blinded soldiers of the Allies whose lives would be wrecked but for the present widespread movement to aid them."[77]

Media depictions of Sergeant Major Middlemiss skirted a fine line between depicting him as a tragic figure of dependence worthy of receiving charity, and a dignified and independent white soldier who maintained his masculine identity as a productive and noble head of his household. A November 1916 BRWF event in Worcester, Massachusetts, featured Middlemiss at the city's Poli's Theatre. The local *Worcester Gazette* recalled that Middlemiss "came forward on the arm of his wife. Although a tragic figure, he had a certain dignity of bearing which forbade one's calling him pathetic." Dressed in his military uniform, the article concluded, "he is still a soldier and above all a man."[78] Like the artist's exploitative and infantilizing depictions of blind soldiers being led by children that the fund used for the purposes of raising money, the fund used Middlemiss in a way that embodied tragic sentimentalism. Unlike the artistic renderings, however, Middlemiss was a real person. The fund intended to show that philanthropic aid could make men anew with the assumption that blindness stripped such men of their manhood to begin with, which was evident in other forms of American rehabilitation propaganda.[79] Further, Middlemiss appeared in front of audiences with his wife, symbolizing manhood (re)gained, and therefore the possibility of similar outcomes in other blind men.

For his own part, Middlemiss himself internalized many of the same ableist attitudes American society had assumed about the supposed helplessness of blind individuals.[80] The sergeant major, for example, deflected attention from any physical scars he suffered in war, and instead spoke primarily about the mental anguish of becoming suddenly blind. In one fund speech to a crowd in Waterbury, Connecticut, in October 1916, Middlemiss stated, "For weeks I suffered agony of mind too great for words." He made it clear to the audience that he did not feel much physical pain from his wound at all. "My real suffering" he continued, "came later and was entirely mental. . . . The future looked black and hopeless to me."[81] That Middlemiss's use of the past tense, that the future "looked black and hopeless," assured audiences that their donations would successfully help other men like him.

Sergeant Major Middlemiss's own testimony for the benefit of the BRWF is significant for two reasons. First, he was not the only injured soldier who brought messages of war wounding to American audiences before the official US declaration of war. Historian John Kinder demonstrates how several disabled veterans achieved celebrity status on speaking tours of the United States by discussing the supposed physical and spiritual benefits of war. Canadian disabled vet Private Harold R. Peat, for example, lectured throughout the United States, appeared in a Hollywood film, and wrote a best-selling autobiography. Until the 1930s when he took up the mantle of antiwar sentiment, Peat sought to convince his audiences that his war wounds made him stronger and more manly than he was before the war.[82] Sergeant Major Middlemiss, by contrast, emphasized not the spiritual, physical, and mental rejuvenation of his war wound experience but perpetuated ableist stereotypes of his blindness as debilitating and depressing. Middlemiss and the BRWF assumed the negative aspects of war and blindness to exploit disability for monetary profit.

Middlemiss's testimony on behalf of the BRWF is also significant because it focused almost exclusively on the mental and emotional rather than the physical trauma he experienced. The audience in Waterbury, Connecticut, is left to assume that the young, white soldier had no physical trauma beyond blindness, and that he did not experience physical pain. His body, in fact, was free from physical trauma such as an amputation or a facial disfigurement.[83] Rather than physical pain, Middlemiss's pain was emotional, and stemmed from the psychological shift he experienced after finding out he was blind which, by his own account, seemed to encompass anguish about blindness—feeling that his life was without hope—rather than the violent trauma of a grenade explosion that incapacitated him for months.

Middlemiss's imagery and rhetoric was purposeful. It aligned precisely with F. C. Yohn's drawing of the young, white blinded soldier who had no obvious physical scars and who was emotionally distraught in order to provoke sympathy and generate donations. The BRWF intended to show that the tragedy of Yohn's blinded soldier, like Middlemiss, was rooted in the reality of a body free from trauma and able to compete in the social and economic forces of modern life, but without the use of sight, which according to predominant attitudes about blindness in the early twentieth century and the lack of accessibility in public spaces would have disqualified him from such autonomy. Middlemiss's anguish was caused, therefore, by the sudden acknowledgment of his blindness rooted in culturally entrenched, yet socially constructed ableist views about blind people's dependency, as much as it was by his very real yet unacknowledged physical trauma. The BRWF, therefore, understood that audiences were more apt to react sympathetically to the former rather than the latter.

The BRWF's collaboration with Sergeant Major Middlemiss was part of an extravagant nationwide fundraising effort that included events such as the Allied Bazaar. New York City's Allied Bazaar took place over the course of eleven days beginning on June 3, 1916, at the Grand Central Palace. Its purpose was to benefit blind, starving, and homeless people in Allied countries, and it included exhibits of war materials taken from the Western Front, such as an airplane, shrapnel shells, bullets, gas shells, and models of French artillery guns.[84] Visitors at the art booth purchased paintings and etchings from such artists as John Singer Sargent, Walter Perry, and George Elmer Brown. The philanthropically inclined visitors bid on prized items and experiences such as cars, boats, gold watches, war relics, and round-trip tickets to Bermuda.[85] The bazaar became, quite simply, the singular event in New York City during the summer of 1916.[86]

For all intents and purposes, the bazaar seemed to have only a cursory or superficial relation to war relief, and instead operated in a carnival atmosphere that promoted its entertainment value to visitors. The existence of war relics, for example, bordered on battle voyeurism. Onlookers saw over five thousand war relics including German helmets mangled by bullets,

Vaudeville performers the Dolly Sisters—Rosika and Jansci—selling tickets at the Allied Bazaar Ticket Day in New York City, June 1, 1916, amid a crowd of onlookers. (Library of Congress, Prints & Photographs Division, reproduction number LC-DIG-ggbain-21842)

and an American ambulance complete with a "bloodstained stretcher" that "told of the splendid work that one [American] gift had done in helping the wounded."[87] In the latter example, there was no mention of the wounded or deceased soldier who spattered the blood over the stretcher in his moments of anguish, or whether the individual survived the ordeal. The event also marked specific days for certain nationalities and ethnicities, where items and people were put on full display for entertainment value. On Serbian Day, for example, Serbian refugees, "pretty girls," assisted at the booth of the Serbian Relief Committee.[88]

Blind soldiers figured prominently in the Allied Bazaar. BRWF occupied six booths and a tea garden at the bazaar, where Sergeant Major Middlemiss made daily appeals for blind soldiers, over five hundred "society women and debutantes" offered their services, and famous actors, actresses, and singers volunteered.[89] From the tea garden, Helen Keller also appealed to the sympathies of the crowd to help the young men with their hopes "maimed." Keller's appeal seemed particularly urgent, for without support they would "stand at street corners begging [for] their bread. They [would] stumble through life, guided by a dog or a little child."[90] The BRWF, therefore, differed little from the other fundraising appeals constructed as extravagant displays of disability and dramatic calls for worthy charity and assistance. And in her appearance at the tea garden, Hellen Keller, like Robert Middlemiss, seemed to pay homage to the images that artists such as Yohn and Thulstrup made available for fund use.

The Allied Bazaar was by no means the end, nor even the apex of fundraising efforts on behalf of the BRWF. In mid-1916, the fund organized a mail campaign, sending an appeal to 120,000 influential Americans throughout the United States to aid blind soldiers. The literature emphasized the fund's goal of supporting Arthur Pearson's St. Dunstan's and Holt's Lighthouse in Paris, and read in part, "Self-respecting, able-bodied, passing daily through a living death, these thousands of blinded war victims are being slowly killed, not by their injuries, not by starvation, but by the apparently permanent hopelessness of their situation."[91] The materials assumed that blind soldiers, like the men pictured in the fund's artistic drawings, were able-bodied after their wounds, or that able-body—rather, nondisabled—was the ideal body type of blind soldiers for the sake of emotional appeal and fundraising. The materials also suggested that the depressing nature of their wound stemmed from the assumption that their blindness restricted them from using their able bodies to their fullest potential. The organization, therefore, positioned blindness as wasting the youth of the men. Such a fate, the BRWF argued, was a daily, slow, and agonizing death.

The BRWF also made it clear to those on the receiving end of its mailing campaign that the agony also extended to the soldiers' families. A circular the fund sent to 65,000 middle- and upper-class women throughout the United States and Canada claimed that "Unless you act [donate] . . . these thousands of women" who depend on the blind soldiers "will be condemned, for the rest of their lives, to an existence of hopeless drudgery and hardship . . . despair and crushing slavery."[92] If blindness did not mean drudgery and hopelessness for the soldier himself, the fund's materials suggested, it was surely going to spell doom for the family members who relied on the soldier.

The BRWF also coordinated with the Federal Council of the Churches of Christ in America to disseminate its stigmatizing messages that assumed blind people's dependency. The council sent an appeal to its affiliated churches and around one hundred thousand clergymen seeking contributions to benefit blind soldiers that read, "The B.F.B. Blind Fund writes that 25,000 are blinded and that at the rate this continues hundreds of thousands will require permanent care, although some of them are taking their own lives." The council suggested to its affiliates that they should make special appeals during Sunday church services after giving presentations of the fund's mission.[93] The fund-clergy partnership suggests that the relief organization went to great lengths to maintain its status as the preeminent war relief organization by appealing to many strands of American society. And such appeals to religious institutions differed little from other fund literature in that it portrayed blindness as an unimaginable fate and a burden, with blindness—rather than physical trauma—being the primary cause of emotional suffering that required divine aid.

Additionally, the appeal to the Federal Council makes no attempt to convey an accurate presentation of the real numbers of men who were blind as a result of the war. Winifred Holt had previously inflated the numbers of blind soldiers in the war zone in 1915, though her estimates were elevated by the hundreds. The fund regularly inflated numbers even further, presumably for the sake of urgency. The combined total of British, French, American, and German soldiers permanently blind from their service in World War I barely exceeded 13,000.[94] This is a far smaller number than the 50,000 that the fund's Philadelphia chapter stated that it needed to provide aid for in its appeal to the public in October 1916, just two years into the war.[95]

The BRWF gave very little aid to actual blind soldiers proportionate to the fundraising levels it sustained by the end of 1916 when it became the subject of scrutiny. One citizen of Worcester, Massachusetts, was skeptical about the organization when he wrote to his local newspaper, the *Worcester News,* that through the organization the "English government is begging money" and that "the flock of gullibles" in Worcester was tricked into contributing "close to $2,000" in one week through the "begging expedition" and the "begging tour." "The poverty story," the writer continued, "hinges on a blind soldier, Sergt.-Major Robert Middlemiss." The anonymous writer challenged a seemingly credulous and ableist organization by critiquing the fund's ableist stories it told for monetary gain with equally ableist characterizations of Middlemiss as a blind beggar and suggesting Middlemiss's continued dependence despite his rehabilitation.[96] The writer then called into question the fund's fiscal responsibility in light of the reality that Middlemiss was on track to send 150,000 circulars in one batch, all of which cost money to print and mail. The writer estimated that the total cost for mailing the one group of circulars could have easily been around $6,000.[97]

The writer was not entirely wrong by pointing out that something was awry. By the BRWF's own account, it had raised over $250,000 by the end of 1916, which had been sitting in "various banking institutions" collecting interest. This lack of urgency in sending money to aid blind soldiers was a far cry from the fund's own urgent appeals to public charity. The fact that the organization hoped to build permanent institutions partially accounted for the reason why it had not spent its money on soldiers by the end of 1916. The organization by that time had, however, spent over $81,000 on operating expenses, likely due to the many extravagant fundraising events and public talks in which they paid for travel and hotel rooms for Middlemiss, as well as materials to mail to potential donors. The fund's founders, George and Cora Kessler, contributed $50,000 of their own money toward that total, meaning that almost half of their operating expenses were taken from donations, despite the fund's insistence that every penny went to the soldiers.[98]

The anonymous writer to the *Worcester News* was not the only person turned off by the exploitative nature of the organization's fundraising tactics. The BRWF coordinated with local businesses in a number of American cities within which they placed collection boxes. Banks and stores in cities such as Utica, New York, Philadelphia, and Bangor, Maine, used the boxes to appeal to their customers to "please 'do your bit'" by donating to blind soldiers.[99] Such boxes were ridiculed. One writer mocked a box displayed at Merchants National Bank in Worcester, Massachusetts. The bank placed the box where it would attract the most attention, and "emblazoned" it with "the American flag and a soldier apparently stricken blind, ready to fall." The display, the writer argued, was misleading because the red, white, and blue display led visitors to believe that it was raising money for blind Americans. "A box with a slot in the cover," the writer concluded, "is placed ingratiatingly close to the clever arranged sign and the gullibles are expected to drop coins in 'for the benefit of our blind soldiers.'"[100]

The BRWF also came under scrutiny for other ways it seemingly misled the public. The fund regularly used films to encourage audiences to donate. Such films typically followed impassioned speeches by the Kesslers, and almost always involved a speech from Sergeant Major Middlemiss. The films showed soldiers being blinded in battle and then "taught" to care for themselves, it showed them in vocational training, and then finally returning to their families.[101] The CMBB had given the BRWF permission to film the work that Winifred Holt undertook at the Lighthouse in Paris, after the fund promised to use some of its own donations to support the CMBB's work. But according to the CMBB's president Joseph H. Choate, the BRWF frequently used such films in their fundraising events without giving any money to the organization. Additionally, because of how vague some of the fund's appeals for donations were, Choate argued that he had "frequently heard . . . that persons had sent contributions to the B.F.B. Fund, believing that they were giving" to the CMBB.[102]

By the end of 1916, the CMBB increasingly distanced itself from the BRWF. One way it did so was by distinguishing that the Lighthouses in

France were "spending money to-day" for blind soldiers, which was a clear jab at the fund that had not spent its donors' money on anything but events and mailings. The committee also made clear that they had no intention of setting up permanent institutions, unlike the fund. Indeed, Choate wittingly argued, "We do not believe in shutting the blind men in institutions. . . . We believe in restoring them to their homes, their friends and, so far as possible, their old trades."[103]

Clear differences aside, the BRWF did little to extend meaningful aid to blind soldiers until after the CMBB had discredited some of their practices. In the fund's executive committee meeting in March 1917, the organization noted that it had donated a little over $100,000 to blind relief efforts in France. Around $80,000 went to creating a section to oversee relief work in France. The rest was distributed to French blind relief organizations already in existence, such as the Société des Amis des Soldats Aveugles. The fund also sent 10,000 British pounds to Sir Arthur Pearson for his work at St. Dunstan's. Neither number comes close to the almost half a million dollars the organization had raised by March 1917. And by 1917, the clouds of war seemed to be drifting toward the United States, which convinced the organization to change its name to the American, British, French, and Belgian Permanent Blind Relief War Fund with the goal of eventually aiding newly blind American soldiers. The fund, though, maintained its stance that it wanted to create permanent institutions.[104]

French Soldiers' Experiences

The Committee for Men Blinded in Battle (CMBB) and the Blind Relief War Fund (BRWF) suggested to audiences that blind soldiers in France lived at the Quinze-Vingts institution in the throes of depression and hopelessness—on the verge of suicide even—with little in the way of vocational training or recreation. The CMBB's seemingly catastrophic messaging served the purpose of soliciting donations, for without American money, as the organization's literature suggested, such men would be unable to live fulfilling lives. Yet neither the committee's nor the fund's depictions of blind French soldiers can be considered completely accurate when compared to the men's actual lived experiences.

American reports, especially the ones about Quinze-Vingts, did not necessarily reflect the full reality of blind soldiers themselves. Only sporadic media coverage gives some indication about how the men there actually lived. One article in the *Worcester Post* in Massachusetts, for example, claimed that men were better off at Quinze-Vingts than at home because the culture of the institution and the influence of being with comrades was less depressing than elsewhere. The same article referenced the fact that an Associated Press reporter visited the institution, where French Minister of the Interior Louis-Jean Malvy questioned some of the men whose "laughter was interrupted" by their introductions with the reporter. "One of the youngest of the blind men, a soldier from the Vosges, was here and he was the gayest. His affliction he bore lightly and smilingly" and "declared it to be a 'souvenir of the Germans.'" The atmosphere was so bright, the reporter noted, that some blind soldiers who had returned home asked to come back "where they felt the surroundings more cheerful and agreeable."[105] That this account comes from an American reporter rather than a French reporter suggests that the relatively cheery account was not necessarily meant for propagandistic purposes for French civilians that may have in some way tried to justify the human costs of the war. Even if the account was slightly manufactured, it contradicted what Americans heard from Winifred Holt and the Kesslers.

Pictorial evidence also suggests that the conditions at Quinze-Vingts, and the soldiers' dispositions, may have been less deleterious than contemporary media depictions hinted at. The National Library of France's collection of photographs of blind French soldiers at Quinze-Vingts shows the young men engaged in numerous activities such as training in massage and brush making, which sighted people commonly thought of as blind trades. There are also numerous images that depict more mundane scenes of life at the hospital, such as the men laughing together while sitting on a park bench smoking cigarettes.[106] The evidence of soldiers who sought to return to Quinze-Vingts after being home for a short time, alongside images such as the one included here, suggest that blind French soldiers did not necessarily live such cloistered and depressing lives, but benefitted from the congeniality and comradeship experienced in a place with other soldiers who had similar experiences as them and, therefore, treated them with dignity.[107]

The CMBB either overlooked or ignored these experiences in the service of more compelling imagery for the purposes of funding their new institutions in France, which the organization argued was of dire need to the blind men. The first of the committee's Lighthouses in France was the Phare de Bordeaux, which opened in June 1915. The Phare de Bordeaux was situated in an old chateau adorned with a statue of Jeanne d'Arc, whom the blind soldiers claimed as their patron saint who would lead them through "their battle in the dark to victory and light."[108] The committee also established Lighthouses in Sévres, Vichy, and Paris, the last of which opened in Pope Benedict XV's residence in 1916 with a visit from French President Poincaré and other dignitaries.[109]

Six blind French soldiers sitting on a bench in a park smoking cigarettes. (Bibliothèque nationale de France)

The CMBB's Lighthouses in France marked a distinct change in how American media described blind soldiers, namely that reports attached redemptive stories to the oft-repeated tales of depressed and hopeless blind French soldiers. One Sergeant G, for example, was among the first soldiers at the Phare de France in Paris, and was, according to Holt, "so weak, so hopeless." But after learning braille and a vocation, he found "light through work." Osmin Lagarde also found "light through work." He was blinded in battle in Belgium in 1914, and later trained at one of the Lighthouses in France. In a letter to Holt, he explained that he was "glowing" with "beams of light" because of the work he accomplished.[110]

These stories, and many others like them, served the particular purpose of showing the American public what American dollars could do if channeled through the CMBB. Winifred Holt frequently contributed her own triumphant stories to American newspapers showing before, during, and after tales of blind soldiers who were once hopeless but who, through Holt's aid, (re)gained their manhood and confidence by finding "light through work." Because institutional records do not exist for the Lighthouses in France we do not know if the soldier stories were fictionalized. Holt, though, certainly knew her audience, as she crafted redemption stories to cater to the sensibilities of predominantly middle- and upper-class white Americans.

Some stories demonstrate the particular ways Holt tried to appeal to that segment of the American population, while they also gave some indication of the experiences at the French Lighthouses. For the former, stories meant to highlight the CMBB's work as an appeal for funding from the general public centered on certain soldiers for particular reasons, because they would have resonated with the audience to which Holt wished to speak. For the latter, the records of Elizabeth Parrish Jackson, who was a nurse at the Lighthouse in Bordeaux, include both writing exercises with and letters from blind French soldiers who formed close connections with the young nurse. Taken together, both sets of sources give a more nuanced understanding about the lived experiences at the Lighthouses than what one might get by simply taking the newspaper articles at face value.

Winifred Holt and the CMBB intended to appeal to predominantly white, upper-class Americans who would have sympathized with young, white men blinded in the war—men who could have conceivably been the readers' sons or husbands. While describing her early activities to the committee, for example, Holt cited the existence of a "Blonde Swede" who was "very handsome" and who was blinded, though "without disfiguring him." Instead, the wound "merely closed his eyes for all time, giving an almost Madonna-like appearance to the closed lids."[111] Through her descriptions, Holt sought to lend urgency to her work while also assuaging fears about the traumatic facial wounds that seemed to appear frequently in accounts of soldiers wounded during World War I. Most of Holt's examples were decidedly not about lower-class French soldiers. "We accept here," she noted, "only soldiers of superior intelligence and of sufficient education to profit by the opportunities we offer." She, thus, relayed to upper-class white Americans stories about middle- to upper-class white French soldiers who would benefit from their aid.[112]

Almost all the blind soldiers that Holt highlighted for American audiences about the Lighthouses were about white men, with two exceptions. Holt published an article in *The Survey* in October 1916 about the grand opening of the Paris Phare de France. The story included a large photograph of a group of blind French officers, including a Black soldier standing with Holt, holding the official seal of the French Lighthouse. The article, though, does not give American audiences any further information about his vocational or postwar experiences, even though he stands in the center of the group.[113] Holt's detour around the Black soldier suggests that she understood that white donors were more apt to donate with the understanding that the money went primarily to white soldiers.

The other example of a Black soldier displayed in press materials for the Lighthouse in Paris included Private Gene. Gene was originally from the southern United States and had been living and working in England in 1914 as a boxer when war broke out. He joined the French army and was blinded in battle. Gene was, according to Will Irwin of the *Saturday Evening Post*, "a great, young black Hercules, a monument of trained muscle."[114] Such rhetoric was not too dissimilar from American wartime discussions that drew on the science of anthropometry to evaluate African Americans' health, body shape, and fitness during the wartime draft.[115] The article, though, differentiated Private Gene from Black Americans in the United States. Gene, for example, "wasn't at all the negro we know at home." Instead, Irwin continued, "War and heroism had given him that air of authority common to all soldiers. . . . He looked you in the eye and answered you straight. . . . The democracy of the French Army had brushed off onto him."[116] Irwin was careful not to upset American racial hierarchies in that he affirmed Gene's heroism was at least in part a byproduct of his association with French military culture, and not his American origins. Aside from the sparse references in newspaper articles, though, most blind French soldiers that appeared in committee-related articles featured white French men of moderate to high social and class status.

Sparse as they may be, records from blind soldiers at the Lighthouse give indications about the men's own experiences. Some sources suggest vibrant and empowering lives, despite the infantilizing and ableist rhetoric of the sighted journalists. Louis C. Cohn of Brooklyn, for example, went to the Lighthouse in Paris in 1916 to establish a braille printing press, through which blind soldiers printed a magazine called *La Lumiere*.[117] No copies of *La Lumiere* have been found, however, and the newspaper reports about the printing endeavor were characteristic of journalistic coverage of blind soldiers in that they were more often about the people providing support services rather than blind soldiers themselves. For example, the *Brooklyn Daily Eagle*, writing about Cohn's experiences in France, referred to blind French soldier Janson de Sailly as one of Cohn's "special pets."[118] Accordingly, one learns far more about Cohn than about the magazine or its creators.

Blind French soldiers also claimed their own stories of rehabilitation through writing. Elizabeth Parrish Jackson worked at the Lighthouses in Bordeaux and Paris and formed collegial friendships with blind French soldiers that lasted beyond her time there. One soldier, "P. Cacheux," wrote to Jackson in 1917 about the regular work he was doing as well as his positive feelings toward his former teacher. He wrote to Jackson: "My life is always the same here. I worck [*sic*] again and again. . . . We have an other [*sic*] lady teatcher [*sic*]; shee [*sic*] is an English one who speak well whith [*sic*] a rather good accent. She is a professional one who seem know her affair. But . . . I cant forget you [*sic*] amiability, self-devotion and our good lessons."[119] A soldier named "Languedoc" also had a cordial relationship with Jackson. "I am very well," he wrote to his former instructor, "and my eye continues to improve very slowly; it never stop [*sic*], but hard sun is bad for it. I am seeing better when it is dark weather, and I am glad thinking that autumn comes quickly."[120] As the letters to Elizabeth Parrish Jackson suggest, blind soldiers at the Lighthouses in many cases had positive experiences with instructors and kept them updated on their vocational progress as well as their personal health even after they parted ways. In Languedoc's case, one can also understand how vision loss was not an absolute category, but instead fluctuated in degree, which Holt's own testimonies to American newspapers do not ever suggest.

An anonymous student essay meant to serve as his English practice lesson, which took the form of a letter written to "My Dear ind [*sic*] Great Friend Tommy," indicates that not all soldiers had amicable relationships with their teachers. The soldier acknowledged the dangers British soldiers faced in the war, including "Your front on the battle-fields . . . the balls and shells," but he argued, "It is more terrible for me . . . I must pass under the angry looking of my English teacher when I don't made the 'some sentences' which she asks every lesson. . . . I have so much other things to do that I can not being a job every time. But . . . is furious when I come with my empty hands."[121] The soldier's letter speaks to the reality that nondisabled societies placed significant pressure on wounded soldiers more generally, and blind soldiers more specifically, to effectively train and become socially and economically independent, regardless of the soldier's immediate health circumstances. The letter also suggests that no amount of benevolent newspaper coverage led by Winifred Holt and the CMBB could change the fact that some men at the Lighthouse felt the sting of impatience from some of their instructors.

The CMBB simultaneously relied on ableist depictions of blind soldiers and provided valuable training for such soldiers. Holt and the committee did not abandon wording that assumed blind soldiers to be tragically depressed and hopeless. Such expressions, however, were accompanied by offers of hope at the benevolent hands of the committee and its Lighthouses. The committee was, if nothing else, successful in marshalling the dual messages of tragedy and triumph to American audiences and using those messages—regardless of how harmful they may have been to blind people everywhere—to accept public donations. Combined with the harmful messaging used by the Blind Relief War Fund, the organizations shaped cultural representations of blindness and blind people that persisted well beyond 1917.

Conclusion

Most Americans interacted with World War I on the periphery before 1917, and war relief organizations provided a way for groups of Americans to feel like they were a part of the world-altering event without being truly involved in it by way of state-sponsored violence. That World War I shaped discussions about blindness was evidenced by the fundraising events of American relief organizations such as the Committee for Men Blinded in Battle and the British, French, and Belgian Permanent Blind Relief War Fund. The events provided entertainment value to civilians at the expense of infantilizing blind soldiers who were recovering from traumatic wounds.

Much of what we know about American philanthropy and blind rehabilitation before 1917 comes from media reports and organizational literature. Sparse evidence exists from soldiers' own testimonies, which provide nuance, but these testimonies are often overshadowed by the larger cultural constructions dominated by the Committee for Men Blinded in Battle and the Blind Relief War Fund. The ableist depictions of blind soldiers that such organizations used for the purpose of fundraising caused damage culturally just as the bullets, shells, and diseases caused damage physically. The latter was physical damage that deprived the soldier of his sight. The former was cultural damage that sighted society and blind soldiers alike internalized, which deprived the soldier of compassionate and unwavering support and ignored the inaccessibility of ableist expectations. Ultimately, by presenting dependency and pity as the natural state of blind people rather than something that was socially and culturally constructed, the Committee for Men Blinded in Battle and the Blind Relief War Fund put the issues that came about with blind soldiers—inaccessibility, lack of opportunity, depression and anxiety, stigma, idleness, socioeconomic vulnerability—on the individual, thus absolving society from questioning its role in creating those circumstances.

Both the Committee for Men Blinded in Battle and the American, British, French, and Belgian Blind Relief War Fund jockeyed to position themselves to provide services for blind American soldiers once the United States entered the war. But despite all the campaigning and fundraising, American policymakers looked elsewhere for a model through which to base their rehabilitation efforts. Sir Arthur Pearson—and his militant sense of independence regarding living as a blind person that shaped St. Dunstan's Hostel for Blinded Soldiers and Sailors—influenced the ways American policymakers constructed rehabilitation for blind soldiers, and how those same soldiers experienced rehabilitation in the wake of the harmful fundraising cultures of 1915 and 1916. Discussions about tragedy, dependence, charity, and philanthropy, nonetheless, persisted in the public discourse.

2

"I'll Get Along"

Reporters Reimagine Blind American Soldiers

On Friday, February 8, 1919, a *New York Herald* reporter boarded the medical transport ship *Saxonia* that carried over one thousand disabled American soldiers who were returning from Europe three months after the signing of the Armistice ending World War I. The reporter passed through the crowds of wounded to interview the thirteen blind soldiers on board. The thirteen men included a Black soldier, Major Nelson Hawkins of the 307th Infantry, who was blind in both eyes from a wound he received in the opening weeks of the decisive American engagement, the Meuse-Argonne Offensive. Hawkins's comrade, Corporal Henry Bitter, lost his sight and both of his hands from a grenade explosion. William Whalen of Brooklyn was blinded by an artillery shell in the Argonne Forest. Private Ewald Wegner of Wisconsin lost sight in both eyes from a battle wound and had secured a glass eye "for appearances" while he recovered in France. The blind American soldiers on the *Saxonia* seemed surprisingly jovial to the *New York Herald* reporter. Corporal Bitter was still getting used to life without his eyesight and his hands and joked that he could not wave back to the crowds of civilians who came out to New York Harbor to greet the soldiers upon their arrival to the United States. Another blind soldier said to him, "Well, you can shake a foot, can't you!" Bitter laughed and kicked the side of the ship in place of a hand wave. The other blind soldiers teased Ewald Wegner about his prosthetic, insisting "that he tell them what he saw 'through his one glass eye.'" Wegner joked back. On the voyage, he "continually pointed out imaginary things" to his blind comrades, including "phantom ships, icebergs, and a Hun raider."[1]

Except for a passing remark made by the *New York Herald* reporter that the men were "pathetic sufferers" because they could not see the picturesque ocean trip home, the tone the newspaper struck about the blind men was remarkably different from stories American newspapers had published before US entry into World War I. Despite American philanthropic organizations' ableist pronouncements about blind French soldiers before 1917, when blind American soldiers returned from Europe national conversations shifted to a decidedly positive tone. William Whalen, for example, had "no complaint to voice," and quipped to a *Brooklyn Times* reporter who also seemed eager to interview the blind soldiers on the *Saxonia,* "I'll get along."[2] Rather than depict sad or hopeless blind men, American media presented the men as independent, ambitious, happy, and hard working.

First introduced by sporadic newspaper and magazine articles such as the *New York Herald*'s piece that opened this chapter, other American media outlets latched onto the image of the blind soldier as a motivator. Some of the first Americans blind from their service in the war, for example, were featured in the US Surgeon General's official magazine *Carry On: A Magazine on the Reconstruction of Disabled Soldiers and Sailors. Carry On* chronicled wounded, disabled, and sick American soldiers through their rehabilitation in American hospitals, including Army General Hospital No. 7, or "Evergreen," in Baltimore, Maryland.[3] Fiction and nonfiction accounts about blind soldiers also appeared in popular magazines such as *Harper's Monthly, Ladies' Home Journal,* and *Collier's.* The literature in *Carry On* and other magazines preceded a yet more significant media project called the *Evergreen Review*, which chronicled the work of the Red Cross Institute for the Blind, which took over Evergreen after the US Army closed General Hospital No. 7 in late 1919.

Taken together the journals, newspapers, and magazines that featured blind American soldiers after 1917 aimed to rewrite assumptions about blind soldiers that earlier stories about French soldiers conveyed. This rewriting claimed that, like their French counterparts, the American soldiers were almost exclusively blinded by artillery or bullets in battle, despite institutional records that noted otherwise. Unlike their French counterparts, however, these depictions chronicled American soldiers who were not too mentally or physically traumatized to lose out on the benefits of physical reconstruction and vocational rehabilitation. Instead of being hopeless and depressed or condemned to a life of suffering, the stories suggested, blind Americans were competent, independent, and happy. Such stories were defined by the needs of the postwar rehabilitation state rather than the thoughts and feelings of the blind soldiers themselves. And though the messages about US soldiers differed from the ones that Americans printed about French soldiers, the authors of both narratives depended on a similar ableist notion of blindness as an almost insurmountable impairment in order to celebrate the successes—or potential successes—of their subjects.

The Myths and Realities of *Carry On*'s Blind Heroes

The first blind American soldiers to return home provided the US government and media an opportunity to reeducate the public about blindness and to inform them about rehabilitation's promises to make such men economically self-sufficient and happy. Rehabilitation officials, as the historian Beth Linker demonstrates, used positive propaganda images and stories in such publications as *Carry On* to make disability appear to be a temporary setback that government rehabilitation could ultimately fix.[4] Whereas the hundreds of thousands of disabled American soldiers may have seemed too abstract a number for the average reader to cope with, individual blind soldiers provided fewer, and therefore easier, examples to track that had the potential to display rehabilitation's successes.

The shift in public American conversations about blind soldiers evidenced in *Carry On* happened within the context of changing demands of the US wartime state. Woodrow Wilson's administration facilitated, coerced, and manufactured the patriotic commitment necessary for a sometimes divided nation to wage a world war. On April 13, 1917—less than a week removed from US entry into the war—the Wilson administration tasked muckraker journalist George Creel to coordinate the federal government's propaganda through the Committee on Public Information, creating publicly sanctioned channels of information in support of the war.[5] Two months later, Congress passed the Espionage Act, providing the federal government with unprecedented authority to suppress antiwar sentiment through hefty fines and imprisonment.[6] The Espionage Act found a powerful ally in US Attorney General Thomas W. Gregory, who vigorously enforced the legislation by cracking down on dissent.[7] Given that the federal government criminalized dissent and shaped public opinion to enforce support for the war, it is of little surprise that *Carry On* shifted conversations so as to not undermine the US war effort through emotionally charged stories about depressed blind soldiers apparently condemned to a life of misery.

Carry On was edited and published by the US Army Surgeon General and the American Red Cross between June 1918 and July 1919—the formative period of American rehabilitation. The publication featured motivational articles by American rehabilitation leaders such as Douglas McMurtrie, the director of the Red Cross Institute for Crippled and Disabled Men, and military leaders such as Colonel Frank Billings, as well as stories about disabled soldiers who had "carried on" and had therefore successfully "overcome" their disability or disabilities by becoming medically healed and economically self-sufficient. The magazine included stories about amputees, psychologically traumatized soldiers, blind, deaf, and tubercular soldiers meant to inspire both the public and other disabled or sick veterans. Postwar literature such as *Carry On* ultimately aimed to convince disabled soldiers and the American public that vocational rehabilitation and hospital-based reconstruction was a worthy investment.

World War I–era rehabilitation was a system in stark contrast to the nineteenth-century pensions and assistance from soldiers' institutions that veterans of the American Civil War received.[8] American progressives targeted Civil War–era pensions as another form of inefficiency in modern industrial life in need of reform.[9] Civil War pensions, which took care of wounded soldiers at public expense with no expectation of rehabilitation, ballooned in size by the turn of the century. Progressives during World War I advocated for medical care and vocational training rehabilitation to potentially reduce or erase cash payments for veterans, motivated by a belief that the government should "rebuild" disabled veterans so that they could produce wealth and contribute to society.[10] Responsibility for veterans moved from the Pension Bureau to the War Risk Insurance Bureau (WRIB), which was primarily responsible for loss or damage to US ships during the war. The bureau provided allotments to dependents in exchange for a contribution from their wages, while the government provided disability insurance at subsidized rates.[11] While the WRIB based disability compensation on how impairments reduced a veterans' capacity for wage labor, the Federal Board for Vocational Education oversaw vocational training with the aim of producing economically self-sufficient wage earners.[12]

First World War rehabilitation was ultimately driven by a belief in modern medicine, an optimism about "curing" disability, and a fear of creating a generation of unproductive young male veterans. It was also a system defined by a belief that male veterans could and should take up their roles as male breadwinners of families.[13] As an official US Army Surgeon General publication, then, *Carry On* disseminated important state-sanctioned information to American readers about a new and potentially positive direction in veterans' benefits by highlighting redemptive stories about soldiers who benefited from rehabilitation and took up positions as productive heads of households.

Carry On was one of the first media outlets that included stories about blind American soldiers. William Zimmerman was the first blind American soldier to return from the war in Europe. Zimmerman joined the US Army in 1910 and served in the Philippines and then took part in the Pancho Villa expedition in New Mexico before serving in France during World War I. In November 1917, while transporting munitions near the Western Front, Zimmerman's truck skidded and turned over, pinning him underneath, fracturing bones and hemorrhaging his optic nerves, resulting in blindness in both eyes.[14] In May 1918, Zimmerman was the first American soldier to enter US Army General Hospital No. 7, or Evergreen—the singular US government rehabilitation hospital for blind soldiers—where he took courses in braille, became a massage therapist, and then worked at Fort McHenry where he provided massage therapy to other wounded soldiers. *Carry On* noted that Zimmerman was motivated to pursue a successful career because he needed to provide for his girlfriend. "You see," he said during his vocational training in 1918, "I have got to get a job now, because they sent for my girl to come . . . here [to Baltimore] to see me and she said, 'Bill, if you make good I am going to marry you.' Well, blindness is a handicap of course but it's not going to stop me."[15]

Carry On was not alone in finding William Zimmerman compelling. Between 1918 and 1921 the Harris & Ewing Photography company traveled from Washington, DC, and took a series of photographs at Evergreen to chronicle the blind soldiers in their training. The photographs from 1918 repeatedly focused on Zimmerman. One image showed Zimmerman smiling as he stood beside either a family member or a visitor to the institute. In another photograph, Zimmerman stood in the center of a small group of blind soldiers and two women reconstruction aides. Zimmerman was also photographed walking with his cane independently around the perimeter of Evergreen. Whether the photographers focused on Zimmerman more than other soldiers because of their own interest in him, or because the hospital staff purposefully emphasized him to convey a clear message of blind soldier independence is unclear. What is clear is that Harris & Ewing Photography, like the editors of *Carry On,* thought Zimmerman was a compelling image of postwar rehabilitation success that differed markedly from the narratives Americans heard about French blind soldiers before 1917.

William Zimmerman's story in *Carry On* is significant not only because he was the first blind American soldier to enter rehabilitation and to gain widespread attention, but also because he embodied the erroneous American assumption that blind soldiers remained physically unscarred. The British, French, and Belgian Permanent Blind Relief War Fund's fundraising events had included artwork from artists such as F. C. Yohn that emphasized similar themes of bodily wholeness, which was part of the reason why Sergeant-Major Robert Middlemiss—who was blinded at the Battle of Gallipoli by a grenade explosion but had no visible disfigurement—was so compelling to American audiences. Zimmerman, like Middlemiss, brought the image of the blind veteran home to American civilians in a way that mediated sensory loss with aesthetic appeal.

Carry On's coverage of Zimmerman also suggested that most, if not all, blind soldiers lost their sight due to a wound received in battle. Physical

William Zimmerman walks confidently with a cane around the perimeter of Evergreen in front of a stone wall. (Library of Congress, Prints & Photographs Division, photograph by Harris & Ewing, LC-DIG-hec-11701)

trauma was surely the most common reason for blindness, as fragments from shell explosions or bullets regularly tore through the soldiers' eyes along with other parts of the head, causing partial or total blindness along with deafness, loss of taste or smell, and extreme psychological distress. Though some of the early cases may have been caused by explosions, they were not all received during battle. Corporal Henry Bitter, who appeared on the *Saxonia,* was blinded and lost both of his hands when a grenade accidentally exploded in front of him as he was training new American recruits behind the front.[16]

Numerous blind American soldiers who arrived at Evergreen in the early months of its existence lost their sight from illness. Some became partially or totally blind from illnesses such as conjunctivitis—inflammation of the eye.[17] Private Charles Burnett became blind after contracting typhoid-pneumonia. Frank Pyle's blindness came after he contracted cerebro-spinal meningitis.[18] Sylvester Boston, a Black soldier from Virginia, lost his sight in November 1918 from glaucoma.[19] Ultimately, three soldiers at Evergreen were blind after bouts of meningitis, and one was blind after contracting gonorrheal ophthalmia.[20] Despite newspaper articles that placed Corporal

The main building at US Army General Hospital No. 7—Evergreen. (Library of Congress, Prints & Photographs Division, American National Red Cross photograph collection, LC-DIG-anrc-02464)

Otis Speed in the category of "wounded," his eyesight had actually weakened gradually during the war until the army classified him as blind.[21] According to an Evergreen ophthalmologist, at least six soldiers were blind from toxic amblyopia, or wood alcohol poisoning.[22] Such numbers suggest wider variations of causes for blindness than *Carry On* and newspaper stories about combat blindness—being war blinded—suggest.

Additionally, blindness was not an absolute category where one's vision was unchanged or where one was either completely blind or completely sighted. Soldiers were completely blind, partially blind, or somewhere in between. Sometimes a soldier found that his sight had improved somewhat through rehabilitation, but more often such men found that their sight deteriorated as the months progressed. This left many men in an emotionally and physically precarious situation. The ambiguities of blindness and the realities that many blind soldiers were not, in fact, blinded soldiers—a phrase which conveyed the notion that they were blinded in combat—were left unexplored in American media.

Also left unexplored by *Carry On* writers was the fact that early attendance in vocational training classes suffered in part because soldiers were "very much troubled" about the uncertain and sometimes fluctuating conditions of their eyes, and hopeful that a miraculous scientific breakthrough would restore their sight. Evergreen's Education Director Harold Molter referenced that the men's deleterious mental conditions resulted from disappointment at not being operated on when they entered Evergreen, which suggests that US Army personnel may have at least transferred soldiers to the school based on the premise that they would have an operation to restore their sight upon arrival, which was not the case.[23]

Psychiatric records also suggest complex psychological realities for the newly blind men, which was not evident in the early stories of men like William Zimmerman. Almost all the patients who arrived at Evergreen with battle wounds had recently undergone operations at the nearby US Army General Hospital at Fort McHenry, and some such men had lingering delirium while recovering from ether "in which they imagined themselves fighting in the trenches or carrying on in some violent war activity," according to one psychiatrist.[24] Half of the soldiers also suffered from some kind of "psychoneurosis," including concussion, exhaustion, shock, irritability, nervousness, or delirium. Evergreen's psychiatrist explained that there was a "remarkable freedom . . . from symptoms of a purely hysterical nature" and that "those patients who have developed psychiatric conditions such as paranoid ideas, have been cases of constitutional psychopathy or have sustained organic damage to the brain."[25] Around two-thirds of the blind soldiers admitted to US Army General Hospital No. 7 also had their sense of smell totally or partially destroyed, and many had their senses of taste and hearing damaged.[26]

William Zimmerman was featured in *Carry On,* then, based on the erroneous assumption that he represented the majority of blind soldiers in that he had not sustained a severe visible physical wound, that he had seen battle in the trenches, and because he clearly traced his blindness to a physical wound sustained in combat. Many, but by no means all, of the soldiers at Evergreen were blinded in battle, and many were partially blind—possessing limited vision in both eyes or in one eye—rather than completely blind. A not inconsequential number of soldiers at Evergreen were blind either through preexisting illness that was aggravated by their military service or from illness or environmental circumstances related to their military service. Most of the soldiers at Evergreen had wounds in addition to blindness, including other sensory wounds, amputations, and severe psychological trauma. These points are significant because most stories that military authorities or newspapers told about blind soldiers at Evergreen either played down these facts or ignored them altogether, which suggests that media outlets were mindful of how the images they chose to report would be received by readers. The *New York Herald*'s reference to Henry Bitter's missing hands is an outlier. More common were depictions of physically whole blind soldiers.

Zimmerman also appeared in *Carry On* because the media regularly used blind soldiers to symbolize the worst wound one could sustain, but that American soldiers had the capability to overcome such supposed calamity. Newspapers and magazines focused on blind(ed) soldiers because they were compelling and because of the emotional appeal of the injury, which was explored in the previous chapter. Such figures had, according to public appeals for sympathy, heroically and tragically lost their sight from shell explosions or bullets, and despite having a body miraculously free of scarring—which was not always true—they were left unable to see with their eyes and therefore could not use their bodies to their full potential. In contrast to the pre-1917 American news stories about blind soldiers, however, the post-1917 stories struck a resoundingly positive tone. New York soldier George Calvert, for example, was blinded in battle by a shell fragment, but he assured Americans back home, "Don't let any of the home folks worry about me. Uncle Sam is going to train me so that I shall be about as useful as I was before I went over."[27] Figures such as William Zimmerman and George Calvert elicited similar emotions from the American public that blind French soldiers had, but also quickly reassured the public that they were different and were indeed carrying on. By highlighting such soldiers and their positive reactions to their blindness, magazines and newspapers sought to convey to other wounded soldiers the message that if blinded soldiers could do it with a wound worse than any other wound, so could you.

Zimmerman also proved compelling to *Carry On* editors because of the socioeconomic roles he occupied. One significant aim of rehabilitation was for the soldier patient to work hard to fulfill his role as the breadwinner of the family. Rehabilitationists, Linker has argued, envisioned the workplace (and not the sheltered workshop or a pension) as ensuring a stable and well-ordered life through which married men could provide for their family, and wage earning defined manhood.[28] *Carry On* made this point explicit through its "Creed of the Disabled Soldier," printed in the March, June, and July 1919 editions of the magazine.[29] The "Creed" argued that it was the goal of every disabled soldier "Once more to be useful—to see pity in the eyes of my friends replaced with commendation—to work, produce, provide, and to feel that I have a place in the world—seeking no favors and given none—a MAN among MEN in spite of this physical handicap."[30] "Seen in this way," writes Linker, "economic dependency—often linked overtly and metaphorically to womanliness—came to be understood as the real handicap that thwarted the full physical recovery of the veteran and the fiscal strength of the nation."[31]

The editors of *Carry On* unquestionably drove this point home in the story of William Zimmerman. Zimmerman's primary reason for training hard after being blinded in the war, as he stated in *Carry On,* was to "make good" so that he could marry his girlfriend. *Carry On* placed sexuality and masculinity front and center alongside work when crafting the ideal of the successful veteran. Zimmerman was blind, according to the magazine, but his disability did not stop him from having a fulfilling relationship with a woman. Zimmerman, though, got the girl because he succeeded in vocational training and secured a job with a steady income. The fact that his story was compelling enough to be featured in the first edition of *Carry On* in June 1918 reinforces the ways that Americans refocused imagery about blind soldiers away from dependence and depression to emphasize independence and happiness.

A key figure in this conceptual transition from dependence to independence was Sir Arthur Pearson, who American rehabilitation authorities turned to as a mentor when planning Evergreen. Pearson was a British publisher before he lost his sight in 1913 from glaucoma, upon which time he became affiliated with the National Institute for the Blind in England and served as that organization's president. Shortly after the beginning of World War I, Pearson organized St. Dunstan's Hostel for Blinded Soldiers and Sailors.[32] St. Dunstan's trained newly blind British and Canadian military personnel, offered vocational training, and provided recreational activities for the men while they learned how to live as newly blind individuals. By the end of the war, it had provided services for over 1,833 soldiers and sailors.[33] Despite his association with the British, French, and Belgian Blind Relief War Fund before 1917—with its promotional materials that depicted blind soldiers as inherently helpless, depressed, and condemned to a life of suffering—Pearson operated with an almost militant insistence that blind soldiers be as independent as possible and to openly display that independence to the public.[34]

The most evident example of Pearson's philosophy toward blind people that shaped his views about British and American wartime rehabilitation came from his "Hints for the Newly Blinded," a pamphlet meant for blind individuals to help them acclimate to their recent loss of sight. Pearson wrote, for example, that he liked to get around without any physical contact between himself and his seeing aid, so long as the seeing aid gave a warning before coming to a curb or an obstacle. Pearson also urged that blind people should avoid using walking sticks, especially indoors, which "should be absolutely barred" because it signified a lack of independence.

Another way to signal independence to seeing people, according to Pearson, was avoiding "the habit of stooping over and feeling a seat" before sitting down, which "gives an impression of helplessness and inefficiency to the onlooker." His other "hints" included personal hygiene recommendations, because according to Pearson looking untidy "goes a long way toward giving the impression of helplessness."[35]

Pearson built his philosophy of portraying independence to the seeing public into the physical environment of St. Dunstan's. For example, wooden boards on the walkways throughout the premises signified obstacles, such as stairs. "A board means danger," Pearson told a reporter from the *Outlook for the Blind*. "It tells me . . . that I am at the top of the stairs and will tell me when I am at the bottom." There were also railings throughout the buildings. "Just before we come to the end of this railing," Pearson continued, "my hand meets a little raised button. That tells me that I must turn to the right!"[36] Ever insistent on suggesting blind independence, though, Pearson made sure that his audience knew that blind veterans did not really rely too much on the handrails. "You will see them getting about quite well without" them, he said.[37] His opposition to aids even extended to the burgeoning guide dog movement. "I had a feeling," Pearson wrote, "that a dog at the end of the string was apt to remind one a little too much of the blind beggar with his tapping stick and shuffling gait."[38]

Pearson's resistance to the use of mobility aids aligned with his sense that his duty as a major public figure and representative of blind service organizations was to counter popular assumptions about blindness, such as blind people having a natural state of dependence or social isolation.[39] His disability politics suggested that blindness was merely a temporary state to be overcome, and that, as historians Julie Anderson and Neil Pemberton write, "the idea of independence for blind people only ever resulted from their conformity to the sighted world's convention of mobility."[40] To succeed in Arthur Pearson's world, blind soldiers had to judge their progress by how well they hid the fact that they were blind.

St. Dunstan's adopted Sir Arthur Pearson's culture of independence, and because Evergreen was still in the early stages of its operation when *Carry On* began publishing stories about rehabilitation, the US Surgeon General magazine featured numerous articles and images about Pearson and blind soldiers at St. Dunstan's to suggest to American readers how Evergreen might operate when more blind Americans arrived. The October 1918 issue, for example, included an image of St. Dunstan's front gates and a photograph that depicted blind soldiers at St. Dunstan's with the caption "Are They Downhearted? No!"[41] Directly beneath the latter image was an article about blind French veterans titled, "Beggars No More," concluding that war "is damnable and death is the least of its tolls. But at least the blind and maimed are no longer in the hideous predicament of a century ago."[42] The title of the article was not coincidental, as *Carry On* likely understood the role public assumptions about blind beggars could have played in shaping expectations about blind American veterans.[43] Rather than being passive recipients of charity, blind soldiers actively went "Over the Top," in rehabilitation. Instead of charging in battle over No Man's Land, as one January 1919 *Carry On* article suggested, the blind soldiers gleefully played leapfrog and "other boyhood games." Ultimately, the magazine explicitly conveyed to the reader that "pity is not always necessary" because blind soldiers "are the cheerfullest of all" and worked for their success.[44]

Carry On's insistence that blind soldiers relied less on charity or social welfare provisions such as pensions and more on vocational training to secure self-supporting employment was in line with prevailing currents in American conversations about blindness by 1919. While blind activists had made significant headway toward securing pension programs, increased funding for workshops, and social services for blind people and administered by blind people, by the early twentieth-century powerful organizations such as the American Foundation for the Blind lobbied against pensions and strictly in favor of vocational training led and administered by professional social workers.[45] All too often, however, sighted people's insistence on vocational training has converted the issues faced by blind people into individual problems requiring grit and hard work rather than problems resulting from broader structural, cultural, and social issues such as ableism, inaccessibility, and poverty. Blind people, then, perversely became more dependent on social workers and meagre benefits as sighted reformers argued that such antipension changes would make blind people more independent and satisfied. *Carry On* propagated messages about the supposedly unambiguous benefits of vocational training.

Carry On contributor and vocational education researcher for the US Army Clarkson Dye visited St. Dunstan's to see the vocational-driven satisfaction for himself in preparation for more American soldiers returning to the United States blind. Dye told *Carry On*'s readers about St. Dunstan's student-soldier "R," who was a mechanic before the war, and whose former employers said they could not rehire him because of his blindness. Arthur Pearson arranged for the young student to learn everything he could about the science of heating system mechanics, as well as typewriting and braille, while Pearson persuaded the employers to give him another chance at work. Within four months, according to Dye, "R" directed a staff of engineers and mechanics and made three times the wages he made before the war.

"This blind man," Dye concluded, had achieved "victory over blindness" because he learned "how to use his brain" and direct the labor of others.[46] The message *Carry On* hoped to convey to its readers through the story about "R" and St. Dunstan's was that with proper training and wise guidance from vocational training officials blind soldiers were actually better off and *more* independent than they had been before the war, and that American soldiers could expect the same kind of success.

While *Carry On* educated readers about St. Dunstan's work with blind soldiers, Sir Arthur Pearson extended his influence over the new Evergreen institution in Baltimore.[47] Pearson arrived in North America in January 1919 to tour Canada and the United States and visit the new American hospital for blind soldiers. Pearson addressed students and staff at Evergreen on January 16, 1919, and made the ideological connections between the two institutes clear—as well as Evergreen constituents' dissimilarity from French blind soldiers. In his speech, Pearson promised the soldiers and staff that the more independent the soldiers could be in civilian life the better, and that rehabilitation should ultimately serve that goal.[48] It was Pearson's influence that significantly shaped Evergreen's development in its early months. Authorities, for example, felt that Pearson's messages were so important that when the thirteen blind soldiers who opened this chapter arrived in New York and had missed Pearson's important talk at Evergreen, the US Army arranged for the men to meet him elsewhere before he returned to England. In February 1919, the thirteen American soldiers from the *Saxonia* sat for a private lecture from Arthur Pearson at Debarkation Hospital No. 5 in New York City, which was situated in the Grand Central Palace that had been home to American philanthropic events for blind French soldiers before 1917.[49]

American military authorities, therefore, used *Carry On* and the ideas of Sir Arthur Pearson to explain to American civilians how blind American soldiers differed from the ableist messages they had heard about French soldiers before 1917. American soldiers were unlike their French counterparts, the magazine suggested, because they had grit and determination, were backed by American rehabilitation reformers, and would ultimately become self-supporting through their own hard work. *Carry On* featured America's first blind soldiers such as William Zimmerman who stood tall and confident with no visible scars, and who embodied many of the criteria Pearson described in his "Hints to the Newly Blinded." The magazine's references to Pearson made clear the connections the US government was trying to make between St. Dunstan's and Evergreen about the new institute that was to train American soldiers blinded in the war. *Carry On* was not alone in its infatuation with blind soldiers.

Sir Arthur Pearson seated with blind American soldiers in a large gymnasium at Evergreen, January 1919. (Library of Congress, Prints & Photographs Division, American National Red Cross Collection, LC-DIG-anrc-02834)

American Magazines Replicate *Carry On*

Between August 1917 and October 1919 blind soldiers proliferated throughout popular American magazines. By mid-1919, when many American magazines published stories about blind soldiers, US fighting in World War I had been over for six months, and the new work of bringing hundreds of thousands of soldiers back to the United States was underway. Over 200,000 US soldiers were wounded, sick, or disabled, and about 120,000 disabled soldiers had passed through the US Army's rehabilitation program.[50] This meant that American publications had a plethora of subjects to profile in their magazines, journals, and newspapers, including numerous blind soldiers both real and imagined.

Some of the stories published after World War I sought to depict the actual experiences of blind soldiers in rehabilitation. In January 1919 William Zimmerman took a reporter from the *New York Times Magazine* on a tour of US Army General Hospital No. 7. Zimmerman, who was apparently doomed by his "personal tragedy" to "the long prospect of darkened years

[and] . . . hopelessness," stunned the reporter with his "confidence as one who steps boldly and happily out into the world, and who bore no sign of being a hospital patient." Zimmerman embodied the "spirit of Evergreen," going about his day with "perfect normality," enjoying a cigarette, reading in the library, and dancing with women. "Ultimately," the reporter concluded, "Zimmerman is not a man who is 'afflicted'; he is a man who has a handicap—and who is overcoming it."[51]

The *New York Times Magazine* reporter was interested in Zimmerman because he was a curiosity and because he provided a convenient overcoming narrative for readers to digest. Zimmerman was not supposed to be happy or confident, because the cultural constructions about blind soldiers that proliferated before 1917 suggested that such people were hopeless and depressed without their ability to see. The reporter found Zimmerman's optimism an oddity precisely because of the reporter's ableist views about blindness that suggested blind people were hopelessly dependent and condemned to a life of isolation. Zimmerman's ability to spiritually overcome supposedly insurmountable mental and physical odds served to motivate others to succeed in their own lives because, as the message suggested, they themselves were not blind.[52]

Blind soldier overcoming narratives showed up elsewhere in postwar literature. *Collier's: The National Weekly* reporter Samuel Hopkins Adams toured Evergreen where he met many of America's first blind soldiers, including William Zimmerman. The product of Adams's tour was an article titled "Blinks" that appeared in the June 1919 issue of the national magazine, which gave readers an inside view of the daily lives of Evergreen soldiers during rehabilitation, while at the same time providing something of a morality tale about hard work and the US Army's ability to reconstruct its wounded soldiers. The story first introduced blind soldier "Sid" who descended from a large staircase in Evergreen's lounge area to inform his fellow "blinks," as the men called themselves, that the doctor pronounced him completely blind in both eyes. "Welcome to the Band of Blinks! Good for Sid!" the others said in response. "It was a bewildering conversation for a layman to listen to," wrote Adams. "The members of the group below appeared to be congratulating the newcomer on having been declared stone blind."[53] Samuel Adams's story seems to suggest that what he witnessed at Evergreen challenged his perception of blind people as being inherently dependent and unquestionably depressed about their lack of sight.

Adams's story is, first and foremost, a redemptive morality tale. It centered around a blind sailor who arrived at Evergreen and could not get used to life as a blind man. As the story opens in Evergreen's comfortable living room where blind soldiers are sitting in luxurious chairs keeping each

A group of blind white American soldiers sitting on leather chairs in the wood-paneled living room of Evergreen as a fellow blind soldier descends the staircase, November 1921. (Library of Congress, Prints & Photographs Division, American National Red Cross Collection, LC-DIG-anrc-14605)

other company, the sailor is off to the side and despondent, a "melancholy wreck," until William Zimmerman invites the sailor to follow him around campus. Adams juxtaposed the two men who seemed to be completely opposite in their outlook. Zimmerman was "a strapping, upstanding, fine-looking young sergeant" who stood upright, "look[ed] you square in the eye . . . a man among men, who in half an hour's association makes you actually forget his disability." By contrast, the sailor was "slow, uncertain, shuffling" with "slumped shoulders" and "malaise of the spirit within." It was only after his association with Zimmerman, and hearing about the many activities and general busyness of the soldiers at Evergreen, that the sailor made a marked transformation into a more confident person. Zimmerman, according to Adams, had "a power for morale among his fellows."

Adams felt that from his short time visiting Evergreen, and through his interactions with William Zimmerman and the sailor, he had come to understand the "psychology of the newly blinded." On the one hand, confident blind soldiers were more idealistic, and passionately carried out their rehabilitation with "courage, patience, determination, [and] cheerfulness." At the opposite extreme were the men who "remain bewildered, anxious, timid, a helpless traveler in a strange land" who would eventually "fall into the apathy of self-distrust and become a mere inert, tragic dependent upon the Government pension" unless "carefully handled." The story ended as Zimmerman stood up from his chair, "stretched his powerful, clean-built form" and gave one last appeal to the audience: "We fellow blinks . . . it's a great life if you don't weaken it."

Blind soldier George Calvert added to Adams's morality tale about the "psychology of the newly blinded" and the individual's need to remain determined rather than despondent. Calvert exclaimed that work was important for him while he was going through vocational training, as it empowered him. Further, he suggested that pensions could be potentially ruinous for a person's life. "What good is it to you," he stated, "when you don't have the feel of working for it." Calvert cited the story of a school friend named Benny who became blind after a fireworks explosion at a Fourth of July picnic. Benny had a family that catered to his every need, providing him with a car and chauffeur, numerous trips, and a guide dog. "They did everything for him but teach him a job." One day, Benny brushed his teeth, but instead of using toothpaste, he used a "chloroform mixture," and he died as a result.[54] Calvert concluded that if only he had been trained properly, if he had been at Evergreen and learned to be a self-sufficient blind person, he would have been trained to know that the bottle was chloroform, and he would have lived. Samuel Hopkins Adams's "Blinks" sought to bring William Zimmerman and his comrades beyond the pages of *Carry On* to a broader reading population, while also providing reassurance to war-weary Americans that wounds could be overcome through grit, hard work, and positive reinforcement. "Blinks" did not want the public's sympathy or a government pension, as Calvert suggested. Instead, according to *Collier's* messaging, blind American soldiers *actively* determined their own destinies.

Blind soldiers also became the subjects of popular fiction and lent similar morality tales as the one in which Adams published in *Collier's*. Maria Thompson Daviess's series titled "Doctor Matt: The Feminine Adventures of a Young Physician" was published in *Ladies' Home Journal* between August 1917 and February 1918. "Doctor Matt" was a fictional story about the young, white, and relatively wealthy Johns Hopkins University–trained Doctor Matthew Ashmeade who volunteered as a medic with the American Expeditionary Forces in France during World War I. Ashmeade was blinded in one eye from an enemy bayonet, and he returned to Hillsboro, Tennessee, to his mother Ann, his fiancée Daphny, and his friend Helen, as well as his medical practice as one of the only physicians in his hometown.

The story follows Dr. Ashmeade as he gets caught up in other people's romantic gossip and relationship problems, all the while neglecting to deal with the fact that his own fiancée, Daphny, disowned him because of his visible facial scar and partial blindness. The series culminates with Daphny returning to Ashmeade only after he falls in love with his friend Helen, who openly embraces the doctor's war wound. After the couple's public embrace, Daphny decides that Doctor Matt's scar and war wound was actually a sign of his masculinity rather than something to be afraid or ashamed of.

Harper's Monthly also published its own fictional story about a blind soldier. Beth Bradford Gilchrist's "Eyes That See" was a fictional short story about a white, "broad-shouldered, blue-eyed young [New England] lawyer" named John Huling, who left behind his sister Ada, his fiancée Grace Dewey, and his sister's friend Molly Burt when he enlisted to serve in World War I. During the war Huling served in Chateau-Thierry and St. Mihiel before he was blinded in battle. He returns to an overly sympathetic mother and fiancée, whose responses to the young soldier's blindness range from utter grief to emphatic but performative optimism. Naturally, as Gilchrist suggests, John Huling gravitates instead to—and ultimately falls in love with—Molly Burt, who treats him with dignity and respect, almost ignoring his disability altogether.

"Doctor Matt" and "Eyes That See" are significant for a number of reasons, the first of which was the ways that hometowns first received the news of Matt Ashmeade's and John Huling's blindness. In both stories, the news was met first with tragic pessimism, followed by reassurance from the wounded men themselves. Beth Gilchrist introduced John Huling's status as a blind veteran in ways that suggested tragedy. John, for example, came home "stumbling in a world of darkness."[55] Gilchrist narrated that John "didn't mind what the war did to him, so long as it killed him, if it was going to kill him, completely" instead of leaving him with a disability.[56] Blindness, Gilchrist implied, was a fate worse than death, and John was stuck in a physical purgatory between life and death. The town's reaction to John's blindness added to his sense of tragedy. Townspeople were shocked at the sight of him "feeling his way clumsily with a cane." They spoke to him in a way that signified their sorrow and compassion. Even John's loved ones, who transitioned frequently from crying to "super-cheer" proved no less frustrating to the young man.[57]

Doctor Matt Ashmeade did not come home to a town overly sympathetic to his blindness. By contrast, almost without hesitation the people of Hillsboro, Tennessee, gave Ashmeade plenty of business treating patients as if he had never left for the war in the first place. It was Doctor Matt's loved ones who reacted with sorrow. Matt's mother Ann Ashmeade stated upon hearing the news of her son's blindness, "No, oh no, I can't bear that! I can't have him—him broken. . . . What of [Matt's fiancée] Daphny? That is his tragedy. What shall we do?"[58] Ann and Matt's friend Helen worried about how best to tell Daphny, with fear that they might "crush a butterfly" over the news.[59] When Doctor Matt decided to tell Daphny himself, her response was sheer fright. "No! No!" she cried as she ran away.[60] Matthew Ashmeade displayed internalized ableism toward his blindness by justifying Daphny's response, when he reassured his mother, "Mother, the love of a woman is not for the maimed."[61]

Neither "Eyes That See" nor "Doctor Matt" allowed readers to get too comfortable with the tragic view of their respective protagonists. Doctor Matt shrugged off his recent dismissal from his fiancée Daphny. "It is best," he said to his mother Ann, "I have work to do and I must travel light."[62] Indeed, Matthew Ashmeade's story is one of tending to other people's needs in a professional and self-assuring manner. Bert Winn was a Hillsboro resident who fell from a ladder, became disabled, and was shut away in his mother's house because she feared the town's reaction to her son's disfigurement. Matt empathized with Bert who, as he argued, went through a similar experience of an overbearing mother trying to shield a son from social prejudice because of disability. Ultimately, Doctor Matt explained, "I operated on [my mother] and cured her" of the limiting beliefs about his disability, and "I am going to operate on your mother" as well.[63] To prove Bert's abilities to live like other kids his age, Matthew brought him to a local baseball game. Matthew Ashmeade's rehabilitation of Bert Winn's disability signified a change in limiting beliefs about disability.

The character of Doctor Matt Ashmeade is like other cultural constructions of blind people in that he served less as a sex symbol or a sexual character and more as someone who existed to help other characters learn about their own views of the world. The fact that Daphny disowned Ashmeade made little difference to the young doctor. It was more important to him that he got to work fixing other people, and this included other people's relationships. This was the case not only with Bert Winn and his mother, but also with numerous other characters who seek him out to help with their troubled relationships.[64] Blind characters are rarely depicted as sexual, and more often they serve as sidekicks to the protagonist's own story of personal revelation.[65]

By contrast, John Huling, who spent significantly more effort battling his town's sorrowful reception upon his return home to New England from Europe, dispelled the audience's sense of tragedy about his blindness by focusing on his personal romantic relationships. John's fiancée Grace was steadfast in her devotion to him, unlike Matthew Ashmeade's fiancée

Daphny. Grace had, as Huling reasoned, "dedicated herself to service," which suggested that women's role in veteran rehabilitation was primarily one of support for disabled men. Huling grew tired of Grace's compassion and found the company of Molly Burt far more satisfying. Molly treated him with "admiration and fellowship" rather than pity and unease. She made it clear that her frustration matched John's regarding how people looked at and treated him. "It makes me boil," she stated, "to hear how they speak to him. Just as though they were sorry for him—*sorry* for a man like that!"[66] Molly's affect was affirming and empowering. She made it her mission to convince John that he could return to his former profession of law. He found himself wanting to spend more time with her because of her unwavering optimism, rather than those who made him feel sorrow. A turning point in their relationship came when John saved Molly from a dangerous, wild dog by running up to it and hitting it to scare it away. Ultimately, the two fell in love and John Huling made the conscious decision to leave Grace for Molly.

The messages in "Eyes That See" and "Doctor Matt" about the ways the two blind soldiers returned home served two competing narratives. Gilchrist and Daviess clearly tried to make readers feel sorrow for John Huling and Dr. Matthew Ashmeade. The many reactions to them in the respective stories, and the descriptions of them as clumsy and stumbling through darkness mirrored cultural constructions of blindness described in the previous chapter. By describing Huling's and Ashmeade's interactions with their families and towns in such a way, the authors were hoping readers might evaluate how they would react in a similar situation, if someone they knew came home from war as a blind veteran. Ultimately, then, both blind characters served supporting roles in what was supposed to be the psychological transformation of the reader. The message was clear: readers should not make men like Huling or Ashmeade feel hopeless, special, or out of the ordinary. They should, instead, follow Molly's and Helen's lead and fulfill the men's sense of longing for "equality and fraternity." Additionally, Gilchrist and Daviess aimed to show the men as having agency over their own lives, rather than being hopeless or dependent.

A second correlating theme of "Eyes That See" and "Doctor Matt" is that women served as auxiliary figures in the rehabilitation of blind soldiers. Molly's character existed to empower John by suggesting that he return to law and become a self-respecting breadwinner. The women in Doctor Matt's story served to affirm his masculinity in other ways. Matt's continuous involvement in women's lives and dealing with other people's relationships served to affirm his fundamental difference from women. He seemed out of place gossiping about other people with Helen or his mother

Ann, and consistently returned to work, finding new ways to heal the town's residents. Though Daviess titled the series "The Feminine Adventures of a Young Physician," she sought to use the feminine adventures to mark Matthew Ashmeade as fundamentally masculine and out of place in such adventures, always on the lookout for ways to get back to serious work and assert his independence. Additionally, it was the guidance of Molly and Helen that led to personal transformations in the two blind men. John's transformation was represented through his frustration with and ultimate disaffection from Grace Dewey because of her condescending sympathy. Matthew Ashmeade's transformation came through Helen's pleading with him to relinquish his internalized ableist belief that disabled men were undeserving of love. Ultimately, both men fell in love, became rehabilitation successes, and served as engaging stories of morality and transformation that could benefit real American blind soldiers and their families.

Taken together, "Blinks," "Eyes That See," and "Doctor Matt" described very different blind soldiers than what Americans were accustomed to before 1917, while at times still relying on familiar ableist rhetorical devices for the sake of storytelling. The sailor at Evergreen had to be melancholy about his blindness for William Zimmerman to give him a sense of purpose. John Huling's and Matthew Ashmeade's personal and social redemptions depended in part on their loved ones greeting them with sympathy and sorrow about their blindness. The stories aimed to convince American readers that blindness could be overcome, and that the sighted public had to examine their own beliefs that shaped their interactions with blind veterans should they meet one someday. Above all, though, the preceding stories introduced blind American soldiers to a large audience just as Evergreen was undergoing significant changes, taking in larger numbers of blind soldiers, and creating a means of storytelling in its own right.

The *Evergreen Review* Puts "Overcoming" Blindness at Center Stage

Evergreen underwent numerous institutional changes in fall 1919, the most significant of which was the closure of US Army General Hospital No. 7, which meant the demobilization of blind soldiers into blind veterans and the transfer of all Evergreen operations to the Red Cross Institute for the Blind that had been, up until that point, an auxiliary organization that aided the US Army with recreational activities for the soldiers. Free from military discipline by the end of 1919, newly demobilized veterans at the Red Cross Institute for the Blind experienced notable changes in their daily lives. New educational opportunities, better sleeping and eating arrangements, and postrehabilitation outreach programs made life palatable and aligned more concretely with Sir Arthur Pearson's model of independence-at-all-costs.

Culturally speaking, the most significant change at Evergreen was the Red Cross Institute for the Blind's publication of *Evergreen Review*, which was a rehabilitation magazine that kept interested sighted readers up to date with daily life at the institute for a small monthly subscription fee. The *Evergreen Review* is significant in part because it provides important although triumphalist and self-congratulating depictions of daily life at Evergreen during its formative years between 1919 and 1920. Photographs of the institute's grounds and stories about blind veterans training in agriculture, commercial sales, woodworking, and other vocational pursuits as well as engaging in sporting events with their blind comrades were further extensions of *Carry On*'s early work to sell rehabilitation to the American public.

The *Evergreen Review* is also significant because the assistant director of the Red Cross Institute for the Blind, and the person who was a central figure in the publication of the *Evergreen Review*, was Charles F. F. Campbell. Charles Campbell founded *Outlook for the Blind*, a publication by sighted people that disseminated stories about blind people to change public perceptions about blindness and raise money.[67] The *Evergreen Review* was likewise meant for sighted readers and supporters of Evergreen and, therefore, the Red Cross carefully curated the images it disseminated to its audiences. The publication is nonetheless important because of the images its editors presented to the public as well as the images or stories the magazine chose not to present, as will be made clear.

Two themes stand out in the ways that the *Evergreen Review* tried to appeal to its sighted readers because of how similar they were to earlier media representations of blind soldiers. First, the *Evergreen Review* documented the regular appearances of famous people who visited Evergreen to signify the men's elevated social capital as blind veterans who had widespread sympathetic appeal from the upper echelons of society. Second, the regular column titled "Who's Who among Our Buddies" chronicled blind veterans who succeeded after their vocational training. The *Evergreen Review* ultimately aimed to convey to its readers that blind veterans were unquestionably socioeconomically independent worker-citizens who had little or no problem acclimating to postwar America.

The numerous famous individuals who visited Evergreen and appeared in the *Evergreen Review* left little doubt that blind soldiers were worthy of the sighted public's attention. Visitors included the queen of Belgium who arrived at the end of 1919, and who was particularly interested in sending a Belgian attaché to study vocational training methods that could be later applied to blind Belgian soldiers.[68] Elizabeth Baker, the wife of US Secretary of War Newton Baker, was so inspired by a conversation she had about the institute with Sir Arthur Pearson and the Red Cross Institute for the Blind's head Dr. James Bordley that she visited Evergreen on February 14, 1920. Baker's visit was memorable because she brought with her seventy-five braille watches to give to the blind veterans so they could tell time through their sense of touch.[69] On April 13, 1920, General John Pershing—the commanding general of the American Expeditionary Forces during World War I—visited Evergreen and spoke to the blind veterans there and reported feeling "inspiration" from seeing them in vocational training.[70]

Unquestionably the most important visits to Evergreen were from Helen Keller. Keller's interactions with the men suggested that she understood their work in "overcoming" their disabilities, and that the men's experiences should ultimately serve to inspire other disabled soldiers who were not blind. Keller visited Evergreen in 1918, in February 1919, and again in March 1920. Keller stated in her speech to blind soldiers on February 25, 1919, that the hardest part of being blind was the loss of "personal liberty," but that through the cultivation of the other senses, through alert minds and courageous hearts, the blind soldiers "shall find plenty of interesting adventures in Darkland." She encouraged her audience to "console yourselves with work, get busy, put your mind on the job at hand. . . . Every triumph you win will help other fellows who are handicapped to make good," and that their greatest victory in life as blind soldiers-turned-civilians was not living a fulfilling life, but inspiring other disabled people "with confidence in themselves and their capabilities."[71]

Keller's interactions with the blind soldiers also suggest that she understood that Evergreen catered exclusively to battle blind(ed) soldiers who were deserving of the full sympathy of society based on their sense of self-sacrifice. When she returned to Evergreen in March 1920 and was asked about her February 1919 visit to the institute, Keller said, "It was one of the most wonderful experiences of my life." "It was inspiring to see the work," she continued, "and the courage shown by the blinded soldiers in overcoming the greatest difficulties." "Those fine fellows," Keller concluded, "are going over the top of blindness just as splendidly as they went over the top in France."[72]

The queen of Belgium, General John Pershing, and Helen Keller lent a sense of authority and urgency to Evergreen in similar ways that celebrities—including Helen Keller—worked alongside the British, French, and Belgian Blind Relief War Fund. Their visits to Evergreen increased public awareness and support for blind American soldiers. Unlike the celebrity associations of previous years, however, the visitors at Evergreen focused on inspirational narratives of soldiers overcoming their disabilities and argued that though blind soldiers had an almost insurmountable disability, they conquered their disabilities through sheer individual will. This was especially the case with Keller, whose own identity and public acclaim rested in part on the public's perception that she heroically overcame her disability.[73]

The *Evergreen Review*'s "Who's Who among Our Buddies" series performed a similar function of inspiration. As Evergreen was a vocational training institution, much of the *Evergreen Review* highlighted the lives of blind veterans who were training for or who had already succeeded in their work. Harvey Gilbert was profiled in the magazine after he opened his Victory Store No. 2 in Perryville, Maryland, in December 1919. Gilbert's Victory Store No. 2 was modeled after Victory Store No. 1, a model training store opened at Evergreen under the direction of the Red Cross Institute for the Blind. The store trained blind veterans in commercial sales, carrying such items as candy, tobacco, and toiletries. When Gilbert opened his own store in Perryville, he welcomed around two hundred customers who purchased a total of $157 worth of merchandise. Gilbert—who "brailled" every shelf in his store—sold the tobacco and candy during the early rush, and his wife sold the other products. The two proved to be "hard-working . . . reliable people who will make good whatever the difficulties."[74]

The *Evergreen Review* highlighted Harvey Gilbert's store opening because his experiences underscored patterns of successful vocational rehabilitation that the Red Cross Institute for the Blind hoped to replicate. First, Gilbert succeeded in part because of the steadfast support of his wife, who worked diligently in the store by his side. He did not necessarily *need* her help, as the article suggested, because his knowledge of braille combined with his training in sales made his independence almost assured. Evergreen's Commercial Department emphasized other men who received help from family or friends. Harry Willian, for example, leaned on help from his sister, Mabel. Willian's eyesight failed while in army training, and he ultimately took courses in insurance sales in the Commercial Department. The Red Cross encouraged Willian's sister Mabel to train with him at Evergreen, and in May 1919, Mabel and Harry started work at the Mutual Benefit Life Insurance Company of New Jersey's Baltimore location.[75]

Roy Mason Chapman and Cecil Allen relied on each other as they ventured out on their own. Chapman and Allen were both blinded in France. They met at Base Hospital No. 8 in Savenay before they took the transatlantic voyage to Evergreen together. The two studied braille and took commercial classes, and when they left Evergreen in January 1920 they opened Chapman, Allen & Company bookstore in Grand Junction, Colorado, near Roy Chapman's home. They were not completely on their own in Colorado. The head of the Commercial Department accompanied them and helped them with their grand opening, and even remained there for several weeks afterward to ensure its immediate stability. The store, according to the *Evergreen Review*, opened on February 1, 1920, and had "three months of good business" thereafter.[76]

Despite the *Evergreen Review's* carefully crafted messaging, it would be a mistake to suggest that all the Commercial Department graduates succeeded. The *Evergreen Review* met James Riddervold's story with enthusiasm. Riddervold was a Norwegian immigrant who joined the American Expeditionary Forces and was blinded in battle just two days before the November 11, 1918, Armistice. He entered Evergreen in April 1919 where he studied sales before opening his own store in Cambridge, Massachusetts, where he sold tea and coffee. Riddervold prided himself in his new venture and wrote to his former comrades who were still training at Evergreen that they needed to get rid of the assumption that because they were blind "the world should lie at their feet." "The sooner they get that out of their heads," he concluded, "the better it will be for them and for others with whom they come into contact."[77]

James Riddervold did not remain so steadfast in his ideas of rugged individualism. By April 1921, Riddervold's Cambridge tea and coffee business struggled to make ends meet. "I keep my own accounts and sell my products," he stated. "I deliver goods anywhere in Greater Boston free of charge . . . I am striving to make myself an asset to society and not a liability." Nonetheless, Riddervold recruited the services of "fine [Cambridge] women [who were] lending the helping hand of lofty sisterhood to a worthy brother struggling against a great misfortune." Records do not exist explaining why Riddervold's business struggled, but Riddervold claimed that it was the "laggard public"—a public that was unwilling to give him a fair shot and sufficient support by purchasing from his store—that stood between himself and independence.[78] Wittingly or not, Riddervold identified ableism—public unwillingness to support a disabled person—as the chief reason for his struggles, rather than his individual work ethic. The Cambridge women's efforts, the newspaper publicity, or possible business changes Riddervold made ultimately turned his coffee and tea company around, for by the end of the year it was profitable again.[79]

Harvey Gilbert's Victory Store No. 2 also struggled and, like Riddervold, his struggles did not appear in the pages of the *Evergreen Review*. Gilbert's story instead continued in the pages of the *Baltimore Evening Sun*, which reported on blind veterans who were seeking money to fund a permanent home for blind veterans who were struggling economically toward the end of 1924. Gilbert spoke about his life after Evergreen: "I went home in 1920 and set up in business. . . . I found everyone very sympathetic but they did not patronize my store and I went broke. I had just enough money to get back here and decided to come and stay."[80] Like James Riddervold, Harvey Gilbert blamed his store's failure not on a lack of training but on sighted society's unwillingness to patronize his store and ultimately a lack of confidence in his abilities because of his blindness.

Despite the realities faced by Harvey Gilbert and James Riddervold, Evergreen put in place significant measures to help its predominantly young white men succeed. L. W. Wallace, the director of the Red Cross Institute for the Blind, spoke at the Kiwanis Club in New Haven, Connecticut, in May 1920 about the work the Red Cross was doing for blind veterans, in which he outlined some of the ways the institute facilitated business development. The Red Cross, for example, lent up to $1,000 worth of low-interest loans to encourage men to open businesses of their own. As the experiences of Roy Mason Chapman and Cecil Allen suggest, the institute sent a representative to the veteran's hometown, picked out a location for the business, worked with the banks to arrange the lease, and formed an advisory board of "prominent citizens" of the town to look after the business after it was established.[81] Far from being left to their own devices, the blind veterans had significant levels of support.

Evergreen sought to facilitate the remaining veterans' transition into self-sufficient business owners, and this goal was not confined to commercial sales. Evergreen's car repair training shop opened in September 1919, and students repaired tires from US Army trucks. A garage called Evergreen Tire Repair Shop opened near Evergreen in July 1920, owned and managed by the institution, which provided work for the veterans who repaired vehicles for the public.[82] Louis Kersting was a graduate of the car and tire repair program. Kersting, who was completely blinded in France by an artillery explosion, left Evergreen in June 1920, and in August the Federal Board for Vocational Education sent a Red Cross Institute for the Blind instructor to Hope, North Dakota, to help him start Victory Tire Repair Shop. "His reports show," the *Evergreen Review* claimed, "that he has been doing a profitable business. And, what is more, there hasn't been a single job come back for adjustment."[83] Evergreen's tire repair shop was a commercial business that the Red Cross established to facilitate business contracts between veterans and the public, which was a thread also evident elsewhere in the Industrial Department. After blinded veterans expressed their desire to become cigar makers, the Red Cross Institute for the Blind created a cigar factory and shop called Factory No. 563, opened in February 1920. The veterans named their product "Our Buddy Cigars," and early reports showed that the men produced 15,000 cigars by May 1920, many of which the men in the Commercial Department sold in Victory Store No. 1.[84]

The Red Cross Institute for the Blind's industrial practices—where blind veteran cigar makers worked in insulated workshops to produce cigars that were eventually sold by blind veterans in the Evergreen store—were similar to the sheltered workshops that institutions for blind civilians had established. As historian Kim Nielsen writes, sheltered workshops ultimately employed people with disabilities apart from nondisabled workers, often at low wages, with "the assumption that people with disabilities could not survive in the outside world and needed a special, protected, environment."[85] Samuel Gridley Howe had established the first workshop for blind workers in 1840 at the Perkins Institution and Massachusetts Asylum for the Blind. The institution trained workers in manual trades such as broom-making, chair-caning, and hand weaving, and acted as an intermediary by providing supplies to workers and then supplying finished goods to potential buyers. By 1908 there were sixteen workshops in existence that employed close to 600 blind American workers who made on average $3 per week per person.[86]

While workshops employed blind workers in trades that the sighted American public traditionally thought of as "blind trades," there were certainly blind workers who did not work in workshops and instead worked alongside sighted workers. Such was the case with civilian Gerald Ensing, a blind factory demonstrator and member of the Grand Rapids Association for the Blind in Michigan. Ensing's job as a factory demonstrator in 1918 was to visit factories and exhibit the kinds of jobs blind workers could undertake at any given worksite.[87] The exigencies of World War I also created opportunities for blind people to move out of workshops. Hundreds of blind civilians were employed in war factories, though only a small number retained those positions after the Armistice.[88] Despite blind people's clear and demonstrated abilities as efficient workers, the Red Cross Institute for the Blind still decided to create a quasi-workshop system, and still had blind veterans caning chairs and weaving baskets, which suggests that World War I may not have been the watershed moment in blind people's economic liberation that those involved in Evergreen had hoped for.

In some instances, the Red Cross coordinated job placement for blind veterans to work alongside sighted civilians. One example was Ernest Bayliss, who had worked in Detroit before the war in various capacities at car companies and a large drug manufacturer. After a shell explosion blinded him, Bayliss trained in the Industrial Department, and the Red Cross coordinated a job placement for him at Frederick Stearn & Company in Detroit drying bottles meant for medication. The institute constructed a wooden model of the machine he was to use, which enabled him to train even before leaving Evergreen. Once proficient, he was hired by Stearn & Company, and a Red Cross staff member spent a week with him in Detroit to ensure he was settled in his new role, where he performed at the same pace as his sighted counterparts.[89] Despite Bayliss's successful job placement, the Red Cross made no effort to suggest that all blind people could work proficiently alongside their sighted counterparts—and therefore away from the "blind trades" in sheltered workshops—given the necessary accessibility measures.

The systems the Red Cross Institute for the Blind installed for blind veterans were comprehensive and contributed to some of the successes that men blind from war service achieved. The *Evergreen Review* documented numerous men who trained in the Commercial Department's Victory Store. Those same men also counted on the support of Red Cross agents who scouted locations for stores in the veterans' own hometowns, took care of the bank paperwork, and spent time with veterans to ensure the stores opened without issues. Red Cross support did not guarantee success, however. Some veterans still struggled, as the experiences of James Riddervold suggest. But Riddervold's challenges did not make it into the pages of the *Evergreen Review*. Nor did Evergreen editors or administrators make the more revolutionary argument that accessibility measures might also enable blind civilians to live and work independently, as their preoccupation rested on identifying blind veterans as singularly worthy of public support as well as inspiringly overcoming their disabilities.

Conclusion

US Army officials had grand expectations for US Army General Hospital No. 7 when the thirteen blind soldiers who disembarked from the *Saxonia* in New York City arrived in Baltimore for vocational rehabilitation. Blind American soldiers, as rehabilitation leaders and media authorities suggested, were not going to be the helpless and dependent men that Americans had envisioned from stories about French blind soldiers. Instead, Evergreen officials looked to Sir Arthur Pearson's example of independence displayed at England's St. Dunstan's Hostel for Blinded Soldiers and Sailors. Early stories about Evergreen men overwhelmingly emphasized the men's work ethic and their battlefield wounds, even if hospital records indicate that not all Evergreen men were battlefield casualties, nor were they all soldiers to begin with. Additionally, media representations suggested that blind soldiers were unquestionably cheerful and optimistic about their futures and stood as inspirational figures to other people with disabilities because many Americans considered blindness as a disability that, more than many other disabilities, hindered one's ability to take an active part in life.

The literature in *Carry On*, the *Evergreen Review*, and the various newspapers and magazines that spotlighted blind soldiers and veterans represents a significant attempt to shift conversations about blindness to better align with the needs of wartime rehabilitation. In so doing, such literature overshadowed the complex physical and vocational realities experienced by many blind veterans. Evergreen was more than just a vocational training school for blind veterans, and the inspiring narratives that accompanied stories of the veterans' successful economic outcomes accompanied similarly inspiring stories about men forming social bonds within the institute's walls. Inspiring stories about the men's social lives abounded in American newspapers, yet also sanitized more complex lived experiences at the Red Cross Institute for the Blind, as the next chapter will demonstrate.

3

Gender, Race, and Belonging at Evergreen and Beyond

Frank Pyle liked to joke about his blindness. Writing for the *American Legion Weekly* in 1920, the blind veteran who lost his sight from spinal meningitis while in Brest, France, described how he and his comrades at Evergreen called themselves "blinks." One of the many stories that he wrote for a predominantly sighted veteran audience had to do with the numerous prosthetic eyes that accumulated at Evergreen during vocational rehabilitation. "One morning," Pyle wrote, "I heard one of the [blind] men calling for the nurse." The nurse found the "blink" searching for his prosthetic eyes that he had taken out the previous night before going to bed. That morning, according to Pyle, "He told the nurse he could not see to go to breakfast without them." Pyle explained that the "blinks" regularly misplaced their prosthetic eyes, and one day an Evergreen administrator even had to announce in the mess hall that he had found multiple glass eyes that needed to be claimed. "This caused quite a laugh and we 'blinks' proceeded to investigate." Pyle concluded, "One private spoke up and said, 'I had a good eye, but I left it over in France.'"[1]

Frank Pyle's article, "The Funny Side of a Tremendous Handicap," is significant for many reasons. It provides a glimpse into the daily lives of blind soldiers beyond the propagandistic pages of the *Evergreen Review* and *Carry On* magazines that sought to depict the men in uncomplicated and sanitized ways to elicit sympathy or inspiration. Pyle's story suggests that the lives of blind soldiers and veterans were richer and more complex, and that their experiences transcended the singular tragic or overcoming narratives so frequently used in stories written by sighted reporters about blind soldiers. Pyle's article is also important because it is one of the few publications written by a blind veteran—a man who worked to construct his own identity as a blind man, free from the restraints of societal ableism—instead of the more typical triumphalist narratives written by sighted observers. Pyle's joking and lighthearted manner of speaking about his blindness and his interactions with other blind veterans at Evergreen suggest that the men led fulfilling lives, and that there was a sense of masculine camaraderie among many of the predominantly white men there that was sometimes lost or diminished in the articles in *Carry On* and the *Evergreen Review.*

All these reasons make Pyle's article a good starting point to investigate the everyday lives of blind soldiers and veterans. This chapter shows that the official stories from *Carry On* and *Evergreen Review* overshadowed the reality that blind soldiers and veterans lived complex lives. That complexity is best understood by examining their own words and experiences reflected in newspaper interviews and personal narrative writing, and reading some sighted observers' literature with a critical lens. The men at Evergreen formed bonds through leisure activities that enabled them to showcase their masculinity while at times trying to pass as sighted or masquerade as totally blind.[2] They met women and they got married and had children, fulfilling roles traditionally assigned to men.

One's ability to fit in at Evergreen—as was evidenced by the lighthearted jovial atmosphere that Pyle conveyed—was also highly contingent on whether the veteran was white or Black, and whether the veteran conformed to the motivational ethos that Evergreen staff tried to cultivate during vocational rehabilitation. The experiences of a group of about half a dozen blind Black veterans who were effectively barred from the institution once the Red Cross took control in 1919 demonstrate that white racism excluded Black veterans. There were also some soldiers who, despite being white, had trouble fitting in, and understanding their exclusion gives important insight into the privileged status of white blind veterans.

These markers of inclusion and exclusion at Evergreen ultimately depended on the men's abilities either to conform to or to challenge what disability scholar Tobin Siebers calls the ideology of ability. Siebers argues that the ideology of ability dictates that *ability* rather than *disability* is the norm, and the ideology of ability therefore represses disability.[3] Narrative stories about blind veterans conformed to the ideology of ability because the writers assumed that blind veterans were transformed for the better when they had overcome their disability and conformed to ability norms by passing as sighted, unless, as Pyle shows, they masqueraded and claimed their disability in ways that felt comfortable to them. This chapter will show that white and Black blind soldiers indeed did both, and sometimes did neither. Understanding the ways that blind soldiers wrote narratives about their own lived experiences demystifies and complicates the stories so prevalent in *Carry On* and *Evergreen Review.*

Blind Soldiers Adjust to Being Blind

Frank Pyle was not alone in approaching his blindness with a sense of comedic levity. Rosanna Thorndike served as a reconstruction aide at Base Hospital No. 8 in Savenay, where many blind American soldiers first encountered rehabilitation services. There, Thorndike accompanied thirty-five soldiers through their earliest days of blindness in which they spent time in classes, writing, doing basketry, eating, and taking walks. In their afternoon walks, Thorndike recalled after her return to the United States in 1919, "The boys were always joking about themselves and they called themselves the 'blind rats.'" They called the orderlies "the one-eyed-pilots." This started when men who had lost only one eye helped soldiers blind in both eyes (by serving as orderlies). "So, in boarding-school style," Thorndike continued, "we took our afternoon walks with the rats [and] the one-eyed pilots." As they walked through the streets of Savenay with their canes, the "one-eyed pilots" had to keep the "rats" from walking into trees. The blind soldiers joked about their navigational challenges and all the while played games to guess whether a man or a woman had walked by them on the sidewalk.[4]

Savenay reconstruction aides also noted the optimism and determination with which some of the blind soldiers approached the early days of their reconstruction. One such soldier was Ewald Wegner. Wegner's war had ended when a shell explosion blinded him and wounded his arm, but despite his trauma he was eager to begin his rehabilitation as soon as he arrived at the US base hospital. According to one reconstruction aide who treated blind soldiers there, Wegner was "always the first to arrive at [the] evening readings [and he] learned Braille rapidly" by practicing with stories provided by Winifred Holt's Committee for Men Blinded in Battle.[5]

Ewald Wegner's eagerness to acclimate to blindness and learn braille was not the universal reaction. Blind soldiers under US Army jurisdiction had to deal with prolonged health issues directly related to their war wounds, and as a result some of them had been pessimistic when American reconstruction aides at Savenay encouraged them to begin training in braille almost immediately upon their arrival. Uncertainty about rehabilitation was certainly a reality that Michael Aaronsohn felt after he was blinded in battle. Aaronsohn arrived in Savenay alongside Ewald Wegner. Unlike Wegner, Aaronsohn felt the perpetual need to shield his grief about his sudden blindness from sighted onlookers by smiling. "That smile!" Aaronsohn wrote in his semi-autobiographical novel *Broken Lights*. "Would anyone ever understand its meaning? That smile . . . was an armor of defense, a shield against that most loathsome of human feelings, pity. He must smile to deceive. He must smile to ward off the barbs of pity. For no one, no one must perceive the anguish of his soul."[6] Aaronsohn, who demonstrated that blind soldiers indeed feel emotionally jarred by their sudden blindness, at once contemplated the grief he felt and his perceived need to hide that grief from sighted aides. Aaronsohn likewise recognized that some of his blind comrades considered the sighted civilian reconstruction aides with a sense of disdain and distrust because they "knew very little about their problems [as blind men]."[7]

Blind soldiers were in no less agreement about reconstruction when they arrived at Evergreen in Baltimore. The US Army administration at Evergreen had to encourage patients to go to class rather than rely on the eager spirit displayed by Ewald Wegner in Savenay. Vocational rehabilitation authorities, for example, had to suggest to the newly arrived men that they could earn "large sums of money" through their vocational training, therefore providing an economic incentive to go to class. When one of the staff members suggested to the blind soldiers that they should learn braille, some of the men were discouraged, and their attitudes toward the civilian instructors, according to one report, were "far from desirable."[8]

The low morale that many blind soldiers felt as a result of emotional, psychological, and physical adjustment to blindness was compounded by their intense desire to be discharged from the service. Evergreen soldier patients at US Army General Hospital No. 7 before 1919 were just that: they were soldiers. Their status as soldiers meant that they did not receive as much money in compensation as they would have if they had been immediately discharged from the service and were classified as veterans. This was a significant issue for many of the men because it meant that they were entitled to $100 per month for life if they were blind in both eyes, plus insurance payments of $57.50 per month, and that they were not getting these payments because they were still classified as "soldiers."[9] Instead, the blind soldiers received the meager army pay of $30 per month, all the while in some cases worrying about providing for dependents.[10] Their prolonged status as soldiers eroded patient morale to the point that some of the blind soldiers petitioned the War Department for discharge and benefits, though they ultimately did not become veterans until the Red Cross took over operations in 1919.[11]

Morale improved slightly when Evergreen hired a recreational leader to fill free time with extracurricular activities. Ethel Potter, Evergreen's first recreational leader, organized numerous events such as holiday parties and elegant dinners. The men had access to a newly built swimming pool, roller skating, bowling, and gymnastics.[12] Evergreen's second recreational leader, W. V. Thomas, arranged athletic programs with nearby Fort McHenry, which was the site of a second major Baltimore hospital. One such program included a visit from the "physical culture expert" named Matysek, who toured area hospitals and demonstrated to the blind soldiers at Evergreen "his wonderful features of strength."[13] Hospital staff invited middle-class white women from Baltimore to serve as dancing partners for the blind soldiers at regularly scheduled dances. Potter and the institute's women reconstruction aides, as well as local civilians interested in lending support, read to the men on a regular basis in the comfortable reading room, as most of the soldiers had not yet cultivated sufficient skill in braille to read the very limited number of braille books that the hospital had at its disposal. Finally, Potter and her colleagues arranged to have local civilian volunteers take the men on car rides or to social events throughout the city of Baltimore.[14]

Enthusiasm certainly increased with the connections made between Evergreen and Baltimore civilians, but so too did sighted people's objectification

A blind white soldier bowling at Evergreen, ca. 1918. (Library of Congress, Prints & Photographs Division, photograph by Harris & Ewing, LC-DIG-hec-11700)

of the blind soldiers. When a *New York Times* reporter visited Evergreen in January 1919, the reporter was greeted and given a tour by educational director Harold Whitehead. After pointing to William Zimmerman as the best example of a blind soldier who was "overcoming" his disability, Whitehead discussed the many ways that Zimmerman's comrades had also displayed their "normality," thus seeking to rebut nondisabled civilians' assumptions about blind people as helpless dependents. The evidence of normality that Harold Whitehead presented to the *New York Times* reporter included the fact that the men read, they bowled, and they danced. "They have girls out from Baltimore," the article continued, "and they have parties as gay and as normal as any Yale Prom," undoubtedly appealing to readers with an image of the men as straight, white, and middle-to-upper class. Major Nathaniel Ardan, the commanding officer of US Army General Hospital No. 7, chimed in: "It would do your heart good to see them turkey trot!"[15] It is unclear whether Ardan found entertainment watching blind soldiers at Evergreen, or if he saw inspiration in them. It is clear, however, that blind soldiers may have been regularly observed and objectified for doing mundane tasks that would not have gained an audience had the subjects been sighted.

The Evergreen Field Day, which took place on September 11, 1920, shortly after students and staff returned from summer vacation, demonstrates that blind veterans were at times active participants in their own objectification. The field day included athletic competitions, a picnic lunch, dinner, and an evening dance. Athletic events took place on the open grass field adjacent to the gymnasium and the music building, which was surrounded by covered handrail walkways that connected each building and that enabled blind soldiers to traverse the campus. The day began with a vivacious opening ceremony. Blind soldier Oscar Lentz and Marjorie Wallace—the daughter of L. W. Wallace, the general manager of the Red Cross Institute for the Blind—were the first to enter the field holding an Evergreen banner. Behind the two leaders came a dozen other soldiers in costumes. Arthur Crane dressed as a police officer. William Roberts, dubbed by the soldiers as the "Queen of the Day," dressed in a regal ceremonial queen's gown and rode in on a chariot accompanied by a team of four "husky slaves." James O'Hara dressed as a "chorus girl" and did a hula dance for the crowd as he entered the arena.[16]

Behind the "mirth-provoking masqueraders" were the "gladiators" who competed in the athletic events.[17] One gladiator, William Walker, performed a "strong man stunt." After driving a six-inch spike into a wooden plank and wrapping the nail with a piece of cloth, he "held [the spike] between his teeth and bent it back and forth until it broke, exactly as if it had

A blind white soldier at Evergreen using a pommel horse in an enclosed field, ca. 1918. (Library of Congress, Prints & Photographs Division, photograph by Harris & Ewing, LC-DIG-hec-11695)

been beaten back and forth with a hammer." Not to be outdone, James O'Hara—the "chorus girl"—performed a strong man stunt in his dress by strenuously lifting two fake 500-pound weights above his head, only to be shown up by a six-year-old boy who carried the weights away with little effort.[18] The main event was the tug-of-war competition between barracks 15 and barracks 16. Though 15 won the first match, barracks 16 wanted a rematch. "There can be no question," wrote the *Evergreen Review,* "that at this moment a conscious spirit of healthy rivalry was born between the inhabitants of barracks No. 16, jokingly known as the 'roughnecks' and those of barracks No. 15, who are supposed to be so much softer than their brothers, that they have been called the 'pussyfoots.'"[19]

Evergreen's field day was in some ways like Nathaniel Ardan's objectification of blind soldiers in his interview with the *New York Times* reporter. In both cases, nondisabled people were observing disabled people for entertainment. However, while there is no evidence to determine whether blind soldiers played an active or passive role in Ardan observing their dancing, blind soldiers organized, planned, and acted or competed in the activities of the field day. Additionally, they did so in a way that, as Tobin Siebers argues, masqueraded their identity—in this case, they masqueraded masculinity or femininity to deflect their status as blind men. William Roberts played the part of the "Queen of the Day," while the "roughnecks" and the "pussyfoots" displayed their masculine vigor to see which group was strongest. And the case of James O'Hara, who dressed as a chorus girl and performed a strenuous, albeit fake weightlifting routine, signified the simultaneous masquerading of masculinity and femininity in the service of displacing the gaze that nondisabled people normally directed at the men because of their disability. Gender identity and sex, as will be discussed in greater detail, factored significantly in blind soldiers' and veterans' journeys through rehabilitation and also enabled them to manage public perceptions of their disability.

Twenty-eight-year-old Frank Pyle, who trained as a Dictaphone operator at Evergreen around the time Ethel Potter began her work as recreational leader, consciously met nondisabled peoples' objectification in his own unique way and wrote in jest about what he considered well-meaning early interactions with the Baltimore public. In his typical comedic prose, Pyle compared his experiences at Evergreen to that of a caged animal and wrote to the *American Legion Weekly* about how Baltimore civilians regularly visited the rehabilitation hospital on Sundays to take the men for car rides, bring them to the theater, or give them presents. One of his comrades had written home one Sunday that "this is the day the people come out and feed the blind apes peanuts."[20] Pyle's comical disdain for being objectified also led him and other soldiers to jokingly mislead their observers about the war and their own wounds. When one woman asked Pyle how he had lost his vision—he had been blinded from spinal meningitis while in the army—he joked, "I was leaning up against a[n artillery] barrage when it went over with me," or, "I was watching the soldiers go across [no man's land] and the strain was too much for my sight," or, "I tried to stop a[n artillery] shell from exploding in front of a Y.M.C.A. man who had lost his way."[21]

There is a lot to unpack from Frank Pyle's ironic and at times self-deprecating humor. His writing was a clear response to the overwhelming influx of civilians who arrived at Evergreen in hopes of "cheering up" or motivating the blind veterans without necessarily trying to understand their experiences or get to know them as individuals. Blind American soldiers were popular symbols of wartime sacrifice in 1920s Baltimore much like their French counterparts to American audiences in 1916 New York City. Civilians wanted to help such men replenish their own wells of middle-class morality. Civilians also assumed that the blind soldiers, like their predecessors in the French Army, were nothing if not completely depressed and

Civilian visitors on a tour of Evergreen. (Library of Congress, Prints & Photographs Division, photograph by Harris & Ewing, LC-DIG-hec-11699)

in need of daily cheer to begin with. Siebers argues that one hallmark of an ableist society is that disabled people are often required to make their bodies (or minds) conform to the social prejudices of the nondisabled. The blind veterans in this instance were expected to be helpless and inferior.[22] Pyle was certainly conscious of such prejudices from men and women who seemed unlikely to get to know him beyond the performative generosity of an occasional visit.

Amid the flood of well-meaning civilians who arrived at Evergreen, Frank Pyle used his elevated social status as a blind veteran to his advantage. He knew that veterans had social capital. He also knew that the civilian driving him around Baltimore expected a good war story, which he was ready to deliver even if the story was fiction. Civilians expected all the veterans at Evergreen to have glorious stories of being blinded in battle, yet Pyle was blind from spinal meningitis. Nonetheless, Pyle took advantage of civilian battle voyeurism when he claimed that his blindness was a result of "leaning up against a barrage when it went over with me."

Pyle's writing also suggests that blind soldiers simultaneously tried to pass as nondisabled and tried to masquerade—overemphasize—their blindness.

Whereas passing refers to a person's efforts to conceal a stigmatized race, gender, sexuality, or disability to avoid the disadvantages that nonmarginalized people typically associate with a marginalized identity, masquerading happens when people either hide one disability by accentuating another disability, or they exaggerate their disability in order to claim their identity and manage the stigma of social difference for themselves rather than concede that power to nondisabled people.[23] Frank Pyle's comrades who had had their eyes traumatized by shrapnel and surgically removed passed by wearing prosthetic eyes, but they also masqueraded by referring to themselves as "blinks" and joking about their prosthetics in ways that may have surprised nondisabled sighted people. The "blink" in Pyle's story who misplaced his prosthetic eyes played an important part in claiming his own disability narrative by purposefully misapplying his prosthesis. This act is what Siebers argues is an important component of "masquerading" one's disability because it "introduces a temporary confusion in the public mind, allowing users a brief moment of freedom in which to assert their independence and individuality."[24]

If the regular crowds of civilians who visited Evergreen made Frank Pyle feel objectified and like a caged animal at the receiving end of nondisabled people's treats, he tried to claim power over his story in ways that suited his comedic personality. In this way, Pyle resisted the dominant narratives about his blindness that necessitated that he act pitiable or dependent for nondisabled civilians. Much like his comrades at Evergreen, Pyle's life and identity was complex. Though he claimed his disability by portraying his interactions with the sighted public in an amusing way, he was slightly more accommodating to gendered and ableist assumptions that their obligation as citizen-soldiers extended into the bedroom, and that as disabled men they were incapable of forming genuine relationships with sexual partners.

Marriage and Sex Help Blind Men "Make Good"

When William Zimmerman began his vocational training at Evergreen, he remarked to *Carry On* reporters that he had to "make good" by becoming economically self-sufficient because that was the only way he could retain the relationship he had cultivated with his girlfriend before the war. "Bill," she wrote to him, "If you make good I am going to marry you."[25] Whether or not this interaction actually happened or it was the creative product of the Surgeon General's office to sell rehabilitation to dispirited disabled male veterans and their families, Zimmerman and the other Evergreen blind soldiers and veterans pursued their vocational training with the expectation that they would need to become breadwinner husbands to fulfill the obligations of masculine postwar citizenship. As will be made clear, gender and sexuality were cornerstones of blind soldier rehabilitation but also served as another method by which the men asserted control over public conversations about their blindness.

Women's inclusion at Evergreen was an outlier when compared to other US Army rehabilitation hospitals. Even when women occupational and physio therapists were accepted for work in rehabilitation hospitals, authorities heavily regulated their use. Women had to have a background in physical education, as the Orthopedic Advisory Council argued, because the women would be more like drill sergeants than sympathetic bedside nurturers.[26] Rehabilitation officials also at times found do-gooder society women or relatives to be "meddlesome," and the US Army Medical Department attempted to keep women out of hospitals. Propaganda depicted society women as "dangerous" and purveyors of unwarranted sympathy, and argued that they kept men from doing the hard work of vocational training.[27] Evergreen, however, was a different story altogether.

That women occupied important roles in blind soldiers' and veterans' rehabilitation was clear from some of the support systems rehabilitation authorities put in place at Evergreen. When Zimmerman was at Evergreen, all blind men slept in the same impersonal military barracks while they trained, but administration still encouraged wives, girlfriends, sisters, or mothers to accompany them through the latter stages of training to help them acclimate to what would become family and work life after Evergreen. To make this possible, the Red Cross Institute for the Blind—which played a supporting role to General Hospital No. 7 until it took over operations in the fall of 1919—subsidized family members who wished to take part in vocational training by lodging them in Baltimore free of charge.[28]

When the Red Cross took over the institute, women's regular presence on the campus convinced administration to reconstruct parts of the campus in ways that would not upset middle-class moral sensibilities. Unquestionably the most striking example of Evergreen's physical changes was the transformation of living arrangements. The large twenty-person barracks that the blind soldiers had previously slept in became smaller, two-person dormitories that afforded the veterans more privacy.[29] Women who wished to visit the men were not allowed into the dorms. Instead, unmarried women had to "call [veterans] by using telephones in the 'double barracks,' [in the] Red Cross House, or in any of the [administrative] offices," at which point the men and women gathered in one of the recreation rooms.[30]

Strict guidelines about men's and women's interactions were only reserved for the single men who lived in the converted barracks, whereas married men lived in special quarters in a two-story building next door, called by the veterans themselves the "Colony of Double Deckerites," "Cupid's Cottage," or "the Love Nest." Cupid's Cottage had a recreation room with chairs and a piano, and in the evening, there was usually a social hour attended by the couples and their friends. Blind veteran James O'Hara, who had hula danced his way through the opening ceremony of Evergreen's field day, recalled that the evening events usually included "songs and stories, and usually . . . some fudge or cake."[31]

O'Hara also commented on the frequency of marriages that took place at Evergreen. By the end of 1920 around a dozen Evergreen men had been married at the institute, and some marriages were between students and staff.[32] Ewald Wegner was "one of the most popular" veterans at Evergreen. He trained in the poultry department where he fell in love with his "attractive instructor," Nettie Gilmore. The two had "flown the coop" after cultivating a relationship from their mutual interest in the chickens.[33] The fact that Wegner married one of his instructors stands in stark contrast to the heavily regulated state of occupational and physio therapists at other rehabilitation hospitals that aimed to desexualize women therapists when they interacted with disabled soldiers.[34] Frank Pyle got married in the middle of rehabilitation, though not to a member of the Evergreen staff. He had arrived at Evergreen in March 1919 and that fall he ventured to Philadelphia, got married, and returned with his new wife and lived in the "Colony of Double Deckerites."[35] By January 1921 between thirty and forty weddings had taken place at Evergreen. The institute was called "The Match Factory," because the men there, according to one newspaper article, "graduate into matrimony almost as fast as they do from their classes in merchandizing, vulcanizing, poultry-raising, cigar-making and the rest of it."[36]

Women who lived at Evergreen with their husbands supported the institute in numerous ways, one of which was in the newly transformed dining room. Responding to the blind men's criticisms of the rigid and unwelcoming atmosphere of the mess hall with its metal tables and military-issued cutlery, the Red Cross created a new, elegant dining room with smaller tables for up to eight people each, with tablecloths, window curtains, and waitresses. The *Evergreen Review* prided itself in the dining services when it claimed that "army rations were transformed into more palatable food."[37] "One lady of the staff or the wife of one of the men [was] usually the hostess," wrote James O'Hara. "For those who do not see, [the women] prepare the food . . . the men do the rest, and need no assistance." O'Hara recalled the ingenuity the veterans had when seeking independence at the family dinner table by envisioning the plate as a clock. "Directly out from you," he wrote, "is 12 o'clock. The side nearest to you is 6 o'clock. To the right is

3 o'clock and to the left is 9 o'clock. . . . Meat is placed at 12 o'clock and spinach at 9 o'clock. As soon as the clock stops, the boys ask to have [the clock] wound up again. This means a second helping."[38] Communal eating reinforced the men's masculine independence and the women's ancillary supporting roles in their postwar lives. The men needed women to set up their successful meals on the plates according to the clock, and building on that, the men themselves ate without help.

Through leisurely reading to the men, women occupied significant roles in blind veteran rehabilitation, although Evergreen had hoped to train blind veterans sufficiently enough in braille so that they could read for themselves. The Evergreen Braille Library, which was organized by braille librarian at the Library of Congress Gertrude Rider, had over 1,000 books. Some veterans found Rider's braille library helpful even after leaving Evergreen. From July to September 1920 Rider sent on average two books per month to each blind veteran who took advantage of the free postage on the books—though there is no indication of how many veterans this was. One anonymous veteran wrote to Rider, "I am almost lost without my Braille." Another wrote, "Although as yet I am a slow reader, I find great pleasure in a good story in Braille."[39]

Despite the size of the Evergreen Braille Library and the ease with which veterans gained access to books, the book selection was limited. American schools and agencies for blind people had only adopted the Revised Braille Grade 1 ½ in 1917 and thus ended the "war of the dots" by standardizing braille type from the numerous grades that had existed before World War I. Before the "war of the dots," blind people had to acclimate to one of five different "codes" of print across the English language, as there was no single standard.[40] The cost of materials to print braille books and labor made their production exceedingly expensive. Whereas the ink version of Mark Twain's *Huckleberry Finn* cost $1.75 to produce in the early 1920s, the same book cost $31.10 to produce in braille.[41] To remedy this, the federal government subsidized the American Printing House for the Blind with $50,000 a year to produce books for blind schoolchildren, but that money was reserved for textbooks. In 1922, a delegation of blind veterans appealed to President Warren Harding to appropriate an additional $50,000 a year for books for their own use. By 1924, that number had increased to $100,000, which went toward publishing sixty-eight different braille books.[42] Ultimately, though, braille books were expensive to produce, and the price limited what Evergreen's library was able to make available for newly blind adult men just learning to read. Many of the books were textbooks that supported the needs of vocational training classes, rather than the popular novels for leisurely reading that so many of the veterans actually wanted, which is part of the reason women read so frequently to them.

Evergreen's braille library was limited also because veterans were not proficient enough to read braille despite their training, and sighted reconstruction aides as well as wives, mothers, and girlfriends regularly stepped in to read ink-based literature.[43] Robert Irwin, who helped form a list of the books to publish for blind veterans at Evergreen, and who would eventually lead the American Foundation for the Blind, commented on the difficulties veterans had with reading braille. "The truth is," he wrote to a colleague in 1925, "our Veteran readers are not anything to brag about" because they were inexperienced in braille, they only had government books for a few months, and they often used their disability compensation to hire readers.[44]

Ewald Wegner did not reach fluency much to the dismay of his aides at the base hospital in Savenay and at Evergreen. His son Robert Wegner recalled that after his father left Evergreen his parents spent a lot of their spare time on the screened-in porch of their house in Gillette, New Jersey. "I remember mother [Nettie Wegner] often reading stories out of the *Saturday Evening Post, Collier's, Country Gentlemen,* and other books and magazines to Ewald," he wrote. "These readings went on all during my life at home."[45] Numerous veterans who ultimately enrolled in college after leaving Evergreen also found that their braille training was insufficient or that institutions were inaccessible and that they provided few or no braille books to begin with.[46] Ultimately, blind veterans invariably ditched braille and relied on women relatives, hired readers, or friends to read to them, at least until the 1930s when the talking (recorded) book offered a less expensive way to bring literature to blind people.[47]

The relationships between blind veterans and their wives were mutually fulfilling and reinforcing, yet were not without cultural stigma that marked the disabled husbands as dependent. The "blinks," according to one article that adopted Frank Pyle's term for the blind veterans, make the "best husbands."[48] Evergreen bride Zoe Beckley even wrote a song about it. "For he sees no faults that other men see!" she wrote, referring to the veteran's blindness as a sign of devotion because he did not judge her physical beauty. The blind man is the best husband, according to Beckley, because he "belongs so COMPLETELY to the girl he marries."[49] Zoe Beckley considered her husband's blindness as a benefit to their marriage in part as a result of her limited conception of disabled sexuality that deprived him of sexual agency in his own right.[50] Women like Beckley argued that blind veterans made the best husbands because they were so devoted to their wives due to their dependence on them and their inability to see other women. This claim rests on the assumption that blind men could not cultivate meaningful romantic relationships on their own accord through serious emotional interpersonal interactions. Therefore, while Beckley understood blindness as an advantage in their relationship, her views nonetheless further stigmatized her blind husband as sexually dependent on her.

One significant stereotype that disability scholar Tobin Siebers has argued oppresses disabled people is "the myth that they do not experience sexual feelings or . . . that they do not have a sexual culture" in their own right.[51] Eugenicists in Britain certainly found the relationships cultivated between seeing women and blinded British veterans at St. Dunstan's astonishing, so much so that the *Eugenics Review* initially suggested that the blind men "might find suitable brides among girls who were physically so unattractive as otherwise to be destined to celibacy." Onlookers who subscribed to the eugenicists' ableist assumptions that blindness disqualified individuals from having fulfilling relationships were subsequently astonished that fifty-five men at St. Dunstan's had married after the war, and almost without exception their brides had been "unusually good looking."[52] As is reflected in the *Eugenics Review* and articles that featured women like Zoe Beckley, nondisabled observers assumed that even though blind American veterans differed from their French counterparts in that they were happily motivated to become economically self-sufficient, their disability still threatened to condemn them to lovelessness. It was the stigma that cast blind veterans as dependent men that called into question their sexuality, but it was their status as veterans (of the masculine occupation of war) that rescued them from the stigma of assuming that they were nonsexual beings.

If there was any doubt on the part of the seeing public that blind veterans had sex, the children conceived at Evergreen dispelled those misconceptions. Ewald and Nettie Wegner had a son and a daughter within months of leaving Evergreen, upon which time they put their vocational training to use by opening a chicken farm in Gillette, New Jersey.[53] Children appeared before training even finished. Marion and Helen were the two daughters of blind veteran Jim McGuire, and joined what the editors of the *Evergreen Review* called the "Roster of Evergreen Babies," which included five born between November 1919 and March 1920.[54] Marion especially enjoyed "showing [her] father the pictures in her bunny book . . . by pressing his finger over them [to] feel the colors."[55] Frank Pyle and his wife were "particularly happy when, in the summer of 1920, the stork brought a tiny boy."[56] Writing in January 1921, Pyle expressed excitement that "a year has now gone by" since the start of Cupid's Cottage, "and we find a dozen tiny soldiers, the sons of war-blinded veterans."[57] The children of Evergreen not only fulfilled blind veterans' own hopes for a family, but they also suggested to the public that blindness did not inhibit the men's ability to create a new generation of abled people.[58]

Discussions about blind veterans and sex here are revealing, as they occurred within a broader wartime and rehabilitation culture averse to sexual interactions between soldiers and women due to the fear of venereal disease and moral corruption. Progressive Era social hygienists and physicians had worked hard to prevent venereal diseases in the American Expeditionary Forces (AEF) through the creation of the Commission on Training Camp Activities (CTCA), which sponsored campaigns aimed at controlling soldiers' sexual desires.[59] General John Pershing, the commander of the AEF in Europe, made contracting a venereal disease punishable by court martial, and the AEF established special convalescent camps to confine men with venereal disease.[60] Authorities at US Army rehabilitation hospitals similarly worried that unsupervised contact with women might lead to moral deprivation or, potentially, venereal disease.[61] Given this context, the US Army and Red Cross's policies regarding blind men's interactions with women seem relatively relaxed, perhaps because of prevailing and erroneous assumptions that blind people were asexual or could not attract romantic partners.

The rhetoric some observers used when speaking about blind veterans and sexuality indeed suggested that the American public assumed the men's *lack* of sexuality, only to be proven wrong by their very real relationships. British eugenicists were surprised that blind veterans found attractive wives. Rhetoric about American veterans also rested on uncertainty regarding the men's sexuality. A Baltimore newspaper told readers about Corporal Harry Keefrider's marriage to Priscilla Connolly, where "war and romance compounded in the right proportions [which formed] the most powerful love potion in the world."[62] Such language assumed that Keefrider did not have sexual agency, that he could not possibly have found love due to his personality, charm, intellect, or looks. Instead, it took a magical potion to make the match happen. Civilian observers made similar assumptions when embracing the name of the home where married couples at Evergreen lived, "Cupid's Cottage." Cupid, after all, used supernatural powers to make love happen between two people who could not possibly have found the connection organically.

Some reports considered the personal narratives of those involved and suggested that the relationships between blind veterans and their wives were deep connections that were mutually beneficial. John Harrel's wife looked forward to returning to their home state of Arkansas where they were to open an insurance business. She said, "He's got the knowledge and I have the Eyes! We both got each other—and we can't fail."[63] Nettie Wegner helped significantly in her and Ewald's Gillette, New Jersey, chicken farm. "Mother was always his eyes," wrote their son Robert, "and treated him like a king. She did all the book keeping [*sic*] for the chicken business," all while Ewald maintained the coal stoves that heated the chicken coops, counted the chickens every evening, fed the chickens, and turned the eggs.[64]

Even though many of these romances were genuine emotional connections between two adults with agency—as the Wegners and the Harrels demonstrate—news stories regularly ignored the men's sexual agency by framing the relationships as a "challenge" for women to live up to their sexual "responsibility" to the men. Reporter Helen Hoffman wrote in the *Boston Herald* about the "duty" women had to fulfill their "supreme sacrifice" by marrying blind veterans. Among those who fulfilled this calling was the instructor of the blind French soldier Paul Thuet, whom she married shortly after meeting him. In a letter to the British, French, and Belgian Blind Relief War Fund, the unnamed instructor concluded that her marriage to Thuet was a better decision than marrying an "ordinary healthy man" because "there are more opportunities of showing him kindness and attention. Such a marriage," she continued, "does not need much courage as people say about us, but much love." While Thuet's wife acknowledged that her loving connection with Paul was a complex relationship with many facets both intrinsic to and independent from his blindness, Helen Hoffman could not conceive of the marriage as anything less than a pity-driven sacrifice on the part of the woman to alleviate the suffering of a poor blind man. Hoffman's goal, it seemed, was to challenge American women to fulfill the same "sacrifice." "Are you, Miss America," she asked, "ready to take a blinded husband?"[65]

Nondisabled reporters rarely portrayed blind veterans' relationships with women as organic or genuine emotional and physical connections. In some circumstances, stories about blind veterans such as Ewald Wegner suggested close and committed relationships between two people that benefited both husband and wife. This was likely the norm, as numerous other blind veterans had seemingly happy long-term marriages. Often, though, newspapers chose to ignore the deep mutual love, and stripped blind veterans of their sexual and emotional agency. Blind veterans did find love, but it came by Cupid's magic arrow, a love potion, or a supreme sacrifice on the part of a woman rather than from kindness, compassion, attraction, and genuine human connection. Not all was as it seemed at Evergreen if readers went solely by what they read in newspapers about the institute. By contrast, life at the institute was decidedly more complex from the beginning. Nowhere was this clearer than with the experiences of Andrew Knebel and Charles Parker Braithwaite.

Trouble behind the Headlines: Jim Crow and the Trouble-Making Tour

Two months before Andrew Knebel joined the ranks of newlyweds at Cupid's Cottage, he was reprimanded for returning to his bed inebriated, waking up almost everyone in his dormitory, and punching a US Army guard in the face who tried to calm Knebel down. Unlike the lengthy newspaper article that reported about Knebel's nuptials, the incident that landed him in Evergreen's locked guard house appeared in no periodical or magazine. The incident report and the haphazard and incomplete trial of Knebel and two of his blind comrades came and went just as the US Army relinquished control of Evergreen to the Red Cross Institute for the Blind. Nonetheless, Knebel's late-night escapade and its lack of public discussion compared to other forms of gendered expression suggest that authorities in charge of rehabilitating blind veterans were aware of the potentially damaging implications of certain forms of recreation and endeavored to shield the men from unsavory public scrutiny. For the blind veterans themselves, Knebel's "trouble making tour," as one official called it, demonstrated that in addition to dances, marriages, and sports, blind veterans' postwar lives also included alcohol.

The fact that blind veterans drank while at Evergreen is significant in part because, though federal prohibition against alcohol was not yet a reality, the US Army was vigilant against such activities. As historian Nancy K. Bristow demonstrates, Woodrow Wilson's creation of the federal agency the Commission on Training Camp Activities in 1917 was an important step in safeguarding young men's morals by protecting them from venereal diseases and alcoholism, and therefore securing the US Army from unnecessary manpower losses.[66] Progressive reformers on the commission understood that shaping the soldier's recreational life and dissuading young men from drinking alcohol was an important step in transforming American culture into the white, urban, middle-class image.[67] Some American mothers even preferred that their sons lose their life in a battlefield death than live a "dishonorable life" consuming alcohol and having sex with prostitutes near US Army camps.[68] The Commission on Training Camp Activities ultimately outlined plans to clean up camp life and surrounding towns, condemned alcohol consumption and prostitution, and encouraged other opportunities for recreation that Progressives deemed more appropriate along the standards of white, middle-class life.[69]

State vigilance against alcohol consumption accompanied broader official fears of veteran misconduct, and such vigilance extended beyond the training camps and into the hospitals.[70] Federal authorities reported on the landscape of vice around US Army hospitals similar to the one at which blind soldiers experienced rehabilitation. In the case of Fort McPherson, Georgia, near Atlanta, an army investigator noted that conditions in hotels and lodging houses were bad, that liquor was sold freely to soldiers, and that "the hotels are still infested with prostitutes" where "the bell boys demand $1.00 for each engagement they make for the women."[71] Officials at US Army General Hospital No. 3 in Colonia, New Jersey, noted toward the end of 1918 that there was no prostitution in the nearby towns, but "there had been several cases of drunkenness among the patients" and that the lack of strict discipline at the hospital compared to camps in France was likely a factor in the high numbers of patients caught drunk.[72] To counteract the situation, hospitals put in place measures to prevent drunkenness, including collaborating with metropolitan police departments and giving out "honor cards" signifying that a patient was morally worthy of receiving a pass to a nearby city.[73]

Evergreen authorities also tried to dissuade blind soldiers from such activities. Before US Army General Hospital No. 7 disbanded, army authorities placed attendants in wards to restrict gambling and drinking.[74] The hospital also monitored the patients' whereabouts, requiring them to have a pass to leave the hospital. Authorities only permitted the men to go to Baltimore on weeknights from 6:30 p.m. to 10:30 p.m., and no later than midnight on weekends. Patients who lost sight in both eyes were required to have an attendant from the hospital accompany them wherever they went.[75] The men had little respite from army regulations. Sighted US Army Lieutenant J. T. Boyd, who was one of the Evergreen administrators, suggested that to prevent alcohol from entering hospital grounds, the blind soldiers should be searched as they entered the hospital from their leave in the city, and that "plain clothes detectives follow" them while they were away.[76]

Despite measures meant to impose middle-class morality on individual soldiers by policing their activities, disabled patients at hospitals in Baltimore and elsewhere drank, fought, and clashed with civilians. In March 1919, two patients were arrested at the Pennsylvania Railroad Station for being drunk, resisting arrest, and attempting to incite a riot.[77] Five months later two patients from the same hospital were arrested at the same railroad station for "raising a disturbance and insulting girls" and then charging at a police officer with their crutches.[78] In May 1920 a group of soldiers from the Medical Department at Fort McHenry fought a group of civilians in Baltimore, wrestled a pistol from one of the civilians, and fired several shots over the gathering crowd.[79] Though the last case may not have been hospital patients, there is ample evidence that measures the US Army put in place to rein in drinking and disorderly conduct did not completely succeed.

Evergreen encountered similar problems, which precipitated hospital administrator J. T. Boyd to investigate how blind patients found access to liquor. His informant, "Mr. Seabold . . . a very reliable, good citizen of the neighborhood," had taken a particular interest in investigating the matter. Seabold told Boyd about rumors that some of the patients obtained liquor "around the car barn through an intermediary, either boys or the employees of the railway company." Seabold also had knowledge given to him from a military police officer in Baltimore who came across a "very drunk" blind soldier in the city, and after the soldier created a disturbance, "two well dressed ladies came up and said they knew the soldier; an automobile suddenly drove up, [and] the ladies whisked the soldier away."[80]

Another incident took place on April 30, 1919, when two white blind soldiers were at the J. L. Wall Bar around the corner from Evergreen and had been "fighting with a negro." The soldiers were "more or less drunk," and one had a scratch on his face "showing that he had been in a fight." Both men were arrested and were brought back to the hospital.[81] There is no indication in the report about what instigated the altercation but considering two white men fought a Black man in early twentieth-century Baltimore, racism likely played a part. What is clear is that blind soldiers drank frequently, that drinking sometimes led to violence, and that authorities understood this to be a symptom of deteriorating morality among disabled soldiers who magazines such as *Carry On* professed were nothing less than happy, independent, and on the way to living productive and moral lives.

While there is no indication that detectives followed intoxicated blind soldiers through Baltimore's streets, hospital staff did search patients when they returned from the city, as blind soldier Andrew Knebel's disciplinary case makes clear. On the night of May 7, 1919, blind patients George Graves, Andrew Knebel, and John McGrath left their barracks for Baltimore just before midnight. Knebel and Graves returned drunk around two in the morning and found that the military police had searched their friend McGrath, placing him under arrest in the guard house for being drunk and disorderly. Upon hearing about their friend, Knebel and Graves finished their bottles of liquor and embarked on what one hospital guard called a "trouble making tour," waking up all the patients with "boistrousness [*sic*] and singing," breaking windows, and turning beds over that had their blind comrades still lying in them.

The violence escalated. The guard on duty tried to reason with the two men to go to bed, but they refused. Lieutenant James Bryant of the US Army Medical Corps arrived to find the men hitting the beds with their canes. Authorities later realized that the men had weighted down the ends of their canes with lead so that they were more lethal and could be used

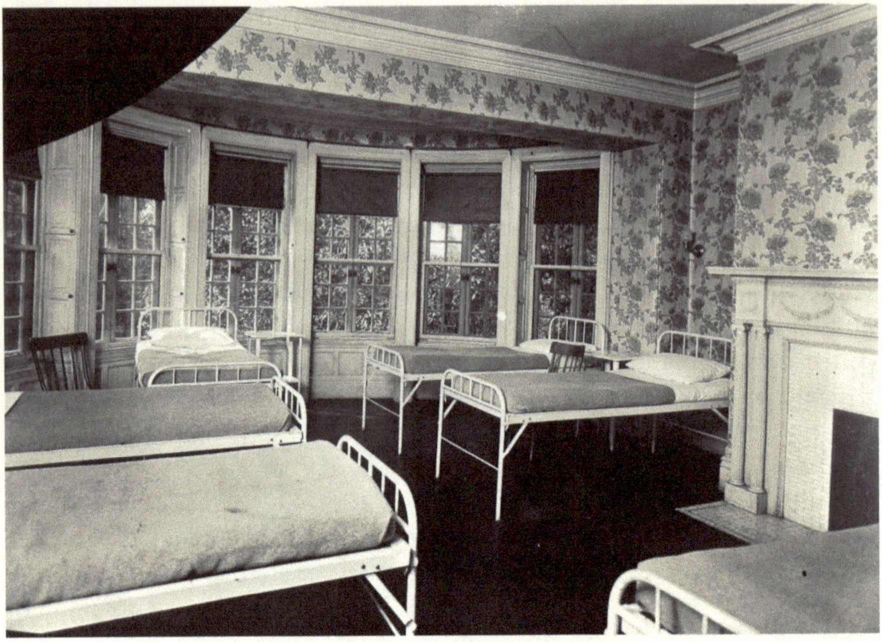

A ward at Evergreen, ca. November 1918. (Library of Congress, Prints & Photographs Division, American National Red Cross Collection, LC-DIG-anrc-02468)

as weapons. When Bryant repeated a previous plea to go to bed, the men yelled, "Hell no, we are not going to bed. . . . You are not big enough to put us to bed." When the guards asked Knebel for his cane, he refused. Guards attempted to take it by force, and in the scuffle, Knebel punched Bryant, to which Knebel admitted that he "probably . . . swung at him . . . but [did] not remember hitting him." After Bryant ordered the two men to the guard house, Graves stated that he "would kill the first man" who touched either him or Knebel. Knebel took off his shirt and provoked Bryant to fight him by calling him "all the names he could think of." Bryant grabbed Knebel by the neck and with the guards proceeded to the guard house. On the way to the guard house, Knebel broke away and punched Bryant in the face, after which time the guards tied his hands and feet. Once they had finally arrived at the guard house, McGrath, who had been arrested earlier that night, jumped on one of the guards to attempt an escape. Once Knebel, McGrath, and Graves were locked in the guard house, Knebel broke out all the windows in a failed attempt to break free.[82]

Andrew Knebel's "trouble making tour" would not have bode well for an institution that professed it was training the most deserving of America's disabled veterans for lives of successful civilian citizenship. Like Frank Pyle, Knebel resisted the dominant narratives about his blindness that cast him as happy, socially interdependent with a supportive wife, and economically productive. Both men wrote their own narratives. Whereas Pyle literally wrote his narrative in a comical way that may have caught nondisabled civilians off guard by portraying blindness with unexpected humor, Knebel metaphorically wrote his narrative through liquor bottles and punches. What may have seemed to hospital administrators as a threat to middle-class morality might suggest, to modern observers, an effort by Knebel to take control of his story while trying to break free of the limitations of military restrictions and middle-class standards of morality.

Andrew Knebel's "trouble making tour" suggests that there was much about daily life at Evergreen that the white administrators hoped to shield from public perception, and the same can be said for the experiences of Black soldiers. Media representations of successfully rehabilitated blind veterans almost exclusively depicted white veterans for white readers.[83] Americans' assumptions about blind soldier whiteness extended as far back as the artistic efforts of F. C. Yohn and Emil Fuchs who drew their idealized white soldiers blinded in combat for the commercial benefit of the British, French, and Belgian Blind Relief War Fund, and when writers suggested that British Sergeant Robert Middlemiss was "typical of the many blinded soldiers" of the war.[84] *Carry On* similarly emphasized white soldier William Zimmerman as its "typical" blind soldier, while the "buddies" *Evergreen Review* profiled as "typical" of the successfully rehabilitated blind soldier were all white. And when Evergreen forwarded to the US government names of ideal blind candidates for the Liberty Loan Drive, all five names—including William Zimmerman—were white men.[85] White blind soldiers and veterans thus benefitted from the privilege of their skin color from the very beginning of their wounds.

Black veterans by contrast felt the sting of racism during and after World War I. Close to 400,000 African Americans were conscripted into the armed forces for World War I, and most served in noncombat units, working as cooks or laborers, while around 38,000 served in combat on the Western Front.[86] Those who returned with war wounds or illnesses from their service encountered structural racism in medicine and rehabilitation at a time when heightened racial tensions and race riots defined the postwar United States.[87] Southern white representatives in charge of disability benefits neglected to forward necessary evidence to the United States Veterans' Bureau to complete Black servicemen's claims.[88] Federal Board for Vocational Education policies, as historian Paul Lawrie has argued, "regularly devalued, deskilled, and institutionalized disabled African American veterans and dismissed their claims to rehabilitation as spurious attempts to unjustly profit from their 'natural inferiority.'"[89] Institutional racism combined with cultural racism, as rehabilitation propaganda that shaped public perceptions about disabled veterans was overwhelmingly white in content.[90] Rehabilitation policy, therefore, marginalized disabled Black veterans in many American hospitals that were under federal jurisdiction.[91]

Blind soldiers and veterans encountered racism in much the same way as their sighted counterparts, though references to Black veterans at Evergreen are sparse and incomplete. There were at least five blind Black soldiers who arrived at US Army General Hospital No. 7 before the institute's late 1919 transfer to the Red Cross. One reference was the *New York Herald* reporter who boarded the *Saxonia* in February 1919 and emphasized the collegiality between blind Black soldier Nelson Hawkins and his white comrades Henry Bitter, William Whalen, and Ewald Wegner when they were on their way to Evergreen.[92] Military records from Evergreen also referenced Black soldiers. They demonstrate that the US Army kept recreation segregated at US Army General Hospital No. 7. For religious services, white soldiers had access to a hospital-approved Catholic priest and a Jewish rabbi, while "Colored clergymen," wrote the hospital's commanding officer, "have been given a permanent pass to the Hospital."[93]

The US Army also maintained a separate and segregated schedule for recreation at Evergreen while Black community members extended gratitude and social opportunities to Black Evergreen soldiers. Black soldiers obtained theater and concert tickets on separate nights from their white counterparts. A specific "Schedule for Colored Soldiers on Post" noted that after segregated Sunday church services, blind Black soldiers went to "dinner in one of the church people's homes."[94] This happened in February 1919, when a "Mrs. Pauline Jackson Helm" brought Black Evergreen soldiers to church, "after which they enjoyed a splendid dinner at the home of Mrs. [Chito] Henry," followed by a social hour.[95] Black community members in Baltimore and elsewhere, therefore, recognized the marginalization that Black soldiers experienced due to white racism in the wards and, in turn, provided recreation opportunities away from institutions.[96] The only evidence that suggested recreational integration was the fact that Black soldiers used the gymnasium "along with the other patients."[97]

The *Evergreen Review* also included references to Black soldiers and veterans. The magazine featured around thirty-five images of blind students in training, many of which were taken during US Army control. Among the images, only two included a Black soldier. One such photograph showed patients learning agriculture and chicken raising, though the single Black man in the image appeared relatively passive. Instead of working, he was standing behind the women reconstruction aides while the white soldiers actively had their hands on the chickens.[98] A second photograph shows blind soldiers sitting in an auditorium listening to a speech given by US General John Pershing. Two Black soldiers are visible in the photograph sitting in the back of the auditorium, whereas much of the image is taken up by the white soldiers and staff.[99] A photograph taken by Harris & Ewing Photography Company during Sir Arthur Pearson's speech to Evergreen students shows a blind Black soldier in the front row (see image on page 60). The *Evergreen Review*'s regular column, "Who's Who among Our Buddies," which highlighted the vocational successes of certain blind veterans during the Red Cross's tenure, did not feature Black veterans.

Despite the posturing that Evergreen officials took to show that Black soldiers received vocational training and took part in events, the experiences of Black soldiers were anything but equal to their white counterparts, especially during the tenure of the Red Cross Institute for the Blind.[100] Of the five Black veterans who had been at the school while it was under US Army control, James Nelson, Nelson Hawkins, Charles Bennett, and Sylvester Boston left Evergreen in the fall of 1919 shortly after the Red Cross assumed control. After the US Army delegated vocational rehabilitation to the Red Cross and the Federal Board for Vocational Education, white administrators significantly marginalized the Black soldiers. According to the *Baltimore Afro-American* newspaper, "Instruction [was] offered the blind soldiers in automobile repair work, the use of the dictaphone, in stenography, reading by the Braille system, typewriting, poultry raising and other useful subjects." However, "the colored students were told that they did not have sufficient education to take up these branches." Black veterans also had to eat in a separate, much smaller dining room.[101]

Charles Parker Braithwaite was the only Black veteran who resisted white racism and remained at the Red Cross Institute for the Blind after the four other men left. Braithwaite had been blinded by a shell explosion in the Argonne Forest in July 1918 when he served in the 369th Infantry Regiment—the "Harlem Hellfighters." Braithwaite refused to eat in the "Jim Crow" room to which the white staff had relegated Black veterans, and Evergreen administration subsequently gave him money to find his meals in Baltimore as an alternative. In an interview with the *Afro-American,* Braithwaite claimed that he had had enough of the racism there, and was returning to his home in Brooklyn, New York. "I can't stand conditions here," he said, "and I am not learning anything. A place has been provided for me in another school. The discriminations here are awful. Why, my room has not even been swept out for a week and my bed linen has not been changed in that time. We have been told that we could not learn anything here, but see the whites well provided for on every hand."[102] Braithwaite found adequate training at the Brooklyn Association for Improving the

Condition of the Poor. The staff there trained him in typewriting, braille, and Dictaphone operation, which were all denied to him at Evergreen even though they were readily available to his white counterparts.[103]

White American media misrepresented Charles Braithwaite's experiences and ignored the racism that forced him to leave Evergreen. The *Brooklyn Daily Eagle* conceded that Braithwaite had served with the "colored troops" under French command, and that he was blinded in combat. The newspaper made no mention of Evergreen. It told its readers that the Brooklyn Association's methods were effective and had been "further sanctioned by Uncle Sam in sending to the association men of total disability" including Braithwaite. Charles Braithwaite, the erroneous account continued, "could live on the pension Uncle Sam allows him, but he is determined to earn a living for himself and his wife."[104] The *Brooklyn Daily Eagle* suggested that Braithwaite made use of "Uncle Sam's" help. He surely took advantage of rehabilitation at least until Red Cross administrators' racism made him feel unwelcome. In no way, though, was Braithwaite sent to the association by Uncle Sam. He went there on his own accord *because* of restrictions against him at Evergreen emplaced by the Red Cross and his fellow blind veterans.

Already marginalized by limiting societal beliefs about blindness, Braithwaite and his Black Evergreen comrades encountered the dual stigma of racism and ableism as they returned home with wounds that were supposed to have earned them special status as war heroes. For Braithwaite, Nelson, Hawkins, Bennett, and Boston, the added barriers of racism made rehabilitation's goals—medical healing, and social and economic independence—far more difficult to achieve. By December 1919, according to the *Afro-American,* local Baltimore Baptist and Methodist ministers condemned the Red Cross for humiliating the blind Black veterans. "There is not a single colored soldier in the Evergreen hospital today," it stated. The situation led the ministers to boycott their support of the Red Cross "as long as it is managed by the same crowd of whites, who drove blind Negro soldiers out of Evergreen Hospital."[105] Unsurprisingly, the Red Cross Institute for the Blind included none of this in the *Evergreen Review,* and other newspapers claimed that Uncle Sam sent Braithwaite to the Brooklyn Association out of goodwill, therefore misrepresenting the racist exclusions that caused him to leave the institute to begin with.[106]

Conclusion

Headlines in American newspapers emphasized blind veterans' masculinity as important markers of their independence. Civilians eagerly peered into the lives of these men to see them carrying on tasks and achieving milestones such as physical development, marriage, and having children, which were as important in their reintegration into society as vocational rehabilitation. Far from being passively objectified by curious onlookers, blind veterans in some cases took advantage of the attention given to them, as the field day and Frank Pyle's writings suggest. These sources ultimately demonstrate that many blind veterans built their own identities by living vibrant and fulfilling lives at Evergreen and beyond. Recreational leaders ensured that the men there had numerous leisure activities in which to partake. Athletic competitions and leisurely swims in the pool were usually accompanied by midday picnics and late-night dinner and dancing. Blind veterans went on dates with women in the city of Baltimore, had fulfilling relationships, got married, and had numerous children. Evergreen seemed to resemble a social club, or in some cases even a college fraternity house, as much as it did a rehabilitation center for vocational training.

As Andrew Knebel's "trouble making tour" and Charles Braithwaite's confrontation of Jim Crow suggest, not all postwar blind veteran experiences conformed to what rehabilitation leaders at Evergreen hoped to display to the public. By returning to his dormitory drunk and punching a guard in the face, Knebel threatened to destabilize the elevated social capital many blind veterans had with the public and jeopardized the subtle equating of independence with morality that the US Army and the Red Cross hoped to convey to the public. Knebel's subsequent treatment, his ultimate acceptance at the institute despite his "trouble making tour," and the positive public reception of his marriage reaffirmed his position as a blind American veteran. By contrast, Charles Braithwaite and other Black veterans experienced no such consideration from white administrators. Instead, white authorities limited Black soldiers' access to even the basic necessities of life such as food and vocational training.

As these stories suggest, there was no uniform blind veteran experience. Health realities varied as much as individual preferences and personalities. How one soldier met rehabilitation may have been very different from how another soldier approached the same training. Understanding the "blind veteran experience" as a monolith does an injustice to the soldiers who lived complex, complicated, challenging, and rewarding lives, and threatens to leave troubling patterns such as racial injustice unexamined. Complicating the myth of the singular blind veteran experience not only makes clear the complexities of blind veterans' individual lives but also problematizes their lives and highlights the ways that blind veterans disagreed among themselves. Nowhere was this clearer than with the development of blind veteran organizations, the subject of chapter 4.

4

The Disability Politics of Blind Veteran Organizations in the United States

The United States Blind Veterans of the World War (USBVWW) organization held its first annual conference in Baltimore, Maryland, in the first week of November 1922. Seventy-five "cheerful" and "smiling" blind veterans arrived at the Southern Hotel for the convention's first day on Monday, November 6, where they heard speeches from Baltimore mayor William Broening and Maryland governor Albert Ritchie, and then had dinner and an evening of dancing. Over the coming days the blind veteran delegates attended events at Evergreen and went on car rides through the city of Baltimore, before the convention culminated in an Armistice Day parade on Saturday, November 11th, which was the four-year anniversary of the 1918 Armistice. At 11 a.m. the veterans and the entire city came to a standstill to commemorate the moment of the signing of the Armistice. The only sound that could be heard was Baltimore City Hall's bells tolling in the distance.[1]

The blind veterans in the parade were invigorated about their new organization and the comradeship it promised to engender, so much so that members quickly emphasized their distinctiveness from other such veterans' organizations. The delegates at the first convention had made it clear that the USBVWW would be more effective at addressing blind veterans' specific needs than the Disabled American Veterans of the World War (DAVWW), the American Legion, or the Veterans of Foreign Wars (VFW). USBVWW Commander Raymond Day argued that point to his comrades at Evergreen two days before the Armistice Day parade. "Boys," he exclaimed to his buddies, "I'm sick to death of the old army organizations. All they do is pass resolutions and hold conventions. Let's not pass any resolutions. When we want something let's go out and get it. Let's make this a regular he-man's society."[2] When the veterans emphatically selected Lieutenant Day as the national commander of the organization the following evening, he further strove to highlight the shared experiences among blind veterans that warranted a separate organization, while also suggesting that American society need not consider them too dependent or disabled. His keynote speech the night of his inauguration was titled, "Sightless, Not Crippled."[3]

As the events of the 1922 convention suggest, the USBVWW was born of an organizational culture meant to distinguish blind veterans as manly, independent, and *not* disabled, but merely unable to see. It is unclear whether this was a concerted reaction to the internalized ableism the men felt because of the cultural messages they had encountered about blindness and dependence in the early twentieth century. It could have also been a bold reaction to public professions of sympathy such as that made by blind US Republican Congressman Thomas Schall of Minnesota who, when he introduced a bill earlier that year to the House of Representatives to incorporate the group of veterans as an official organization, made an impassioned speech on their behalf in which he stated, "No doubt many of those brave blind fellows up there [in the gallery] wish that fate had left them on the battlefield rather than to have returned here sightless."[4]

What is clear—and what this chapter aims to show—is that the social anxieties about blindness, dependency, and worthiness that surfaced throughout the existence of Evergreen, and that shaped public pronouncements of the men's independence, continued to define blind veterans' lived experiences when veterans sought to build their own organizations and define their own image independent of sighted people's assumptions about them. The USBVWW sought to aid all blind veterans, including those who increasingly struggled to carry on as the 1920s progressed. Postwar struggles existed in part because of lack of compensation. Not all blind veterans could definitively connect their blindness to military service, and many veterans were not completely blind and therefore did not receive full disability compensation but were nonetheless held to the same social standards as those who did receive full compensation. By 1925, a small group of blind veterans split into a second organization—the Blind Veterans' Chapter (BVC) of the DAVWW—because of a contentious disagreement with their comrades in the USBVWW about the latter's attempt to open a permanent blind veterans' home and sheltered workshop for those who continued to encounter difficulties making a life for themselves and their families because of socially ingrained ableism and inaccessibility. At the heart of their disagreements were not important conversations about the inaccessibility of American society for all blind people, but instead age-old social anxieties related to blindness and dependence.

Blind Veterans Organize Around Compensation Problems

James Francis Nugent could not count on his disability compensation. Nugent, a shipping clerk from Chicago, served in the US Army from 1903 to 1921. A lengthy and storied military career by any standard, his army service took him as far away as Alaska and the Philippines, though he ultimately did not go to France during the period of war mobilization. Rather than going "over the top" in France, between 1917 and 1918 he helped transport soldiers between US Army camps before they sailed for Europe. After World War I he studied business, and frequently strained his eyes by reading books in dim light. "I noticed that my eyes were not good," Nugent recalled in 1923. "In the fall of 1920 I applied for glasses and in a short time my sight was gone." James Nugent received disability compensation as a blind veteran and entered Evergreen alongside other blind veterans after his discharge from the army in 1921. There, he lived in Cupid's Cottage with his wife while he studied cigar making. In 1923 the Veterans' Bureau suddenly cut off his disability compensation, which had been $100 a month, because it ruled that his blindness was not incurred in the line of duty—in war. "I am 42 years old and blind," Nugent concluded. "I have spent the best years of my life in the army. They gave me compensation once. Now they take it away. What am I going to do, handicapped as I am? Am I to become a beggar?"[5]

The Veterans' Bureau also cut Dewey Geers's compensation in 1923. Geers went blind as a result of an eye infection he received from a dirty towel while stationed at a training camp in Fort Worth, Texas.[6] Similar to James Nugent, Geers had received $100 a month for his disability over the years preceding the bureau ruling, and the comfort of having the steady compensation allowed him to plan to buy a home for his wife and family, as well as purchase a car for his growing business. His case was particularly dire according to Evergreen physician Dr. Marie Ingram, who became an ardent advocate for the blind veterans with compensation issues. According to Ingram, Geers was worthy not necessarily because of his military service, but because "he has not sat down and let his life overcome him. He has shown very real energy and an inspiring repugnance to the role of [the] beggar." Surely, she continued, the cost of compensating all blind veterans equally and consistently would not cost the Veterans' Bureau much—subtly signaling that her conception of disability access and compensation was limited in scope to those society subjectively deemed worthy. By suddenly cutting off Geers's compensation, the Veterans' Bureau "cannot be sure that it will not cut off some very deserving man—and make a pauper of him."[7]

James Nugent and Dewey Geers joined hundreds of thousands of Americans whose disability compensation was tied to shifting grounds of federal legislation. Passed in 1917, the War Risk Insurance Act (WRIA) created disability compensation for disabled veterans of World War I. Progressive reformers hoped the law would deviate significantly from previous forms of war-related disability provisions. Instead of unpredictable Civil War–era pensions, the WRIA was supposed to create predictable benefits that were published in advance of military service. The act, according to historian K. Walter Hickel, replaced pensions with compensation as "soldiers were disabled in the service of their 'employer,' the nation-state." Conceived in the context of, and modeled upon, workers' compensation laws that tied one's disability to the extent to which impairment limited one's earning capacity, the WRIA ultimately proved to be a disappointment in part because it depended on physicians to complete a medical exam and diagnosis, which restricted access to benefits, especially when it proved difficult to connect one's impairment to war service.[8]

Through a series of congressional acts, legislators increasingly adjusted disability compensation to avoid dispensing benefits exclusively to the limited number of veterans who were disabled *and* who could trace their disability directly to war service.[9] Legislation in 1921 created the United States Veterans' Bureau and established the precedent of presumption of service origin for complicated medical conditions such as tuberculosis and neuropsychiatric disorders. The World War Veterans Act of 1924 further expanded access for veterans with tuberculosis.[10] Yet, as Hickel argues, disability was still "a medical construct established by physicians and a social construct established by legislators, administrators, and veterans" and was therefore continuously defined and redefined through the immediate postwar years, giving medical authorities significant control over benefits claims sometimes to deleterious effects for disabled vets.[11] The result was that of the roughly 940,000 compensation claims decided by June 30, 1924, Veterans' Bureau doctors denied over 485,000.[12] Nugent and Geers were part of that statistic.

James Nugent and Dewey Geers were also part of a group of twenty other blind veterans who had their disability compensations cut by the Veterans' Bureau as a result of an internal review meant to limit pensions for disabilities ruled "not in the line of duty" or as a result of "willful misconduct." The ruling that affected the blind vets came from US Comptroller General John Raymond McCarl, who President Warren Harding appointed around the time of the founding of the US Veterans' Bureau in 1921. A lifelong Republican from Iowa, McCarl was a workaholic who regularly looked for ways to cut public spending, which later put him at odds with Franklin Roosevelt's New Deal.[13] Shortly after Harding appointed the new comptroller general,

McCarl reviewed disability compensation claims related to "presumption of soundness" in War Risk Insurance compensation. According to McCarl, full disability compensation was not payable for a disability arising after termination of military service, from willful misconduct during service, or from an infection or disease prior to military service that went undetected on enlistment.[14] In other words, when they entered the service American soldiers were presumed to have been of "sound condition."[15] Ultimately, the decision cut Geers and Nugent off from the compensation around which they had built their lives.

That their compensation was cut so suddenly not only signaled the complexities of the Veterans' Bureau, but was also emblematic of the complicated nature of blind veterans' compensation on a national scale.[16] The Veterans' Bureau did not merely award a single payment to all blind veterans. Rather, it determined disability compensation based on the extent of a veteran's disability and the extent to which that disability limited his capacity to earn an income through wage labor. Veterans blind in both eyes received a compensation of at least $200 per month, a number that increased further if they had one or more missing limbs, but complete blindness in both eyes was a minority of the overall cases of visual disabilities among veterans. A March 1955 Veterans Administration study that looked at compensation for living disabled veterans of American wars—including World War I—listed 2,072 who had lost or lost the use of both eyes and 21,894 veterans who had lost or lost the use of one eye.[17] The percentage of blind veterans in World War I, World War II, and the Korean War who were completely blind in both eyes was, therefore, rather small.

Compensation for the remaining blind and visually impaired veterans was even more complicated than that which completely blind vets received. According to the Veterans' Bureau compensation scale, a disabled veteran who was blind in one eye but with the other eye "normal"—20/20 or 20/40 vision—earned just $35 per month. If the same veteran had moderate loss of sight in the remaining eye—20/100 vision—his compensation increased to $65 per month. If the veteran had "marked loss" of sight in the remaining eye, the compensation increased further to $90 per month. The Veterans' Bureau scale ultimately included compensation that ranged from as much as $200 per month to as little as $10 per month for disabilities that ranged from total blindness in both eyes to blindness in one eye, and different grades of limited vision and light perception in either eye.[18] Compensation was therefore as varied as the biological realities of veterans' eyes.

Blind veterans not only differed with regards to the federal compensation they received based on the extent of their disabilities, but they were also subject to the whims of legislation in the states within which they lived. Depending on where veterans lived in the United States, they may have benefitted from significant funding in the form of bonus bills and tax incentives, or no benefits at all. State legislatures conducted heated debates over bonus bills and other compensation measures, which left a patchwork of uneven benefits at the state level. Massachusetts passed a bonus bill that awarded veterans and reconstruction aides a flat rate of $100 for six months or more of service during World War I.[19] Illinois awarded veterans 50 cents per day of service during the war, up to $300.[20] Veterans in Oregon had a choice of a cash bonus of $15 per month of service during the war that totaled no more than $500, or a loan of between $500 and $3,000 meant to purchase a home or to start a business.[21] Two states, New York and New Jersey, passed legislation granting disability compensation of $500 a year specifically to blind veterans, in addition to property tax exemptions and tuition scholarships for higher education.[22] On the opposite side of the spectrum, at least nine states voted against issuing any bonus to veterans, and over a dozen states did not put a bonus up for a vote to begin with. In Maryland, state courts found the bonus bill unconstitutional.[23] In Indiana, a bonus bill passed both a state referendum and a legislature vote but was ultimately vetoed by the governor in March 1923.[24]

In addition to signaling the inconsistencies in disabled veterans' compensation, James Nugent's and Dewey Geers's sudden reduction of benefits from the Veterans' Bureau also suggests the fact that many veterans could not trace their blindness to combat, a fact observed by Evergreen ophthalmologist Dr. Alan Woods. Woods had arrived at Evergreen in March 1920 as a consulting ophthalmologist and served at the school when it was under Red Cross control as well as when it became Evergreen School for the Blind under the jurisdiction of the Veterans' Bureau in 1921, which lasted until its ultimate closure in 1925. Woods kept records on over 300 blind veterans who he had treated at Evergreen during that period, and his experiences there led him to some important conclusions about the institute and its veterans. Under the Red Cross, Woods argued, Evergreen had "expanded and flourished. . . . The morale of the students was high, the instruction appeared to be good, the men were interested in their work, and the graduates were well trained and proficient in their trades." If the Red Cross had continued its control of Evergreen, Woods concluded, it may have "developed into a second St. Dunstan's."

In stark contrast, he continued, Evergreen's era as a Veterans' Bureau facility marked a "period of decline."[25] The bureau, he argued, was new and had enormous responsibilities providing services for hundreds of thousands of veterans in need at a time when civilians were more likely to want to move on from the war than to linger on in discussions about compensation.

Veterans who resided at Evergreen when it was under bureau control recognized that they did not have the same social capital that blind soldiers had when Evergreen first opened. According to them, "the cream was off the milk." The reason for this, the men claimed, was that when the school was US Army General Hospital No. 7 and Red Cross Institute for the Blind, the blind men were mostly battle casualties "who were the aristocrats and elite of the student body" because civilians understood that their blindness came as a result of fighting in war rather than illness or accident—even if this was not necessarily always the case. "As the school went on," Woods explained with some derision toward his former patients, "the percentage of battle casualties decreased [and] the number of syphilitics and psychoneurotics became greater." Men had too much freedom and independence to consume alcohol or stay out late and cause disorder, which "seriously interfered with the general morale of the institution."[26] The facts that Andrew Knebel's "trouble making tour" happened under General Hospital No. 7, and the Red Cross Institute for the Blind was responsible for the reprehensible Jim Crow policies that barred Black soldiers, are conveniently absent from Woods's nostalgic judgment. Taken together, though, Alan Woods's testimony and the experiences of men like James Nugent and Dewey Geers suggests that as time went on blind veterans struggled due to insufficient pensions and a lack of social capital due in part to their inability to connect their blindness to trench warfare.

In response to these postwar challenges, disabled and nondisabled veterans formed fraternal organizations to create social solidarity and advocate policies to benefit their comrades. American soldiers had founded the American Legion in Paris in 1919 as an organization to represent the interests of all Great War veterans, able-bodied and disabled.[27] The Legion quickly became the largest veterans' organization with close to a million members by 1921, and along with organizations such as the VFW, Legionnaires lobbied the federal government on issues that ranged from maintaining military preparedness to preferential hiring and helping veterans with compensation claims.[28] The DAVWW, the largest postwar organization for war-injured veterans, formed a year after the American Legion.[29] In the United States alone more than 150 veterans' groups served as fraternal organizations, ex-servicemen's clubs, military societies, and government advocacy groups.[30] Disabled veterans' experiences of social reintegration, through the creation of such organizations, was thus in many ways a "collective" experience.[31] The experience of group solidarity among blind American veterans, as will be explored, suggests, however, that there were clear limits to the collective bonds that shaped postwar veterans' organizations.

It was in the context of proliferating veterans' organizations that blind soldiers coalesced into their own organizations. Whereas the American Legion was a mixed organization composed of able-bodied and disabled veterans, and the DAVWW was a composite organization composed of veterans with different disabilities, the organizations for blind veterans were single-population groups, which means that they were composed of veterans sharing the same injury.[32] Single-population disabled veterans' organizations created a kind of solidarity that would have been difficult to manifest in larger organizations such as the American Legion or the DAVWW. "Conditions such as blindness," writes historian David Gerber about the creation of single-population veterans' organizations after World War II, "necessarily involve a comprehensive, and to some extent continuous, life-adjustment, especially when experienced in adulthood after a lifetime of able-bodied activity." Additionally, members of such organizations often claimed that other organizations simply could not understand their particular needs.[33]

The first single-population organization created by blind American soldiers formed in November 1919 when 146 Evergreen students created Evergreen Post No. 5 of the American Legion. Despite being part of the mixed American Legion organization, the Evergreen Post No. 5 was a single-population soldiers' group. And despite propping up its stability on the larger American Legion organization that exists to this day, Evergreen Post No. 5 did not last. Though the post had a membership of over 100 blind veterans at its outset, most of its membership returned home by 1921, and only a handful of those veterans called Baltimore home. The post was quite literally a temporary vocational rehabilitation center, which meant that if it had any long-term stability as a veterans' organization, its members would have been few.

Blind veterans created the USBVWW in the wake of Evergreen Post No. 5 of the American Legion, and one of its first issues was helping veterans with their compensation claims. Yet, as USBVWW commander Raymond Day made clear, the organization could do little to help the likes of Dewey Geers and James Nugent. Day criticized the Veterans' Bureau not for marginalizing such men because of the origins of their blindness, but because of what he saw as inconsistent rulings that first unduly liberalized their compensation and then cut it suddenly. "These rulings," Day argued, "led hundreds of ineligible men to believe they were entitled to Federal aid," which "works a hardship on men cut off summarily" because of "the Government's failure to detect at enlistment disease contracted before entry to service." The leader's solution was to frame a new law granting separate compensation scales to veterans who were blind from illness or accident incurred outside the line of duty, undetected at induction, or from "willful misconduct."[34]

Taken together, the experiences of veterans such as James Nugent and Dewey Geers as well as the complex compensation geography that granted varying degrees of disability pensions to blind veterans in different states suggests that there was no singular set amount of money blind veterans could count on receiving after the war, just as there was no singular blind veteran war experience. A blind veteran from Indiana received far less than a blind veteran from New York, even if both men may have been completely blind in both eyes. Discrepancies abounded even more if either one was blind in one eye or partially blind in either eye. Finally, the Veterans' Bureau's inconsistent rulings regarding compensation left even more questions for blind veterans trying to understand why their pay had diminished. When all these factors combined with inadequate vocational training and ableist attitudes about blindness, Evergreen men fell through the cracks of American social welfare.

The United States Blind Veterans of the World War Seeks a Permanent Home

The USBVWW represented many more veterans than the twenty who had their compensation cut alongside Dewey Geers and James Nugent. Economic and social marginalization led numerous veterans to consider returning to Evergreen after 1922 to make it their home once again. Richard Knigge tried to make a living as a basket maker in Portland, Oregon, but found no market for his baskets once he left Evergreen.[35] George Kocserha left Evergreen and entered the Columbia Theological Seminary in New York. He studied hard and succeeded in classes, "but he was gassed as well as blinded and his health [did not] permit him to continue his course [of study]."[36] One blind veteran at the first convention of the United States Blind Veterans of the World War was particularly discouraged. He had studied vulcanizing at Evergreen, but he did not have enough vision to work in that field, and his compensation was so little that it was hard to care for his family.[37] Henry Coyle of Charleston, Massachusetts, was blinded in service in France. In September 1922 he and his family were starving and living in miserable conditions while his debt piled up because his health necessitated frequent absences from work.[38] Socially and economically marginalized, blind veterans looked to Evergreen for stability in their lives due to lack of support in their own communities or families, the failure of their vocational training to prepare them for practical lives after the military, and because of prolonged health challenges and multiple disabilities sometimes unrelated to blindness.

Blind veterans also hoped to find inspiration and comradeship through the new organization. The *Baltimore Evening Sun* recognized the spirit of comradeship and the inspiration that existed at the first United States Blind Veterans of the World War convention in November 1922. There, one blind veteran arrived "almost helpless" by his loss of sight and was discouraged by his attempts to "get back to normal." According to the *Sun,* "He had not shaved himself since the day he lost his sight. . . . But when he came to the convention and found a man not only blind but with both hands gone performing his daily duty of shaving himself, the big, husky blind man made up his mind to be his own barber again."[39] The message the *Sun* aimed to convey was that the man had fallen through the cracks of the social welfare system that the US government initiated to empower disabled veterans to succeed, but that contact with a close comrade who had multiple disabilities and was presumably worse off was inspiration enough for the man to recognize his own privileged status. He then cleaned up his act.

Despite the USBVWW's goal of making blind veterans' lives better through comradeship and mutual support, its attitudes toward blind veterans' struggles were mixed when it came to disability compensation. On the one hand, the organization's leader Raymond Day campaigned extensively on behalf of the small group of men whose compensation had been cut by the Veterans' Bureau. On the other hand, Day argued that the conflicting rulings by the bureau should be criticized, but not necessarily the original law itself that cut compensation to veterans who were blind due to willful misconduct or due to other injuries or diseases not incurred in the line of duty. The problem Day sought remediation from, therefore, was not the fact that veterans blinded after the war or from willful misconduct were rated differently from veterans blinded during the war, but that the Veterans' Bureau made conflicting rulings about that law. The increasingly liberalized rulings, Day stated in 1923, "led hundreds of ineligible men to believe they were entitled to Federal aid. Now comes the ruling which says a soldier cannot claim as ground for compensation the Government's failure to detect at enlistment disease contracted before entry to service."[40] Day therefore argued that the original law was just, and that those whose blindness was not incurred in the line of duty were justifiably denied compensation. There were legitimate limits to those worthy of a pension.

The issues about compensation were unresolved when the USBVWW met for its second convention in St. Louis, Missouri, in 1923. There, members spoke again of their comrades' continued struggles that included inadequate compensation, confusing federal legislation, and useless vocational training. The men also considered a new topic: establishing a permanent home and vocational training center to replace Evergreen that could help blind veterans find their passion, facilitate employment, and grant loans to men hoping to open businesses.[41] Despite media campaigns to change the ways people saw American blind veterans, what came to be known as "Blind Soldiers' Week" bore striking similarities to the ableist public campaigns held by American philanthropists on behalf of blind French soldiers before 1917.

The USBVWW spearheaded Blind Soldiers' Week in October 1924 just weeks before its third convention. The Baltimore-based campaign was a public donation drive across the United States to help the USBVWW establish a permanent national home and workshop where blind veterans who struggled to carry on and who needed help could live, work, and find comradeship. The USBVWW and its allies placed Blind Soldiers' Week posters around the city of Baltimore. US President Calvin Coolidge issued a proclamation endorsing the week and calling on all patriotic Americans to donate. Baltimore mayor George Cryer and Maryland governor Albert Ritchie also lent support. Ritchie proclaimed the opening day, October 19th, "Blind Soldiers' Sunday." That day the city's religious leaders referenced the campaign in their Sunday sermons. The Service Star Legion, War Mothers of America sponsored entertainment at the New Lyceum Theater while patriotic women gave speeches throughout the city and blind veterans from Evergreen spoke to audiences at City Hall Plaza. The campaign organizers also placed donation booths in hotels and public buildings, and letters of appeal went out to businesses, factories, schools, and department stores soliciting donations.[42]

The USBVWW permanent home campaign is a significant chapter in the histories of blind World War I veterans for many reasons. First, the desire of numerous blind veterans to establish a home reflects the realities that despite cheerful "overcoming" rhetoric in rehabilitation literature such as *Carry On* and *Evergreen Review*, many blind veterans continued to struggle. Second, the methods and messages of dependency and vulnerability used by the USBVWW and its allies were at times strikingly similar to the methods used by the Committee for Men Blinded in Battle and the Blind Relief War Fund in 1915 and 1916, which were methods and messages that the US government sought to avoid in the immediate aftermath of the war when rehabilitating American soldiers. Finally, the permanent home campaign demonstrated that there existed significant disagreement among blind veterans about what supports were necessary for them. While the USBVWW certainly wished to establish the home in response to the very real social and economic marginalization of its members, numerous blind veterans did not agree with the public campaign and created the Blind Veterans' Chapter of the Disabled American Veterans of the World War to mobilize against it. Ironically, anxieties about disability and dependence drove the arguments leveled by both groups of blind American veterans against their opponents.

The campaign for a permanent home began when the USBVWW learned that the Veterans' Bureau would close the vocational training school at Evergreen at the end of June 1925, and that the remaining blind veterans there would be transferred to nearby veterans' hospitals. Disheartened by the news and determined to remain where they were, the veterans proclaimed that they were not sick, but "men who are normal in every way except that they lost their sight." The Veterans' Bureau agreed to help establish a vocational training school where Evergreen students—not hospital patients—could go after the institute closed, and the USBVWW intended to establish a building adjacent to the bureau school to serve as a recreation center and home that would function in similar ways to the Red Cross Institute for the Blind during the lifetime of US Army General Hospital No. 7. USBVWW members felt that the permanent home was necessary because they did not want their lives dependent on the policy changes of new presidential administrations that might decide to defund the Veterans' Bureau or close one of its hospitals.[43]

In addition to fears about policy changes, numerous USBVWW members cited more personal reasons why they wanted to establish a permanent home. Harvey Gilbert had trained at Evergreen in the Commercial Department after he was blinded by a shell in July 1918, but the store he opened after leaving Evergreen eventually went bankrupt—the store that was ironically named "Victory Store No. 2." "I had just enough money to get back here [to Evergreen] and decided to come and stay."[44] Richard Knigge also tried to make a living and was unable to and wrote of his intention to return to Evergreen from his home in Portland, Oregon. Knigge had trained in basket-weaving at Evergreen but found no market for his baskets once he left the institution. "The baskets which find a sale," wrote the *Baltimore Sun,* "bring less than it costs him for material to make them from." George Kocserha also wanted a permanent home. Kocserha left Evergreen and entered the Columbia Theological Seminary in New York, but despite working diligently his lingering health struggles from being gassed during the war forced him to leave the seminary.[45] Harvey Gilbert, Richard Knigge, and George Kocserha wanted a permanent home because they found that their Evergreen training inadequately prepared them to make a living on their own, or because other health problems prevented them from carrying on without sufficient support.

In conceiving of a permanent home, the USBVWW hoped to establish a sheltered workshop in which the blind veterans could work. Workshops such as the first in existence in the United States at the Perkins Institution in Massachusetts produced handmade objects such as brooms, chairs, and baskets manufactured from easily obtainable materials and sold to the public, all aided by the management of sighted administrators.[46] The idea behind workshops was to create the conditions for disabled people's independent work in a supervised fashion, rather than blind adults trying to make a living in the unpredictable world on their own. For blind veterans, this sounded appealing because they struggled to make ends meet in their own communities with the meager training they received from Evergreen and the lack of independent living services available to disabled people at the time. Workshops, though, were increasingly associated with dependency, charity, and low wages, and not all blind veterans wanted to be stigmatized by those associations.

In addition to labor insecurity and inadequate disability compensation, many blind veterans simply wanted companionship from people who understood their lives. Harvey Gilbert preferred living with "other men who are in the same condition as I."[47] Richard Knigge, like his comrade Gilbert, also wanted a sense of comradeship with other blind veterans or, as the *Baltimore Sun* wrote: "He wants to live with his other unfortunate comrades at the proposed new home."[48] Burl Glover studied basket-weaving at Evergreen and recalled, "We blind feel more comfortable among our own kind. . . . It is easier to mix with others in the same condition. The public offers us plenty of sympathy, but they cannot give companionship." L. H. Penfield echoed Glover's hope for companionship. "The blind veterans want a real home," he stated. "Many of us feel that we have no one to take care of us. If we were collected in a place that could be called home, we would be able to help each other. The world gets tired of continually helping a blind man, but we understand each other."[49] The organization's commander Raymond Day also referenced comradeship. "We have a feeling of fellowship," he said. "We like to be together and this home will give us a permanent gathering place."[50]

Burl Glover, L. H. Penfield, Raymond Day, and many other blind veterans hoped to find comradeship at a Baltimore estate called Beechfield. By October 1924, Congress had already appropriated the $350,000 for the Veterans' Bureau training center that the permanent home would supplement.[51] The USBVWW's public campaign to raise one million dollars to purchase the Beechfield estate failed when it was purchased by other interested buyers.[52] By the summer of 1925 the organization had secured an equally luxurious twenty-room clubhouse at 1812 Eutaw Place in Baltimore, though with no physical connection to a Veterans' Bureau vocational training center.[53]

The USBVWW's appeals to secure the Beechfield home would have been familiar to the Blind Relief War Fund. One "well-wisher's" letter to the editor of the *Baltimore Sun* wholeheartedly agreed with the fundraising campaign and shamed the American public for not supporting veterans that they viewed as worthy sufferers. "What of the blind veteran?" wrote the anonymous and concerned citizen. "Ah, have we forgotten? Have we grown callous to suffering?"[54] A Gold Star Mother also lent her support to the "sufferers." "Have the people of Baltimore forgotten the Golden Rule even for those in affliction? . . . Most of these men have no mothers' tender care to take them about. They need a home, where they can live and where they are taken care of according to their affliction." The Gold Star Mother pleaded with the public that the men needed the new home because they were unable to care for themselves and because only through a secluded home specifically made for blind veterans would they find happiness in their life.[55]

In the process of advocating on behalf of blind veterans for a permanent home and sheltered workshop, American civilians did not use blind veterans' own testimonies or arguments to appeal to the public for funding. American civilians also did not distinguish between the problematic assumption that blind veterans were suffering from blindness and the more realistic statement that they were suffering from inadequate vocational training and social support systems while living in an ableist society that cast all disability as a problem. Instead, as the two letters to the editor of the *Baltimore Sun* suggest, Americans reverted to ableist assumptions about blindness as dependence and affliction to capitalize on sympathy. Such rhetoric did not sit well with all blind veterans, which propelled a group to mobilize against the campaign for a permanent home.

The Blind Veterans' Chapter Mobilizes against Their Comrades

A small group of blind veterans created the Blind Veterans' Chapter of the Disabled American Veterans of the World War at the end of 1925 in direct opposition to the United States Blind Veterans of the World War's public campaign to fund a permanent home and workshop. The creation of the BVC signals that the instructiveness in thinking about veterans' organizations as mixed, composite, or single-population does not account for the fissures that existed *within* single-population groups of disabled vets. Despite the fact that blind American veterans had so much in common in terms of their generational, wartime, and injury experiences, they fundamentally disagreed over their political philosophies related to social welfare. The public fundraising efforts on behalf of the USBVWW's permanent home created the conditions for inter-single-population organizational strife.

The BVC was vigorously opposed to both the blind veterans' and the public's use of sympathy for fundraising, which they viewed as nothing less than objectification. The BVC also differed from the USBVWW in how they viewed themselves compared to other World War I veterans. The USBVWW was a stand-alone organization, and its members argued that they had physical and psychological disabilities that were "greater and less understood . . . than any other class of disabled men," which made it imperative for them to remain separate from other disabled veterans' organizations so that they could gain social and political advantages unique to their needs.[56] By contrast, members of the BVC did not want civilians or veterans to think of them as special or uniquely deserving, which is why they formed their organization within the Disabled American Veterans of the World War rather than as a separate organization.

The BVC's conviction that they shared much in common with other disabled veterans meant that the men neglected or downplayed the fact that blind veterans had varied health issues and lived experiences. BVC members, for example, argued that federal pensions for blind veterans sufficiently met their needs, and therefore any campaign for a permanent home was not needed. At one November 1925 BVC event, members claimed that their organization did not desire a home because their members received full disability compensation of around $200 per month, "and they have been very happy in the knowledge of this security."[57] But the BVC's contention that blind veterans did not need any more than the $200 per month in disability compensation from the federal government rested on the problematic and incorrect assumption that all blind veterans received the Veterans' Bureau's full pension because all veterans were completely blind in both eyes.

BVC leadership also ignored the real socioeconomic differences that existed among blind veterans because of the lack of accessible employment opportunities. The USBVWW had responded to such differences when it heeded calls for a permanent home from marginalized blind veterans throughout the United States who had little to no support systems, inadequate vocational training, and too little compensation to live comfortably. By contrast, George Calvert, Michael Inselbuch, and Michael Aaronsohn represented the social and economic privilege that leading figures of the

BVC enjoyed when they mounted their opposition campaign against the USBVWW's permanent home.

Dr. George Calvert, a blind veteran who benefitted from New York State's generous disability benefits, was a good example of how veterans from his state fared better than veterans elsewhere. Calvert had served overseas during the war and was blinded by a piece of an exploding shell, which led to both eyes being enucleated (removed), and he received the full $200 per month in federal disability compensation as well as the relative social privilege usually granted to those who were blinded in battle and not by illness, accident, or willful misconduct.[58] Sometime after his war service and Evergreen rehabilitation, Calvert became a physician and then was elected to the New York State Assembly to represent Onondaga County. Calvert occasionally spoke at the New York State Legislature in Albany, New York, about his comrades who would benefit from the Kiernan Bill, including Bernard Corcoran, Bernard Ward, and James Canavan who were all battlefield casualties and members of the BVC.[59] Written by Calvert, the Kiernan Bill provided an additional $500 a year for life to New York veterans blinded as a result of their war service.[60] George Calvert represented a group of blind veterans who were relatively materially privileged compared to other blind veterans due in part to where they lived.

Calvert also represented a subset of blind veterans who were completely blind because of war wounds and who, as a result, may have been out of touch with the realities of many of the men in the USBVWW with partial blindness who struggled economically and socially. In a 1925 letter to the editor of the *Baltimore Sun*, for example, Calvert argued that if members of the USBVWW really wanted a home, "there is plenty [of] opportunity for them to get one in the same manner the other boys have," such as working hard, using their compensation, and buying their own home.[61] Whether or not Calvert understood that not all blind veterans received the same compensation, had the same level of disability, lived in a state that actively helped veterans purchase homes and start businesses, or had substantial enough familial or economic support to have made individual success far more attainable is unclear. What is clear is that Calvert assumed that success came solely from personal hard work and not the contingent realities of disabled veterans' lives.

Michael Inselbuch was also a well-positioned founder of the BVC who was vocal in his opposition to a permanent home. Inselbuch was gassed in April 1918 while serving with the 26th Division in the Toul sector in northern France. He eventually became the national commander of BVC, which was founded with the help of his wife Louisa Frishmuth. Frishmuth was a wealthy widow of a Philadelphia cigar manufacturer who enlisted in

First Lady Grace Coolidge receives a forget-me-not from Michael Inselbuch, a blind veteran of World War I, at the White House, on October 28, 1925. (Coolidge Family Papers, Vermont Historical Society)

the Red Cross during the war. She was determined and devoted to helping American soldiers blinded in the war. Frishmuth met Michael Inselbuch after he left Evergreen and was taking additional training at the Pennsylvania Institution for the Blind at Overbrook. They married in 1920. Frishmuth was "instrumental in founding the [Blind Veterans'] National Chapter of the Disabled American Veterans [of the World War]," according to Inselbuch.[62] Michael Inselbuch's marriage to Louisa Frishmuth suggests that he also had access to her wealth, and this likely placed him in a similar class status as George Calvert.

Michael Inselbuch's socioeconomic position makes his stance on the permanent home debate unsurprising. Inselbuch believed that the public campaign for a permanent home was primarily a charade by the sighted public on behalf of a small group of misguided blind veterans who did not really know what they wanted or needed. Writing to the *Baltimore Evening Sun,* Inselbuch argued that the blind veterans themselves—those in the BVC—knew best what they needed in life, and that those "well-meaning" people should know that "the proposed institution for the blind is not wanted by the blind. . . . We need not say how embarrassing and humiliating . . . all this publicity and charitable pride [is] at our expense."[63] Other BVC veterans echoed Inselbuch's distaste for the idea of a home "from the proceeds of circuses, concerts and other schemes for private glorification offered to the public in his name."[64] Vice Commander Gustave W., for example, exclaimed, "I am sure the majority of blind veterans will be grateful if this begging is stopped."[65] Such statements suggest that BVC veterans were well-attuned to the showmanship and ableism inherent in fundraising events such as those undertaken on behalf of disabled soldiers, but were also willing to use that ableism to their own advantage in order to discredit their opponents.

Despite the BVC's condemnation of the campaign for what they argued was exploitative and overdramatic, its rank and file did not hesitate to use dramatic sensationalism to their own ends. George Calvert did just that in his testimony in support of the Kiernan Bill in New York, in which he erroneously assumed that all New York State blind veterans who benefitted from the bill were battlefield casualties like himself.[66] "At the time these men sustained their disability," he said, "they were suffering from many days of marching and fighting without adequate food or clothing. Many of them were left for hours on the field of battle with shell after shell breaking near them and machine gun bullet[s] singing over their heads."[67] Calvert thought singularly about battle casualties and complete blindness in both eyes, and not blindness from illness or injury incurred away from the front or after the war, or that some veterans did not receive full disability compensation or encounter a compassionate public. This makes Calvert's opposition to the USBVWW—an organization that included numerous veterans who were socially and economically marginalized in part because they were not battlefield casualties nor were they completely blind—all the more telling. A battlefield casualty, in Calvert's mind, was worthy of compensation.

Calvert's testimony in support of the Kiernan Bill is also important because of who he did not mention in his examples of heroic and worthy blind veterans of New York State. He did not, for example, mention Charles Parker Braithwaite, a Black veteran who lived in Brooklyn and was blinded in battle while serving with the 369th Infantry Division. Other than being Black, Braithwaite fit the description of a battlefield-blinded veteran that Calvert portrayed to the public. Calvert conceded, "It is impossible for me to recount the names of all" blind veterans of New York State, "but, I am only giving the names of those with whom I am personally acquainted as a result of a personal investigation and study of their cases."[68] Charles Braithwaite's absence from Calvert's testimony was an erasure of Braithwaite's military service and sacrifice at a time when Black veterans experienced growing hostility from white Americans throughout the United States.[69] Braithwaite's absence also meant that Calvert was not acquainted with his Black comrades from New York, nor was he necessarily interested enough to find out about them and whether or not they needed extra support from the Kiernan Bill. The names of Black veterans who left Evergreen after confronting racism there are absent from materials relating to the BVC and the USBVWW, including membership rolls.

Braithwaite's absence suggests that Black blind veterans' experiences were not recorded in the same ways as white veterans' experiences and that Black veterans were not integrated into organizations alongside white veterans. Black veterans, therefore, experienced racism and hostility of rehabilitation administrators and physicians in charge of medical examinations for benefits as well as social exclusion by white veterans with similar disabilities.[70] This would stand in stark contrast with the World War II–era Blinded Veterans Association, which took a strong stand against racism and anti-Semitism, as is shown by historian David Gerber.[71] Not affiliated with either organization, potentially resulting from the marginalization he felt during rehabilitation, Charles Braithwaite became member of the segregated George P. Davis Post No. 116 of the American Legion, to which he belonged at least into the early 1930s.[72]

George Calvert's statements in support of the Kiernan Bill and in opposition to the USBVWW's permanent home may have been racially calculated. The Kiernan Bill depended on support from New Yorkers for it to pass, and explaining to white New Yorkers that Black New Yorkers would also benefit with a $500 annuity for life may have proved problematic for the bill's passage in an era when Black veterans more generally struggled for recognition of their service and their rights as citizens of the United States.[73] The comrades who Calvert profiled in his speeches in support of the bill were similar in some ways to the romanticized and exploitative imagery the Committee for Men Blinded in Battle and the Blind Relief War Fund used in their promotional materials to raise money from American audiences for blind French soldiers. Calvert's rhetoric was reserved only for legislative measures that he viewed were legitimate forms of public assistance rendered for heroic service to the nation. Calvert not only saw the permanent home as illegitimate relief, but the very act of creating a home and workshop from public charitable donations threatened to undermine his own image as self-made and successful by highlighting class differences among blind veterans.

Another figure who played a significant role in the BVC—and who stood beside George Calvert at the DAVWW convention in June 1925 as it urged Congress not to appropriate funding for a blind veterans home—was Michael Aaronsohn.[74] Born in 1896, Aaronsohn grew up in poverty in an orphanage. He succeeded in school before serving in the military—Aaronsohn was twenty-two years old when he was wounded in the Meuse-Argonne Offensive by a piece of artillery shrapnel.[75] Physicians in Baltimore recorded that he had both eyes enucleated and that he suffered from "concussion & shock," as well as psychoneurosis, likely from combat trauma.[76] Aaronsohn felt that he had a calling to serve his disabled comrades. He assumed the position of chaplain of the DAVWW, which he retained for six years as he assiduously fought for veterans' rights and visited wounded men in hospitals around the country.

Michael Aaronsohn, or "Fighting Mike" as the press called him, subtly suggested that his success after the war was a result of his overcoming his blindness. Aaronsohn viewed his early days of blindness as a tragedy, one that incapacitated him and threw him into a state of childhood. After his rehabilitation, Aaronsohn wrote, "I came out of the toddling period of childhood and began to walk erect and blithesome." He rejected a "temporary wave" of public sentimentality and sympathy, and instead wanted a "sense of justice" through rehabilitation.[77] But rather than using his antisympathetic stance to fight ableism, highlight social inequities, and argue for a more egalitarian politics of disability in society for all, Aaronsohn more often than not used his platform to show how he succeeded primarily because of his own personal effort.[78]

In his postwar life, Aaronsohn became almost a celebrity veteran. He returned to his schooling after rehabilitation and graduated from the University of Cincinnati and Hebrew Union College. He was prominent in American Jewish life. He became a rabbi in 1923 and gave numerous speeches across the United States. According to his contemporaries, Aaronsohn "symbolized the triumph of the human will over blindness." And while he did have difficulty learning braille, with work he was able to master it so that the "dots bristled with meaning and thoughts."[79] Aaronsohn's story was among the most motivational for veterans and the public alike, as it relied on a message that he overcame his disability through hard work and persistence, and implied in that story was the message that those in the USBVWW who sought a permanent home only needed to work harder so that they, too, would not need "charity."

And yet, Aaronsohn's success story was not what it initially appeared to be. Despite his message of hard work (a message echoed by his friends and in the press), he had a metaphorical leg up when it came to attaining success. First, there was his class background. Aaronsohn stated that most of his reading was through people reading to him, and he found it "necessary to employ three readers a day."[80] One of the readers was his sister Dora, who helped him through the rest of his education at Hebrew Union College.[81] But having three readers meant that Aaronsohn had both the familial stability to allow his sister to aid in his education, and the financial capacity to hire an additional attendant above the one that federal compensation allowed for blind veterans.[82] Perhaps his upbringing in an orphanage that led him to detest public charity influenced what parts of his own success story he wished to highlight. An added bonus was his extensive training with typewriters before the war, a luxury not afforded to every disabled veteran. When he entered rehabilitation, Aaronsohn wrote, "I amazed my companions . . . with the speed and ease with which I was able to swing along on the mechanical keyboard," a feat not as accessible to the other men at Evergreen. In his postwar life Aaronsohn used this to his advantage, and wrote correspondences, papers, sermons, theses, lectures, and at least three books.[83]

Michael Aaronsohn held onto the near-celebrity status that was intimately connected to his perceived ability to overcome war-induced blindness and therefore repudiate the idea of the need for a permanent home as public charity. The status was his identity, and the source of much of his acclaim as he used it as a springboard for his advocacy for other disabled veterans, disabled civilians, and the founding of the Jewish Braille Institute.[84] Aaronsohn, however, constructed and deployed his identity in a way similar to deaf-blind celebrity Helen Keller. While Keller's politics of racial and economic justice were radical, her disability politics were relatively conservative. She depoliticized disability "by relegating it to the realm of coping and personal character." Her disability, argues historian Kim Nielsen, was her public image and her image depended on perpetually overcoming her disability.[85]

Aaronsohn focused not on his existing education or social status, but on the hard work that enabled him perpetually to overcome his blindness and succeed in postwar life. He positioned rehabilitation success as a product of individual effort, and depoliticized the state and social mechanisms that would have enabled true accessibility such as affordable braille books, or inclusive support systems for independent living. Paradoxically, Aaronsohn discounted the public sympathy that allowed for his celebrity status while he averted attention from the class privilege that made success far more likely for him. All of this is significant because like George Calvert and Michael Inselbuch, Aaronsohn's involvement in the BVC and its campaign against the USBVWW's permanent home was based on the idea that some veterans succeeded because of their own hard work and determination, and others failed because of their lack of that hard work and determination, all the while ignoring the very real differences in health, pensions, geographic political realities, and social, racial, and class privileges enjoyed by few.

Figures such as Michael Aaronsohn, Michael Inselbuch, and George Calvert were complex. They certainly wanted to help their fellow disabled comrades. Aaronsohn's chaplaincy work and George Calvert's political career quite clearly shows their devotion to helping others. However, the men often ignored their own social class privileges in service of perpetuating a narrative that through their own hard work they had overcome their disability. In so doing, any alternative veteran experience that included struggle threatened to undermine the success that Aaronsohn, Inselbuch, and Calvert felt they had earned on their own, by highlighting the ways that American ableism, classism, and racism could hinder individual success.

Conclusion

The United States Blind Veterans of the World War and the Blind Veterans' Chapter of the Disabled American Veterans of the World War held opposing views about how best to support blind veterans from World War I. The USBVWW recognized the marginalization some of its members lived with as a result of the circumstances and the extent of their blindness as well as ableist prejudice. The BVC was far less sympathetic to the continued and very real struggles endured by blind veterans. What remains unclear is whether this was because BVC members thought that highlighting struggling blind veterans and mobilizing pity for money was personally degrading and ableist to blind people everywhere, or because it challenged the very basis of their own personal journeys and claims to have "overcome" blindness following the rhetoric put forth by rehabilitationists. Regardless of their stance on a permanent home, few blind veterans used their social standing—their status and identities as disabled veterans—to challenge directly the injustices of a society built in a way that marginalized all blind people.

Epilogue

Frank Schoble and the Persistence of Public Sympathy for Blind Veterans

Lieutenant Frank Schoble Jr. boarded the S.S. *Leviathan* on September 10, 1927, as part of the self-described "Second American Expeditionary Forces"—over 18,000 veterans and their families who traveled on twenty-seven ships to the American Legion convention in Paris.[1] Schoble was a scrappy young man from Pennsylvania, the son of a wealthy hat manufacturer, and a student at the University of Pennsylvania who left school just one year shy of graduation in order to join the US Army and serve in World War I. His service ended when he was blinded in the Argonne Forest by a piece of shrapnel that led to vision loss in both of his eyes.[2] Schoble trained at Evergreen and then returned to the University of Pennsylvania to complete his undergraduate degree, where his friends helped him read his textbooks and his professors gave him oral rather than written exams. Throughout his postwar years Schoble remained fervently committed to veterans' advocacy, which ultimately led him to join the Second A.E.F. to Europe ten years after the onset of his vision impairment.

The American Legion trip expanded beyond the boundaries of Paris that fall. Frank Schoble was part of a smaller delegation of 243 high-ranking Legionnaires who traveled to numerous cities and met with European dignitaries, the list of which included the king and queen of Belgium, King Victor Immanuel III of Italy, and the king and queen of England. The reception that greeted the veterans was sensational when it was not somber and reflective. Almost the entire city of Nice came out to welcome the Legionnaires as the streets were lined with American flags while people shouted, "Vive l'Americain Legion!" By far the biggest ceremony took place in London, where the small delegation of Legionnaires paraded through the city and laid a wreath at the Cenotaph monument as the Big Ben tower's clock gonged in the distance and the city was stilled in commemorative silence.

Lieutenant Frank Schoble Jr. was the center of attention almost everywhere the Legionnaires went. When Schoble and his comrades visited Belgium's Tomb of the Unknown Soldier in Brussels, King Albert and Queen Elizabeth "drew a word of sympathy" specifically to the blind veteran. When the delegation arrived at Buckingham Palace to serve as audience to the king and queen of England, the king moved toward Frank Schoble "to grasp the groping hand of the blond-haired young man," and Queen Mary "stepped [out] from her place and reached for the hand which sought hers" before she stated to the crowd, "It is pitiful it happened—with the war so close to an end," referring to the fact that Schoble was blinded in combat just days before the signing of the Armistice on November 11, 1918.

The event that garnered the most attention about Frank Schoble was the Legionnaires' visit to the Vatican to meet with Pope Pius XI. The delegation gathered in Saint Peter's Square before proceeding into the papal reception chamber where the pope entered, dressed in "pure white [with] a large gold pectoral cross . . . suspended from a gold chain around his neck." Before giving a speech, the pope passed among the kneeling Legionnaires as many of them kissed his ring. Then, suddenly, he stopped at Frank Schoble, who he "singularly blessed." "The Pontiff, placing his hand upon Schoble's blond hair, said: 'May the Lord bless you, dear boy, for what you have done and for what you have suffered. We are sure He will give you strength to undergo deprivation.'"[3]

There is a lot to unpack from Frank Schoble's experiences in Europe in the fall of 1927, the first of which is the fact that he was at the center of highly sympathetic interactions with dignitaries, which suggests that the ableism that so affected blind soldier imagery during the war years had not disappeared. The Belgian and English royals—the very same royals who served as members of the British, French, and Belgian Blind Relief War Fund committees of their respective states—extended their sympathy to Schoble, whom they viewed as being deprived of all that he needed to be happy in life, as if his blindness was somehow worse than death itself. Additionally, the writers who published such accounts replicated the sympathy in their retelling of the events. Stories like Schoble's, written by sighted journalists who employed sympathetic and tragic tropes about blindness—reminiscent of the coverage of philanthropic organizations in 1915—often say more about sighted people's fears of blindness and disability than they do about actual blind people such as Schoble.[4]

The tragic ableist tropes used by American relief organizations in 1915 were also present in the religious symbolism of the media coverage of Schoble. The impulse of Christians to understand blindness as in need of divine intervention stems in part from Jesus's "healing" of a blind man to show the power of God.[5] Schoble embodied the images produced by artists such as F. C. Yohn, whose fundraising poster featured a blind soldier seeking divine aid while on the battlefield. Pope Pius XI and the journalists who wrote about the Vatican visit assumed that Frank Schoble was in need of divine intervention or saintly blessing to help him endure his "suffering" and "deprivation."

The descriptions of the Legionnaires' European tour are missing an important component, namely what Frank Schoble thought of it all. The reader navigates through Europe almost as a fly on the wall, observing sympathetic platitudes toward a veteran whose wound meant that he no longer had the use of his eyes. Schoble occupied center stage in the story by virtue of his war service, but because of the ocularcentric ableist world within which Schoble lived, journalists may not have thought it important to find out what the blind veteran thought or felt about it all. What we know about Schoble's experience, therefore, is somewhat limited. Blind characters in fiction and nonfiction are almost always drawn by sighted writers, and because ocularcentrism depends on understanding sight as the most important of the senses, the knowledge and perspectives of blind people such as Schoble have been "easily dismissed" or considered by sighted people as "downright trivial."[6]

While we can't know what Frank Schoble thought of the press coverage of Pope Pius XI blessing him, we do know Schoble's views about blindness through his work on behalf of blind people. In a September 1920 speech to the Rotary Club in Philadelphia, Schoble argued, "It is not so bad to be blind. Our spirit is not broken. We are cheerful. We are not as sad as pictured, and do not need sympathy, while we appreciate it."[7] Schoble continuously insisted that if blind people were given social and institutional support like he was given, they would also succeed and live fulfilling lives on their own terms.[8] At the Poor Richard Club in Philadelphia, Schoble convincingly argued for a shift in public perception of blind people everywhere. He explained how he was blinded in the war, how he learned to use a typewriter and to read with "raised letters," and how he experienced depression that accompanied his early months while learning to be blind at Evergreen. That depression, however, likely had more to do with societal assumptions about blindness that Schoble internalized than about blindness itself, as Schoble himself concluded, "The blind man is the poorest advertised man in the world, because every blind man who makes a success in spite of his handicap also wants to hide his affliction from people."[9]

Frank Schoble ultimately appreciated the fact that his status as a veteran who was blind brought a certain level of public attention that otherwise may not have existed, but he wanted to use that attention to shift Americans' understanding of blindness as being an almost insurmountable and pitiable experience. Schoble spent much of the early 1920s pleading for a training institution for blind adults so that the benefits he received as a blind veteran touched by war's immensity might be extended in some way to blind civilians who were largely unaffected by the war. In a second speech to the Philadelphia Rotary Club, this time in 1923, Schoble argued that the public really did not care much about blind people until the highly publicized efforts on behalf of blind soldiers during the Great War. He benefited from the public passion to rehabilitate blind soldiers and sailors, and benefitted from the aid of government and welfare workers. "But the question that was raised in my mind," he explained, "is whether or not the soldier is the only blind person who shall benefit." Schoble argued that the entire country would benefit from better services and accessibility for all blind people. And if the blinding of a few hundred soldiers attracted Americans' attention to the needs of the tens of thousands of blind civilians, "I can say from my heart that it is a privilege to be one of that number."[10] His sentiments were overshadowed by the pope's blessings.

There was a paradox at play in Frank Schoble's story and the stories of many other blind veterans like him. Schoble's status as a war veteran made civilian society more willing to consider his testimony about war and his ability to speak on behalf of veterans' issues. Schoble's blindness also enhanced his ability to connect with audiences due in part to the cultural constructions examined in this book that placed blind veterans at the center of sentimental stories of self-sacrifice. His status as a war veteran, however, made him seem uniquely worthy of special consideration from the public in ways that the public might not have extended to blind civilians. Sighted civilians were far less able to dispense with their ableism and tap into Frank Schoble's testimony as a blind person independent of his status as a war veteran. His lived experiences of blindness that he shared with so many civilians could not be detached from his elevated status as a wounded war veteran and limited the extent to which society was able or willing to consider how ableism affected blind people everywhere.

Frank Schoble's disability activism was thus absent from the *American Legion Weekly*'s and newspaper retelling of the Legionnaire's 1927 expedition. Instead, Schoble merely served as a "guide post" in the way that Carl Bronner did when he sat in the balcony and received a sympathetic applause from the US House of Representatives after Edith Nourse Rogers's impassioned speech about Bronner's blindness. If the clouds of World War I had dissipated by 1927, the themes that defined American cultural retellings of blind veterans of the war—themes such as dependence, sentimentality, sacrifice, and darkness—remained unnervingly present. Despite Schoble's successful solidarity with and activism on behalf of his comrades—his lived experiences as a blind veteran—he also became a figure who sighted audiences stripped of his complexities, his uniqueness, and his flaws and then singularly displayed so that sighted readers could revisit their own sense of sacrifice and loss from the Great War and perhaps feel that they had not suffered as much as they liked to think. Ultimately, emotive representations of Schoble—cultural constructions of the blind veteran—prevented sighted Americans from examining their own prejudices and then creating a more just and accessible society for all blind people. If, as David Gerber argues, histories of disabled veterans "help mark the boundaries at which the usual stigmas that have been attached to disability have been eroded," the stories of blind veterans during World War I emphasize the extent to which those boundaries may have remained a significant part of the disability experience.[11]

Notes

Introduction

1. "To Carl Bronner," *Red Cross Courier,* January 21, 1922.

2. "Blind Veteran Is Praised by Harding," *Boston American,* December 12, 1921.

3. "Harding Entertains 2000 Wounded Men: Blind Soldiers Excite His Special Interest," *Boston Globe,* June 9, 1921.

4. For a discussion of Edith Nourse Rogers's veterans' advocacy efforts, see Jessica L. Adler, *Burdens of War: Creating the United States Veterans Health System* (Baltimore: Johns Hopkins University Press, 2017), 158 and 208.

5. This and other quotes about Carl Bronner—and blind veterans of World War I generally—express concerns about manhood, poverty, and social welfare, as will be discussed throughout this book. For a discussion of manhood and state enforcement of the breadwinner role in the family, see Michael Willrich, "Home Slackers: Men, the State, and Welfare in Modern America," *Journal of American History* 87, no. 2 (September 2000): 460–89.

6. "Charles Bronner," *Cincinnati Enquirer,* June 9, 1926, 6; "Congress Has a Heart," *Richmond Item,* June 9, 1926, 1; "A Guide Post," *Davenport (IA) Daily Times,* June 16, 1926, 3; "A Guide Post," *Springfield (MO) News-Leader,* June 16, 1926, 6; "Congress Has a Heart," *San Angelo (TX) Evening Standard,* June 10, 1926, 4; "Whose Is the Debt?" *Pittsburgh Press,* June 13, 1926, 94; "A Hush Falls," *Kansas City Times,* June 4, 1926, 20.

7. "Armless and Blind, He Learns Typewriting," *Washington Times,* November 13, 1921, 14.

8. "Eyes, Hands Lost in Grenade Explosion, Detroit Ex-Sailor Shows World Cheerful Front," *Detroit Free Press,* July 15, 1920, 2.

9. "Happy Over New Operation: Blind and Handless War Victim Sees New Hope Ahead," *Baltimore Sun,* August 22, 1920, 36.

10. "Eyes, Hands Lost in Grenade Explosion," 2.

11. "Wounded Men Full of Grit: Three Interesting Soldier Cases Compiled by War Insurance Bureau," *Brooklyn Citizen,* July 13, 1921, 3.

12. "Blind American War Veterans Assemble Here for Convention: Men, Cheerful and Smiling, Deny They Are Unfortunates," *St. Louis Globe-Democrat,* November 13, 1923, 12; "Blind Veterans Glad to Live at Evergreen" *Baltimore Evening Sun,* October 17, 1924, 37.

13. Douglas C. Baynton, *Defectives in the Land: Disability and Immigration in the Age of Eugenics* (Chicago: University of Chicago Press, 2016), 2; Sarah F. Rose, *No Right to Be Idle: The Invention of Disability, 1840s–1930s* (Chapel Hill: University of North Carolina Press, 2017), 2; Susan Schweik, *The Ugly Laws: Disability in Public* (New York: New York University Press, 2009), 2.

14. See, for example, Theda Skocpol, *Protecting Soldiers and Mothers: The Political Origins of Social Policy in the United States* (Cambridge, MA: Belknap Press of Harvard University Press, 1992).

15. Gwendolyn Mink, *The Wages of Motherhood: Inequality in the Welfare State, 1917–1942* (Ithaca, NY: Cornell University Press, 1995), 4.

16. Willrich, "Home Slackers," 460–72.

17. Baynton, *Defectives in the Land,* 6.

18. Nancy J. Hirschmann and Beth Linker, eds., *Civil Disabilities: Citizenship, Membership, and Belonging* (Philadelphia: University of Pennsylvania Press, 2015), 3–8; Douglas C. Baynton, "Disability and the Justification of Inequality in American History," in *The New Disability History: American Perspectives,* ed. Paul K. Longmore and Lauri Umansky (New York: New York University Press, 2001), 34–36.

19. Adriane Lentz-Smith, *Freedom Struggles: African Americans and World War I* (Cambridge, MA: Harvard University Press, 2009), 1–4.

20. Paul R. D. Lawrie, "'Salvaging the Negro': Race, Rehabilitation, and the Body Politic in World War I America, 1917–1924," in *Disability Histories,* ed. Michael Rembis and Susan Burch (Urbana: University of Illinois Press, 2014), 323–29.

21. John M. Kinder, *Paying with Their Bodies: American War and the Problem of the Disabled Veteran* (Chicago: University of Chicago Press, 2015), 9.

22. M. Leona Godin, *There Plant Eyes: A Personal and Cultural History of Blindness* (New York: Pantheon, 2021), 27. David Bolt, *The Metanarrative of Blindness: A Re-reading of Twentieth-Century Anglophone Writing* (Ann Arbor: University of Michigan Press, 2016), 10–11.

23. Godin, *There Plant Eyes,* xv.

24. Godin, *There Plant Eyes,* ix. Additionally, Bolt uses two other terms: ocularnormativism, meaning "the mass or institutionalized endorsement of visual necessity"; and ophthalmocentrism, meaning "fixations not on vision but on the instrument of vision, as in notions of eyes that are sexy, innocent, hot, cold, hard, soft, kind, evil, honest, lying, and so on." Bolt, *The Metanarrative of Blindness,* 5 and 53.

25. Godin, *There Plant Eyes,* 275.

26. It should be noted that David Bolt and other writers explore the limits of the social model as it pertains to experiencing visual impairment. To demonstrate this fact, Bolt cites Sally French's "The Wind Gets in My Way," which explores how "going out is more difficult on a windy day because the wind makes a noise that obscures the small auditory cues that can be so helpful." The social model that argues disability as a social construct, then, cannot account for real challenges some visually impaired people face with certain tasks. Bolt, *The Metanarrative of Blindness,* 30. For a good recent discussion on the social model of disability, see Paul Longmore, *Telethons: Spectacle, Disability, and the Business of Charity* (New York: Oxford University Press, 2016), xv; Michael Rembis, Catherine Kudlick, and Kim E. Nielsen, "Introduction," in *The Oxford Handbook of Disability History* (New York: Oxford University Press, 2018); Bess Williamson, *Accessible America: A History of Disability and Design* (New York: New York University Press, 2019). There are also numerous chapters in Alice Wong's edited book *Disability Visibility* about the social model of disability. Alice Wong, ed., *Disability Visibility: First-Person Stories from the Twenty-First Century* (New York: Vintage Books, 2020).

27. For a discussion of the medical model, see Catherine Kudlick, "Social History of Medicine and Disability History," in *The Oxford Handbook of Disability History,* ed. Michael Rembis, Catherine Kudlick, and Kim E. Nielsen (New York: Oxford University Press, 2018); Beth Linker, "On the Borderland of Medical and Disability History: A Survey of the Fields," *Bulletin of the History of Medicine* 87 (Winter 2013): 525–26; James W. Trent, *Inventing the Feeble Mind: A History of Mental Retardation in the United States* (Berkeley: University of California Press, 1994).

28. Schweik, *The Ugly Laws,* 1; Rose, *No Right to Be Idle,* 1. For a discussion on the intersection of eugenics and disability, see Michael Rembis, *Defining Deviance: Sex, Science, and Delinquent Girls, 1890–1960* (Urbana: University of Illinois Press, 2011); Michael Rembis, "Disability and the History of Eugenics," in *The Oxford Handbook of Disability History,* ed. Michael Rembis, Catherine Kudlick, and Kim E. Nielsen (New York: Oxford University Press, 2018).

29. Frances Koestler, *The Unseen Minority: A Social History of Blindness in America* (New York: American Foundation for the Blind, 1976), 212.

30. Koestler, *The Unseen Minority,* 212.

31. Koestler, *The Unseen Minority,* 215.

32. Koestler, *The Unseen Minority,* 215–16.

33. Beth Linker, *War's Waste: Rehabilitation in World War I America* (Chicago: University of Chicago Press, 2014), 2–7.

34. In footnote 30 on page 191 of *War's Waste,* Beth Linker noted that "very little has been written about the treatment of war-related sensory disabilities." This note confirmed my interest in pursuing this project in the American context. Exceptions to the relative gap in scholarship on war-related sensory disabilities include Monika Baàr, "Prosthesis for the Body and for the Soul: The Origins of Guide Dog Provisions for Blind Veterans in Interwar Germany," *First World War Studies*

6, no. 1 (2015): 81–98; Corinne Doria, "'From Darkness to the Light': Memoirs of Blind Canadian Veterans of the First and Second World Wars," *Canadian Journal of Disability Studies* 7, no. 3 (2018): 122–44; Serge Marc Durflinger, *Veterans with a Vision: Canada's War Blinded in War and Peace* (Vancouver: UBC Press, 2010); David A. Gerber, "In Search of Al Schmid: War Hero, Blinded Veteran, Everyman," *Journal of American Studies* 29, no. 1 (1995): 1–32; Gregory L. Goodrich and Tom Zampieri, "Evergreen: The First U.S. Veterans' Blind Rehabilitation Center," *Journal of Visual Impairment & Blindness* 133, no. 2 (2019): 180–93; Adam Luptak, "Victory, Defeat, Gender, and Disability: Blind War Veterans in Interwar Czechoslovakia," *Journal of Social History* 53, no. 3 (2020): 604–19; Martina Salvante, "'Thanks to the Great War the Blind Gets the Recognition of His Ability to Act': The Rehabilitation of Blinded Servicemen in Florence," *First World War Studies* 6, no. 1 (2015): 21–35. For discussions on World War I and disabled veterans, consult Adler, *Burdens of War*; Kinder, *Paying with Their Bodies*; Linker, *War's Waste*; Rose, *No Right to Be Idle*.

35. Bolt, *The Metanarrative of Blindness,* 10.

36. Godin, *There Plant Eyes,* xvii.

37. Godin, *There Plant Eyes,* xiii; 278; Bolt, *The Metanarrative of Blindness,* 21.

38. Godin, *There Plant Eyes,* 275.

39. Thanks to Rick Fogarty for helping me organize my thoughts on this point in particular.

40. Bolt, *The Metanarrative of Blindness,* 23.

41. Bolt, *The Metanarrative of Blindness,* 18–34.

42. For consistency, throughout the rest of the book I use the term "soldier" to refer to soldiers and sailors blind from their service unless their status as sailors directly impacted their postwar experiences and public reception.

43. David A. Gerber, "Introduction: Finding Disabled Veterans in History," in *Disabled Veterans in History: Enlarged and Revised Edition,* ed. David A. Gerber (Ann Arbor: University of Michigan Press, 2012), 1.

44. Linker, *War's Waste*, 8–9.

Chapter 1. Blindness Comes Home

1. "Hippodrome Benefits Net $20,000 for Blind," *New York Tribune*, April 24, 1916, War Blind 1916, Volume II, Samuel P. Hayes Research Library, Perkins School for the Blind, Watertown, MA (hereafter SPH).

2. "Hippodrome Dark, Makes Audience Feel Blindness," *New York Herald*, April 24, 1916. War Blind 1916, Volume II, SPH.

3. "$25,000 Is Raised for Europe's Blind: New York Responds to Appeal Made at Great Benefit in Hippodrome," *New York Press*, April 24, 1916. War Blind 1916, Volume II, SPH.

4. "Hippodrome Dark, Makes Audience Feel Blindness"; "$25,000 Is Raised for Europe's Blind."

5. This was similar in some respects to antimilitarists who emphasized the human costs of industrialized warfare to prevent war, as John Kinder argues. Instead, organizations such as the Blind Relief War Fund were highlighting war injury (blindness, in this case) to raise money and not simply to refute war. John M. Kinder, *Paying with Their Bodies: American War and the Problem of the Disabled Veteran* (Chicago: University of Chicago Press, 2015), 41.

6. For a discussion of American humanitarian aid during World War I, consult Kinder, *Paying with Their Bodies*, 51–57; Branden Little, "Commission for Relief in Belgium (CRB)," *1914–1918 Online: International Encyclopedia of the First World War,* ed. Daniel Ute, Peter Gatrell, Oliver Janz, Heather Jones, Jennifer Keene, Alan Kramer, and Bill Nasson (October 2014); Helke Rausch, "The Birth of Transnational U.S. Philanthropy from the Spirit of War: Rockefeller Philanthropists in World War I," *Journal of the Gilded Age and Progressive Era* 17, no. 4 (October 2018); Julia F. Irwin, *Making the World Safe: The American Red Cross and a Nation's Humanitarian Awakening* (New York: Oxford University Press, 2013).

7. Julie Anderson and Neil Pemberton, "Walking Alone: Aiding the War and Civilian Blind in the Inter-war Period," *European Review of History* 14, no. 4 (December 2007): 461. For a discussion on why rehabilitationists focused their attention on children, consult Brad Byron, "A Pupil and a Patient: Hospital-Schools in Progressive America," in *The New Disability History: American Perspectives,* ed. Paul K. Longmore and Lauri Umansky (New York: New York University Press, 2001). For a concise history of the Progressive Era, consult Michael McGerr, *A Fierce Discontent: The Rise and Fall of the Progressive Movement in America, 1870–1920* (New York: Oxford University Press, 2005).

8. Frances Koestler, *The Unseen Minority: A Social History of Blindness in the United States* (New York: American Foundation for the Blind Press, 1976), 50.

9. "Save Baby's Eyes! Save It From Life of Darkness!" *Wilkes-Barre (PA) Times-Leader,* April 13, 1910, Perkins School for the Blind Bound Clippings: Prevention of Blindness, 1910, SPH.

10. "Blindness of Many Needless: Eternal Darkness Is Cost of Carelessness in Early Stages," *Rochester (NY) Times,* March 21, 1910, Perkins School for the Blind Bound Clippings: Prevention of Blindness, 1910, SPH.

11. Thomas A. Krainz, "Transforming the Progressive Era Welfare State: Activists for the Blind and Blind Benefits," *Journal of Policy History* 15, no. 2 (2003): 230.

12. Krainz, "Transforming the Progressive Era Welfare State," 224.

13. Krainz, "Transforming the Progressive Era Welfare State," 233–42.

14. Catherine J. Kudlick, "The Outlook of *The Problem* and the Problem with the *Outlook*: Two Advocacy Journals Reinvent Blind People in Turn-of-the-Century America," in *The New Disability History,* ed. Longmore and Umansky, 192.

15. It is important to note that the American Association of Workers for the Blind also helped undercut the efforts of the blind activists in Colorado's Society of United Workers for the Blind, curtailing their efforts to secure blind

pensions and wresting authority and expertise away from blind people and into the hands of professional social workers. Krainz, "Transforming the Progressive Era Welfare State," 252.

16. Kudlick, "The Outlook of *The Problem* and the Problem with the *Outlook*," 194.

17. John Keegan, *The First World War* (New York: Vintage Books, 1998), 27–35.

18. American propaganda was emotionally charged beyond propaganda related to blind soldiers and civilians. Consult, for example, Fred Spear's poster, *Enlist,* which depicted a woman victim of the German sinking of the *Lusitania,* clutching her baby as she sinks to the bottom of the Atlantic Ocean. The difference between general propaganda and propaganda in service of blind relief organizations was how widespread and emotional such imagery was in service of one singular issue: blind soldiers.

19. "Blind Children of Belgium Aided by Afflicted Here: Little Ones at Lighthouse of New York Association Send Contribution to Be Taken Aboard the Argosy," *New York Herald,* March 27, 1915, War Blind 1915, Volume I, SPH.

20. John Horne and Alan Kramer, *German Atrocities, 1914: A History of Denial* (New Haven: Yale University Press, 2001), 13–15.

21. "Blind Children of Belgium Aided by Afflicted Here."

22. "Belgian Blind Need Physicians' Help," *New York Tribune,* April 8, 1915, War Blind 1915, Volume I, SPH.

23. "Many Blinded By War, Says Winifred Holt: Secretary of Association Here Says Foreign Need Is a Big Drain," *New York Sun,* March 30, 1915, War Blind 1915, Volume I, SPH.

24. "Europe's Blind Worst Tragedy of War, Says Girl from Front: Miss Kathleen Burke, Here Seeking Aid, Describes Harrowing Experiences in Trenches," *New York Telegram,* May 24, 1916, War Blind 1916, Volume II, SPH.

25. Dorothy Canfield Fisher, "The Refugee: A Narrative of the Sufferings of Invaded France," *The Outlook,* September 19, 1917, 87–91.

26. "Sister Beatrice Bartlett Will Speak in This City," *Providence Bulletin,* October 27, 1915, War Blind 1915, Volume I, SPH.

27. Horne and Kramer, *German Atrocities,* 196.

28. Keegan, *The First World War,* 82.

29. Keegan, *The First World War,* 82.

30. Parliamentary Recruiting Committee Poster No.16.W.13068–345: *Remember Belgium: Enlist Today* (Leeds: Henry Jenkinson Ltd), Photograph, http://www.iwm.org.uk/collections/item/object/30258; Ellsworth Young, *Remember Belgium—Buy bonds*—Fourth Liberty Loan, United States Belgium, ca. 1918 (New York: United States Prtg. & Lith. Co), Photograph, http://www.loc.gov/item/96507603/.

31. Horne and Kramer, *German Atrocities,* 194.

32. Horne and Kramer, *German Atrocities,* 111.

33. Horne and Kramer, *German Atrocities,* 35–36.

34. M. Leona Godin, *There Plant Eyes: A Personal and Cultural History of Blindness* (New York: Pantheon, 2021), 18–28.

35. "Sister Beatrice Bartlett Will Speak in This City."

36. David M. Lubin, "Lies That Tell the Truth: American Artists in the Crucible of War," in *World War I and American Art,* ed. Robert Cozzolino, Anne Classen Knutson, and David M. Lubin (Princeton: Princeton University Press, 2016), 35–36.

37. Thomas I. Faith, "Gas Warfare," *1914–1918 Online: International Encyclopedia of the First World War*, January 25, 2016.

38. Gerard Hutchison Cox, "Gas Poisoning in Warfare," *Medical Record* 95, no. 8 (February 22, 1919): 312.

39. Horne and Kramer, *German Atrocities*, 181–83.

40. Pearl James, "Citizen-Consumers in the American Iconosphere during World War I," in *World War I and American Art,* ed. Robert Cozzolino, Anne Classen Knutson, and David M. Lubin (Princeton: Princeton University Press, 2016), 46–47; Mark D. Karau, "Submarines and Submarine Warfare," *1914–1918 Online: International Encyclopedia of the First World War,* ed. Ute Daniel, Peter Gatrell, Oliver Janz, Heather Jones, Jennifer Keene, Alan Kramer, and Bill Nasson; David M. Kennedy, *Over Here: The First World War and American Society* (New York: Oxford University Press, 2004), 5.

41. Erick Trickey, "The Sweetheart of the American Expeditionary Force," *Smithsonian Magazine,* June 5, 2018, https://www.smithsonianmag.com/history/sweetheart-aef-180969241/.

42. "Where Are You, God?" *New Castle (DE) Herald*, July 12, 1915, War Blind 1915, Volume I, SPH.

43. *Nashua (NH) Telegraph,* August 3, 1915, War Blind 1915, Volume I, SPH.

44. Horne and Kramer, *German Atrocities*, 204.

45. Consult, for example, the *Les heros de la Belgique* postcard released in 1916 that shows German soldiers as beasts sitting on the ruins of Louvain waving a flag that reads, "Civilisation, Humanite." *Les heros de la Belgique*, Belgium, 1916, Photograph, http://www.loc.gov/item/2019630570/.

46. For a discussion of histories of blindness in the United States, consult Koestler, *The Unseen Minority.* Koestler's history is a good starting point on histories of blindness. For more recent histories, consult Godin, *There Plant Eyes*; Kim E. Nielsen, *The Radical Lives of Helen Keller* (New York: New York University Press, 2004); Kudlick, "The Outlook of *The Problem* and the Problem with the *Outlook*"; Kim Nielsen, "Helen Keller and the Politics of Civic Fitness," in *The New Disability History,* ed. Longmore and Umansky, 187–213; David A. Gerber, "Blind and Enlightened: The Contested Origins of the Egalitarian Politics of the Blinded Veterans Association," in *The New Disability History,* ed. Longmore and Umansky, 313–334.

47. For a discussion on cultural perceptions of disabled veterans in modern Western societies, as well as public perceptual differences between disabled civilians and disabled veterans, consult David A. Gerber, "Introduction: Finding

Disabled Veterans in History," in *Disabled Veterans in History*, ed. David A. Gerber (Ann Arbor: University of Michigan Press, 2000), 1–24.

48. For a discussion on harmful stereotypes about blindness, consult Koestler, *The Unseen Minority*, 3.

49. Kudlick, "The Outlook of *The Problem* and the Problem with the *Outlook*," 196.

50. "4,000 Blind French Soldiers: That Number in Paris Alone, Writes Winifred Holt," *New York Post*, August 14, 1915, War Blind 1915, Volume I, SPH.

51. Frances Koestler has estimated that 450 Americans, 3,000 British, 2,800 French, and 7,000 German soldiers were blind from their service in the entire war. Koestler, *The Unseen Minority*, 8.

52. H. Randolph Latimer, "Ambition and Apathy in Work for the Blind," *Outlook for the Blind* 13, no. 3 (Autumn 1919): 59–62.

53. In the context of newspaper reports such as this that reached American audiences for fundraising purposes, the term "blinded" was almost always used instead of "blind." "1,000,000 Wounded in French Hospitals: Conditions Worse Now Than Last Winter, Says Harold E. Goad, in Appeal for Funds—Expect 5000 More Totally Blind in Six Months," *Boston Herald*, December 10, 1915, War Blind 1915, Volume I, SPH.

54. "Twelve Thousand Blinded in War," *Boston Journal*, June 21, 1916, War Blind 1916, Volume II, SPH.

55. "Romance and Tragedy of Europe's Broken Men: How Faithful Women Are Marrying the Maimed, Blinded, and Battered Heroes of the Great Conflict in Europe, and the Vast Problem Presented to the Warring Peoples by the Enormous Numbers of Injured Men," Clarksburg (WV) Telegram, October 31, 1915. This article also appeared in newspapers in numerous states.

56. "1,000,000 Wounded in French Hospitals."

57. Part of what David Bolt terms the "metanarrative of blindness" is the "ocularnormative logic that equates life with light and sight, from which it follows that sightlessness may be equated with darkness and death." Consequently, literary tropes perpetuate the assumption that death is preferable to life with a visual impairment. David Bolt, *The Metanarrative of Blindness: A Re-reading of Twentieth-Century Anglophone Writing* (Ann Arbor: University of Michigan Press, 2016), 111–16; Richard Harding Davis, "Blinded in Battle, But Not Made Useless: How the Soldiers of the Allies Who Must Live Forever in Darkness Are Now Taught to Become Independent," *New York Times Magazine*, February 27, 1916, War Blind 1916, Volume II, SPH.

58. "New York Woman in Paris Tells of Helping War's Derelicts," *New York Mail*, September 27, 1915. This article was replicated in several newspapers with different headlines. "War Blind Find New Sight in Toy: Miss Holt Says Ability to Count Domino's Spots Is Dawn of Hope," *New York Tribune*, September 27, 1915; "Blinded Soldiers in Pitiful Plight: Miss Holt Writes of Great Suffering and Bravery," *New York Post*, September 28, 1915, War Blind 1915, Volume I, SPH.

59. Kudklick, "The Outlook of *The Problem* and the Problem with the *Outlook*," 196.

60. "For Blinded Soldiers: American Loses Eyes, Wins Prized Medal for His Bravery," *Gardner News*, April 12, 1915, War Blind 1915, Volume I, SPH.

61. Kenneth Proctor Littauer, "How France Cares for Her Blind Heroes," *Providence Journal*, July 25, 1915, War Blind 1915, Volume I, SPH.

62. "Minutes of Meeting of the Executive and Advisory Committees and Vice-Presidents of the A.B.F.B. Permanent Blind Relief War Fund, held at the Office of Mr. Frank A. Vanderlip, President of the National City Bank, 55 Wall St., on Friday, March 2, at 4 p.m., 1917," War Blind 1917, Volume III, SPH.

63. Littauer, "How France Cares for Her Blind Heroes."

64. "New York Will Aid War-Blinded Men: Committee Organizes with Joseph H. Choate at Head- Second Food Ship to Sail," *New York Tribune*, July 10, 1915, War Blind 1915, Volume I, SPH.

65. Keegan, *The First World War*, 175.

66. Hew Strachan, *The First World War* (New York: Simon & Schuster, 2014), 183.

67. Keegan, *The First World War*, 298–99; Strachan, *The First World War*, 189.

68. "Our History," *Helen Keller International*, www.hki.org/who-we-are/our-history; "Aid for War's Blind Pressingly Needed: Committee of Leading Men Issues a Signed Appeal for Contributions," *New York Times*, April 9, 1916, War Blind 1916, Volume II, SPH.

69. "'A' for America, Now in Blind Relief Fund's Name," *New York World*, February 4, 1916; "American Committee Formed for Permanent Aid to War Blind: Organization Will Co-operate with Similar Bodies in England, France, and Belgium in Supporting Institutions Where Soldiers and Sailors Who Have Lost Their Vision Will Be Taught to Earn a Living," *New York Herald*, February 16, 1916; "Aid For War's Blind Pressingly Needed: Committee of Leading Men Issues a Signed Appeal for Contributions," *New York Times*, April 9, 1916, War Blind 1916, Volume II, SPH.

70. "Artists Respond to Appeal for Soldiers Blinded in War," *New York Herald*, April 17, 1916, War Blind 1916, Volume II, SPH.

71. "Urgent: The Appeal of Appeals For the Young Men Blinded in this War," Pamphlet, B.F.B. Permanent Blind Relief War Fund for Soldiers and Sailors, n.d., War Blind 1916, Volume II, SPH.

72. Koestler, *The Unseen Minority*, 8.

73. "Artists Respond to Appeal for Soldiers Blinded in War"; "'Blinded Soldiers' Hands': New York Artists, Surgeons, and Military Folk Discuss War Relief Picture," *Boston Record*, May 24, 1916, War Blind 1916, Volume II, SPH.

74. "'Blinded Soldiers' Hands.'"

75. Sergeant Major Robert Middlemiss's story bears some resemblance to the creation of the legend of Al Schmid, a blind World War II veteran. We do not know the extent to which Middlemiss struggled with his fame and identity like Schmid did. David A. Gerber, "In Search of Al Schmid: War Hero, Blinded Veteran, Everyman," *Journal of American Studies* 29, no. 1 (April 1995): 1–32.

76. "Blind British Soldier Comes to Help Sightless Comrades," *New York Tribune*, May 13, 1916; "Two Famous Blind Folks Share Joys in Braille: Helen

Keller Writes to Blinded British Soldier That Life Is Rich, Though Dark—What Sergeant Major Robert Middlemiss Is Doing," *Hartford Courant,* July 30, 1916, War Blind 1916, Volume II, SPH.

77. "Seek Aid for Men Blinded in Battle," *Philadelphia Ledger,* October 22, 1916, War Blind 1916, Volume II, SPH.

78. "Sergt. Middlemiss Makes Powerful Plea for Blind: Over $2,000 Contributed by Sympathetic Audience at Poli's," *Worcester (MA) Gazette,* November 13, 1916, War Blind 1916, Volume II, SPH.

79. Beth Linker, *War's Waste: Rehabilitation and World War I America* (Chicago: University of Chicago Press, 2009) 131.

80. Koestler, *The Unseen Minority,* 2–3.

81. "Became Suddenly Blinded in Battle: Sergt Maj Middlemiss to Tell of His Sufferings," *Waterbury (CT) American,* October 25, 1916, War Blind 1916, Volume II, SPH.

82. Kinder, *Paying with Their Bodies,* 59–60.

83. Consult, for example, Susan M. Schweik, *The Ugly Laws: Disability in Public* (New York: New York University Press, 2009).

84. "Bazaar to Show Tools of Death," *New York Tribune,* May 15, 1916; "Great Allied Bazar Planned: New England Contribution to the Exhibition in New York Assigned to a Central Location," *Boston Globe,* May 29, 1916, War Blind 1916, Volume II, SPH.

85. "Bazaar to Show Tools of Death."

86. The bazaar sold over $400,000 in tickets and donations before the doors even opened. "Half Million Aid Bazaar for Allies: Only a Fraction of Those Who Had Tickets Able to Gain Admittance," *New York Sun,* June 4, 1916, War Blind 1916, Volume II, SPH.

87. "Half Million Aid Bazaar for Allies."

88. "Famous Artists Sing for War Fund: Receipts of Allied Bazaar Entertainment Will Go to Battle-Blinded Soldiers," *New York Times,* June 8, 1916, War Blind 1916, Volume II, SPH.

89. "Bazaar to Show Tools of Death"; "$1,500,000 Receipts of Allied Bazaar," *New York Times,* June 20, 1916; "Half Million Aid Bazaar for Allies," War Blind 1916, Volume II, SPH.

90. "Allied Bazaar Ends in Patriotic Blaze," *New York Times,* June 22, 1916, War Blind 1916, Volume II, SPH.

91. "New Fund to Aid Employes Blinded: Jireh Swift, Jr., Named as Sub-Treasurer," *New Bedford (MA) Times,* April 25, 1916, War Blind 1916, Volume II, SPH.

92. "Women of Nation Asked to Aid Blind War Victims," *New York Herald,* April 25, 1916, War Blind 1916, Volume II, SPH.

93. "Church Pleads for War Relief: Story of Blind and Homeless Told in Circulars Sent to Communities," *New York Tribune,* June 14, 1916; *Boston Transcript,* June 17, 1916, War Blind 1916, Volume II, SPH.

94. Koestler, *The Unseen Minority,* 8.

95. "Seek Aid for Men Blinded in Battle," *Philadelphia Ledger,* October 22, 1916, War Blind 1916, Volume II, SPH.

96. For a discussion on the cultural construction of the blind beggar, consult Moshe Barasch, *Blindness: The History of a Mental Image in Western Thought* (New York: Routledge, 2001), 95–96; Koestler, *The Unseen Minority,* 7.

97. "Why Not Take Care of Our Own Blind? Why Send Our Good Coin to Care for England's Blind?" *Worcester (MA) News,* November 15, 1916, War Blind 1916, Volume II, SPH.

98. "B.F.B. Fund Has $270,000: Remarkable Growth of One War Charity—Permanence Its Aim," *New York Times,* December 10, 1916; "Blind Relief Fund All Goes to Victims: Leaders in Work Pay Expenses from Own Purses, Helen Keller Announces," *Washington Times,* July 3, 1916, War Blind 1916, Volume II, SPH.

99. Mabel T. Plaisted, "For Blind Soldiers," *Bangor (ME) Commercial,* August 19, 1916, War Blind 1916, Volume II, SPH.

100. "Why Not Take Care of Our Own Blind?"

101. "Sergt. Middlemiss Makes Powerful Plea for Blind."

102. "Choate Assails B.F.B. War Blind Fund's Methods: Victims Should Be Restored to Homes, Not Shut in Institutions, He Says," *New York Tribune,* December 12, 1916; "Schiff Gives $5,000 to Aid War's Blind," *New York Sun,* December 12, 1916, War Blind 1916, Volume II, SPH.

103. "Choate Assails B.F.B. War Blind Fund's Methods."

104. "Minutes of Meeting of the Executive and Advisory Committees and Vice-Presidents of the A.B.F.B. Permanent Blind Relief War Fund."

105. "Blind Soldiers Choose Trades: Many at Institution in France," *Worcester (MA) Post,* October 22, 1915, War Blind 1915, Volume I, SPH.

106. "Rééducation des soldats aveugles aux Quinze-Vingts [hôpital de Paris, 1916]: [photographie de presse]/[Agence Rol], Bibliothèque nationale de France, département Estampes et photographie, EI-13 (491), Paris, France.

107. An impetus toward group solidarity has been charted by David Gerber with regards to blind veterans after World War I and World War II. David A. Gerber, "Disabled Veterans, the State, and the Experience of Disability in Western Societies, 1914–1950," *Journal of Social History* 36, no. 4 (Summer 2003): 904–5.

108. Winifred Holt, "The Lighthouse for Blinded Soldiers," *The Survey,* October 14, 1916, 43–44; Winifred Holt, *A Report to the Committee for Men Blinded in Battle* (New York: Tudor Press, 1918), 2.

109. Holt, *A Report to the Committee for Men Blinded in Battle,* 16; "New York Woman Aids War-Blinded in Paris: Miss Winifred Holt to Be Given Use of Large House," *Providence Journal,* October 25, 1915, War Blind 1915, Volume I, SPH; "The Lighthouse in France: What Franco-American Committee Has Done for Men Blinded in War," *New York Times,* March 27, 1917; Winifred Holt, *First Lady of the Lighthouse: A Biography of Winnifred Holt Mather,* ed. Edith Holt Bloodgood (New York: New York Association for the Blind, 1952), 112.

110. Winifred Holt, "Blinded Soldiers Find New Hope: Remarkable Cases at the Lighthouse of France Described by Miss Winifred Holt," *New York Sun,* June 25, 1916, War Blind 1916, Volume II, SPH.

111. George Payne, "America's 'Lady of the Lighthouse' Our Gift to France and Her Blind Soldiers: Miss Winifred Holt Has Been Sent to Bordeaux to Lead the Sightless Victims of War into the Light," *New York Tribune,* August 2, 1915, War Blind 1915, Volume I, SPH.

112. Winifred Holt, "The Lighthouse for Blinded Soldiers," *The Survey,* October 14, 1916, War Blind 1916, Volume II, SPH.

113. Holt, "The Lighthouse for Blinded Soldiers."

114. Will Irwin, "Flashes from the War Zone," *Saturday Evening Post,* July 15, 1916, War Blind 1916, Volume II, SPH.

115. Paul R. D. Lawrie, *Forging a Laboring Race: The African American Worker in the Progressive Era* (New York: New York University Press, 2016), 73.

116. Irwin, "Flashes from the War Zone."

117. "This Brooklyn Man Sets Up and Operates First Electric Printing Press for Blind," *Brooklyn Daily Eagle,* January 28, 1917, War Blind 1917, Volume III, SPH.

118. "This Brooklyn Man Sets Up and Operates First Electric Printing Press for Blind."

119. Elizabeth Parris Jackson Papers, 1917–1983, Schlesinger Library, Harvard University.

120. Elizabeth Parris Jackson Papers.

121. Elizabeth Parris Jackson Papers.

Chapter 2. "I'll Get Along"

1. "13 Blind Soldiers Most Cheerful in Shipload of 1,172," *New York Herald,* February 8, 1919, United States War Blind, 1919–1923, Samuel P. Hayes Research Library, Perkins School for the Blind, Watertown, MA (hereafter SPH).

2. "Blind Brooklyn Soldier Back: Private W. T. Whalen Also Minus Left Hand," *Brooklyn Times,* February 8, 1919, United States War Blind, 1919–1923, SPH.

3. For the sake of clarity and brevity, I will be using the term "Evergreen" to refer to US Army General Hospital No. 7 throughout this chapter.

4. Beth Linker, *War's Waste: Rehabilitation in World War I America* (Chicago: University of Chicago Press, 2011), 141.

5. David M. Kennedy, *Over Here: The First World War and American Society* (New York: Oxford University Press, 2004), 60–61.

6. For a detailed study of coercive patriotism and citizenship during World War I, see Christopher Capozzola, *Uncle Sam Wants You: World War I and the Making of the Modern American Citizen* (New York: Oxford University Press, 2008); Kennedy, *Over Here,* 26.

7. Kennedy, *Over Here,* 78.

8. For a discussion of American Civil War–era soldiers' pensions and institutions in the context of the burgeoning American administrative state and partisan

politics, see Patrick J. Kelly, *Creating a National Home: Building the Veterans' Welfare State, 1860–1900* (Cambridge, MA: Harvard University Press, 1997); Richard L. McCormick, "The Party Period and Public Policy: An Exploratory Hypothesis," *Journal of American History* 66, no. 2 (September 1979): 279–98; Stephen Skowronek, *Building a New American State: The Expansion of National Administrative Capacities, 1877–1920* (New York: Cambridge University Press, 1982).

9. For a concise discussion of the Progressive Era, see Michael McGerr, *A Fierce Discontent: The Rise and Fall of the Progressive Movement in America, 1870–1920* (New York: Free Press, 2003).

10. Linker, *War's Waste,* 2.

11. Linker, *War's Waste,* 30.

12. Linker, *War's Waste,* 164; Sarah F. Rose, *No Right to Be Idle: The Invention of Disability, 1840s-1930s* (Chapel Hill: University of North Carolina Press, 2017), 194–96.

13. Jessica L. Adler, *Burdens of War: Creating the United States Veterans Health System* (Baltimore: Johns Hopkins University Press, 2017), 25.

14. "Who's Who among Our Buddies," *Evergreen Review* 1, no. 2 (February 1920): 23.

15. W. H. Zimmerman, "Our First Blinded Soldier: He Is Being Re-educated and Will Make Good," *Carry On: A Magazine on the Reconstruction of Disabled Soldiers and Sailors* 1, no. 1 (June 1918): 13.

16. List of patients who are totally blind at U.S.A. General Hospital No. 7, March 8, 1919, RG 112, Series UD 8, Box 916, Folder 705—Patients, National Archives, College Park, MD (hereafter National Archives).

17. N. I. Ardan to the Surgeon General, "Statistical Report," February 8, 1919, RG 112, Series 31 (K), Box 206, Folder 314.7-2 (G.H. #7) K, National Archives.

18. List of patients who are totally blind at U.S.A. General Hospital No. 7, March 8, 1919.

19. "Brief History, Neurological Diagnosis, and Prognosis in the Permanent Patients, U.S.A. General Hospital No. 7," 20, RG 112, Series NM 31 (K), Box 206, Folder 314.7-2 (G.H. #7) K, National Archives.

20. C. C. Wholey, "Brief Preliminary Report on Blinded Soldiers at U.S.A. General Hospital, No. 7, Roland Park, Baltimore, Md.," n.d., RG 112, Series UD 8, Box 913, Folder: "Historical Data," National Archives.

21. "The *Mercy* Brings Her Last Wounded Home from France," *New York Tribune,* May 26, 1919; "700 Lame, Blind, and Halt Soldiers at Merry Feast," *New York World,* May 30, 1919, United States War Blind, 1919–1923, SPH.

22. Alan C. Woods, "The Story of the Red Cross Institute for the Blind (1918–1925) in Relation to the Present Problem of the War Blinded," *American Journal of Ophthalmology* 26, no. 10 (October 1943): 1015. Daniel Carbone was the case of wood-alcohol blindness mentioned by Woods. Carbone was on temporary leave from Camp Dix visiting family in Long Branch, New Jersey, when he drank what physicians called "Black Jack," which was wood alcohol with "coloring fluid" mixed in. "Camp Dix Soldier Goes Blind from Drinking 'Black Jack' Mixture," *Long Branch (NJ) Daily Record,* August 2, 1919, 1.

23. Harold Molter, Acting Educational Director, to the Commanding Officer, "History of Educational Department," April 22, 1919, RG 112, Series NM-31 (K), National Archives.

24. Wholey, "Brief Preliminary Report."

25. Wholey, "Brief Preliminary Report."

26. Wholey, "Brief Preliminary Report."

27. "Blind and Cheerful: Soldiers Reach Home," *Springfield (MA) Republican,* October 14, 1918, United States War Blind, 1917–1918, Volume 1, SPH.

28. Linker, *War's Waste,* 4.

29. The "Creed" is also referenced elsewhere. Consult John M. Kinder, *Paying with Their Bodies: American War and the Problem of the Disabled Veteran* (Chicago: University of Chicago Press, 2015), 122; Linker, *War's Waste,* 4.

30. Linker, *War's Waste,* 4; "The Creed of the Disabled Soldier," *Carry On* 1, no. 6 (March 1919).

31. Linker, *War's Waste,* 4.

32. "Sir Arthur Pearson," Blind Veterans UK, https://www.blindveterans.org.uk/about/our-history/sir-arthur-pearson/.

33. Julie Anderson and Neil Pemberton, "Walking Alone: Aiding the War and Civilian Blind in the Inter-war Period," *European Review of History* 14, no. 4 (December 2007): 460.

34. Anderson and Pemberton describe Pearson's regimen using adjectives such as "military style." Anderson and Pemberton, "Walking Alone," 465.

35. "8,000 Blind Soldiers to Self Help: U.S. to Follow Pearson's Plan for War's Blind," *New York Morning Sun,* January 26, 1919, United States War Blind, 1917–1918, SPH.

36. Hayden Church, "American's London Home Now Hostel for the Soldier Blind," *Philadelphia Ledger,* November 7, 1915, World War Blind, 1915, SPH.

37. Sir Arthur Pearson, "Address Delivered at Evergreen, January 15, 1919," *The Outlook* 13, no. 1 (Spring 1919): 22.

38. Anderson and Pemberton, "Walking Alone," 463.

39. Anderson and Pemberton, "Walking Alone," 463.

40. Anderson and Pemberton, "Walking Alone," 463–65.

41. *Carry On* 1, no. 4 (October/November 1918): 6–17.

42. Gertrude Atherton, "Beggars No More," *Carry On* 1, no. 4 (October/November 1918): 17–20.

43. Anderson and Pemberton demonstrate that, in the case of St. Dunstan's, veterans' fears of being associated with "idle" and "weak" civilian blind people drove their resistance to mobility aids. Anderson and Pemberton, "Walking Alone," 470.

44. *Carry On* 1, no. 5 (January 1919): 26.

45. Thomas Krainz, "Transforming the Progressive Era Welfare State: Activists for the Blind and Blind Benefits," *Journal of Policy History* 15, no. 2 (2003): 250–52.

46. Clarkson Dye, "Vocational Guidance for the Blind," *Carry On* 1, no. 8 (May 1919): 29–30.

47. An evident philosophical difference between Evergreen and St. Dunstan's was that, unlike Pearson's vehement aversion to dark-tinted glasses and white

canes, numerous American soldiers at Evergreen wore dark-tinted glasses and used canes (albeit not white). There is no indication whether these differences were intentional or not, and institutional records are relatively absent any mention about mobility aids.

48. "Brings Cheer to Blind: Sir Arthur Pearson Delivers His Message at Evergreen," *Baltimore Sun,* January 17, 1919, United States War Blind, 1919–1923, SPH.

49. "13 Blind Soldiers Hear Pearson Talk: Sightless British Publicist Cheers Patients in Hospital Here," *New York Sun,* February 14, 1919.

50. Linker, *War's Waste,* 8.

51. "Joy in Life for The Blind: Self-Confidence Restored to the Soldier Patients in General Hospital 7, Near Baltimore—Dancing as an Aid in Overcoming Awkwardness and Diffidence," *New York Times,* January 26, 1919, War Blind Collection, 1919–1921, SPH.

52. For a discussion of disability and overcoming as inspiration, see M. Leona Godin, *There Plant Eyes: A Personal and Cultural History of Blindness* (New York: Pantheon, 2021), xv.

53. Samuel Hopkins Adams, "Blinks," *Collier's: The National Weekly* (June 1919): 13.

54. Adams, "Blinks," 46.

55. Beth Bradford Gilchrist, "Eyes That See," *Harper's Monthly* (October 1919): 630.

56. Gilchrist, "Eyes That See," 630.

57. Gilchrist, "Eyes That See," 631.

58. Maria Thompson Daviess, "Doctor Matt: The Feminine Adventures of a Young Physician, Part 1: The Dividend of Love," *Ladies' Home Journal* (August 1917): 19.

59. Daviess, "Doctor Matt, Part 1," 65.

60. Daviess, "Doctor Matt, Part 1," 65.

61. Daviess, "Doctor Matt, Part 1," 65.

62. Daviess, "Doctor Matt, Part 1," 65.

63. Maria Thompson Daviess, "Doctor Matt: The Feminine Adventures of a Young Physician, Part II: The Kidnaping of Bert Winn," *Ladies' Home Journal* (September 1917): 76.

64. See, for example, the story about Alfred Gault and Helen, or Maude Brockton and Horace Menefee. Maria Thompson Daviess, "Doctor Matt: The Feminine Adventures of a Young Physician, Part III: The Jilting of Impressionable Maude," *Ladies' Home Journal* (October 1917): 20.

65. David Bolt, *The Metanarrative of Blindness: A Re-reading of Twentieth-Century Anglophone Writing* (Ann Arbor: University of Michigan Press, 2014), 51; Godin, *There Plant Eyes,* 190–92.

66. Gilchrist, "Eyes That See," 634.

67. Catherine J. Kudlick, "The Outlook of *The Problem* and the Problem with the *Outlook:* Two Advocacy Journals Reinvent Blind People in Turn-of-the-Century America," in *The New Disability History: American Perspectives,* ed.

Paul K. Longmore and Lauri Umansky (New York: New York University Press, 2001), 188–96.

68. "Visit of the Queen of Belgium," *Evergreen Review* 1, no. 1 (January 1920): 3.

69. "Mrs. Newton D. Baker's Visit to the Institute for the Blind," *Evergreen Review* 1, no. 3 (March 1920): 27.

70. "General Pershing's Talk at the Red Cross Institute for the Blind, Baltimore, MD., April 13, 1920," *Evergreen Review* 1, no. 5 (May 1920): 43.

71. "Helen Keller's Address at Evergreen, February 25, 1919," *Evergreen Review* 1, no. 4 (April 1920): 35.

72. "Helen Keller's Impression of the Red Cross Institute for the Blind," *Evergreen Review* 1, no. 4 (April 1920): 40.

73. Kim E. Nielsen, *The Radical Lives of Helen Keller* (New York: New York University Press, 2004), 12.

74. "Victory Shop No. 2, Perryville, Md.," *Evergreen Review* 1, no. 2 (February 1920): 24.

75. "Who's Who among Our Buddies: Harry C. Willian," *Evergreen Review* 1, no. 2 (February 1920): 22.

76. "Who's Who among Our Buddies: Roy Mason Chapman," *Evergreen Review* 1, no. 4 (April 1920): 36–37; "Who's Who among Our Buddies: Cecil Edward Allen," *Evergreen Review* 1, no. 4 (April 1920): 37–38.

77. "Who's Who among Our Buddies: James F. Riddervold," *Evergreen Review* 1, no. 3 (March 1920), 29–30.

78. Ethel M. Baker, "Blind Soldier Demonstrates That He Is a Live One: Riddervold Manages His Own Business—Says Only a Laggard Public Stands between War Blinded and Independence," *Boston Herald,* April 10, 1921.

79. "'Will to Win,' Brings Success to Disabled Vets," *Boston Post,* November 13, 1921.

80. "Blinded, Gassed Veterans Illustrate Need of Home: Many Find It Impossible to Earn Living and Are Glad to Stay at Evergreen—Volunteers Needed for $1,000,000 Campaign," *Baltimore Evening Sun,* October 17, 1924, 46.

81. "Tells of Work Now Being Done for War Blind," *New Haven (CT) Journal,* May 20, 1920.

82. "Vulcanizing for Blinded Soldiers," *Evergreen Review* 1, no. 8 (August 1920): 68–71; "Blinded Veterans Open Own Business," *New York Sun,* September 20, 1920.

83. "Who's Who among Our Buddies: Louis H. Kersting," *Evergreen Review* 1, no. 11 (November 1920): 98.

84. "'Our Buddy' Cigars," *Evergreen Review* 1, no. 5 (May 1920): 45–46.

85. Kim E. Nielsen, *A Disability History of the United States* (Boston: Beacon Press, 2012), 176.

86. Frances Koestler, *The Unseen Minority: A Social History of Blindness in the United States* (New York: American Foundation for the Blind Press, 1976), 210.

87. "Current Events," *Outlook for the Blind* 12, no. 1 (Spring 1918): 26.

88. Koestler, *The Unseen Minority,* 210.

89. "Who's Who among Our Buddies: Ernest Bayliss," *Evergreen Review* 1, no. 3 (March 1920): 30–31.

Chapter 3. Gender, Race, and Belonging at Evergreen and Beyond

1. F. Raymond Pyle, "The Funny Side of a Tremendous Handicap: A Man Blinded in the Service Proves That a 'Blink' Can See a Joke as Well as Anybody," *American Legion Weekly* 2, no. 17 (May 21, 1920): 6.

2. Passing and masquerading will be discussed in greater detail in the body of the chapter. But for a discussion of both, see Jeffrey A. Brune and Daniel J. Wilson, *Disability and Passing: Blurring the Lines of Identity* (Philadelphia: Temple University Press, 2013); Tobin Siebers, *Disability Theory* (Ann Arbor: University of Michigan Press, 2008).

3. Siebers, *Disability Theory,* 111.

4. "Girl Returns with 9 Blind: Rosanna Thorndike Tells of Work with Sightless Soldiers," *Boston American,* May 25, 1919.

5. Historical Division, Office of the Surgeon General, "History of the Hospital Center—Savenay," 289–94, RG 112, Series NM-31 (Y), Box 33, Folder 314.7–2 (A.E.F.) Y, National Archives.

6. Michael Aaronsohn, *Broken Lights* (Cincinnati, OH: Johnson & Hardin Company, 1946), 270.

7. Aaronsohn, *Broken Lights,* 274.

8. Harold Molter, Acting Educational Director, to the Commanding Officer, "History of Educational Department," April 22, 1919, RG 112, Series NM-31 (K), National Archives, College Park, MD (hereafter National Archives).

9. "Evergreen—School for Blind Soldiers," *The Outlook* 13, no. 1 (Spring 1919): 1.

10. "Red Cross Institute for the Blind," *The Outlook* 13, no. 2 (Summer 1919): 43.

11. Petition from Blinded Soldiers to the Secretary of War, January 31, 1919, RG 112, Series UD 8, Box 915, Folder: 004.6: Insurance, National Archives.

12. "Suggestions for Recreation Department for U.S.A. General Hospital #7," January 14, 1919, RG 112, Series UD 8, Box 916, Folder 353.8—Athletics & Amusements, National Archives; Ethel Priscilla Potter, "Equipment Recommended for Recreation Building," RG 112, Series UD 8, Box 916, Folder 353.8—Athletics & Amusements, National Archives.

13. W. V. Thomas to N. I. Ardan, January 3, 1919, RG 112, Series UD 8, Box 916, Folder 353.8—Athletics & Amusements, National Archives.

14. Lawrence Bradley, "Philadelphia Aids U.S. in Instructing Sightless Soldiers," *Philadelphia Press,* January 12, 1919, United States War Blind, 1917–1918, Samuel P. Hayes Research Library, Perkins School for the Blind, Watertown, MA (hereafter SPH); Harold Molter, Acting Educational Director, to the

Commanding Officer, "History of Educational Department," April 22, 1919, RG 112, Series NM-31 (K), Box 206, Folder 353.1 U.S.A. Gen. Hosp. #7 Roland Park, Baltimore, Md., National Archives.

15. "Joy in Life for the Blind: Self-Confidence Restored to the Soldier Patients in General Hospital 7, Near Baltimore—Dancing as an Aid in Overcoming Awkwardness and Diffidence," *New York Times,* January 26, 1919, War Blind Collection, 1919–1921, SPH.

16. "Field Day at Evergreen," *Evergreen Review* 1, no. 9 (September 1920): 75–77; "Blind Soldiers Stage Contest in Athletics," *Baltimore Sun,* September 12, 1920, 10.

17. "Field Day at Evergreen," 75–77.

18. "Blind Soldiers Stage Contest," 10.

19. "Field Day at Evergreen," 75; Evan P. Sullivan, "Finding 'the Man behind the Handicap': Gender, Rehabilitation, and the War Blind of the First World War," in *War and Veterans: Treatment and Reintegration of Soldiers in Post-War Societies,* ed. Frank Jacob and Stefan Karner (Boston: Verlag Ferdinand Schöningh, 2020), 86.

20. Pyle, "The Funny Side of a Tremendous Handicap," 6.

21. Pyle, "The Funny Side of a Tremendous Handicap," 6.

22. Siebers, *Disability Theory,* 109.

23. Brune and Wilson, *Disability and Passing,* 1; Siebers, *Disability Theory,* 105.

24. Siebers, *Disability Theory,* 110–11.

25. W. H. Zimmerman, "Our First Blinded Soldier: He Is Being Re-educated and Will Make Good," *Carry On: A Magazine on the Reconstruction of Disabled Soldiers and Sailors* 1, no. 1 (June 1918): 13.

26. Beth Linker, *War's Waste: Rehabilitation and World War I America* (Chicago: University of Chicago Press, 2011), 64.

27. Linker, *War's Waste,* 132.

28. Alan C. Woods, "The Story of the Red Cross Institute for the Blind (1918–1925) in Relation to the Present Problem of the War Blinded," *American Journal of Ophthalmology* 26, no. 10 (October 1943): 1013.

29. "The Past Year at the Red Cross Institute for the Blind," *Evergreen Review* 1, no. 6 (June 1920): 52.

30. "The Federal Board and the Red Cross Institute for the Blind," *Evergreen Review* 1, no. 10 (October 1920): 88; Sullivan, "Finding 'the Man behind the Handicap,'" 90.

31. "A Visit to Evergreen by Letter," *Evergreen Review* 1, no. 12 (December 1920): 100.

32. "A Visit to Evergreen by Letter," 100.

33. "Blind Soldier Elopes," *Washington Post,* August 5, 1919; Sullivan, "Finding 'the Man behind the Handicap,'" 92.

34. Linker, *War's Waste,* 64.

35. "Who's Who among Our Buddies: F. Raymond Pyle," *Evergreen Review* 1, no. 11 (November 1920): 97–98.

36. "Blind Soldiers and Brides Living in Cupid's Cottage," *Palm Beach Post*, January 5, 1921, 8; "A Visit to Evergreen by Letter," 100; Sullivan, "Finding 'the Man behind the Handicap,'" 92.

37. "The Past Year at the Red Cross Institute for the Blind," 52.

38. "A Visit to Evergreen by Letter," 100–101.

39. "Braille Books for the Men at Home," *Evergreen Review* 1, no. 9 (September 1920): 80.

40. Frances A. Koestler, *The Unseen Minority: A Social History of Blindness in the United States* (New York: American Foundation for the Blind Press, 1976), 37 and 96.

41. Koestler, *The Unseen Minority*, 81.

42. There is no indication of what books the American Printing House for the Blind published with the Veterans' Bureau funding. Koestler, *The Unseen Minority*, 81.

43. "A Visit to Evergreen by Letter," 102.

44. Koestler, *The Unseen Minority*, 82.

45. Memories: Robert E. Wegner, http://robertwegner.net/default.asp, accessed February 5, 2022.

46. Frank Schrepfer studied at Harvard and had his roommate read textbooks to him, while Frank Schoble had friends read him his textbooks while a student at the University of Pennsylvania. Schoble also had his professors give him oral quizzes rather than having him read and write. "Blind, But Is Student at Harvard: Ex-Soldier Wishes to Become Landscape Architect," *Boston Post*, January 31, 1922, United States War Blind, 1919–1923, SPH; "Frank Schoble, Blind Soldier, Captures College Prize: Former Framingham Man Praised by Marshal Foch and General Pershing for Plucky Fight," *Framingham (MA) News*, March 10, 1923, United States War Blind, 1919–1923, SPH.

47. Koestler, *The Unseen Minority*, 130–32.

48. "Blind Soldiers and Brides Living in Cupid's Cottage," 8; "A Visit to Evergreen by Letter," 100; Sullivan, "Finding 'the Man behind the Handicap,'" 92.

49. "Blind Soldiers and Brides Living in Cupid's Cottage," 8; "A Visit to Evergreen by Letter," 100.

50. Tobin Siebers argues that disabled people constitute a "sexual minority," and that one might represent disabled sexuality as a positive contribution to the future by reconceiving sexuality apart from ability and imagining the sexual benefit of a given impairment, claiming it as a sexual advantage. Here, Zoe Beckley sees the disability as an advantage in her relationship, but in a way that further stigmatizes the disability. Siebers, *Disability Theory*, 136–42.

51. Siebers, *Disability Theory*, 138.

52. "Blind Pick Pretty Brides," *New York World*, October 14, 1917, War Blind Bound Clippings, 1917, SPH; Sullivan, "Finding 'the Man behind the Handicap,'" 91.

53. Memories: Robert E. Wegner, http://robertwegner.net/default.asp, accessed April 30, 2021.

54. "Roster of Evergreen Babies," *Evergreen Review* 1, no. 4 (April 1920): 40; Zoe Beckley, "'Blink' Makes Good Husband: Wives Tell Why They Married Blind Heroes," *Haverhill (MA) Gazette,* January 6, 1920.

55. Beckley, "'Blink' Makes Good Husband."

56. "Who's Who among Our Buddies: F. Raymond Pyle," 97.

57. F. R. Pyle, "Cupid's Cabin Is Established at Blind Institute," *Bridgeport (CT) Times,* January 1, 1921.

58. Siebers argues that "sex is the action by which most people believe that ability is reproduced . . . and ability remains the category by which sexual reproduction as such is evaluated." Siebers, *Disability Theory,* 139–40.

59. Allan M. Brandt, *No Magic Bullet: A Social History of Venereal Disease in the United States Since 1880* (New York: Oxford University Press, 1985), 59–64; Nancy K. Bristow, *Making Men Moral: Social Engineering during the Great War* (New York: New York University Press, 1996).

60. Brandt, *No Magic Bullet,* 101–16.

61. Evan P. Sullivan, "Making Good: World War I, Disability, and the Senses in American Rehabilitation" (PhD diss., University at Albany, 2020), 83–86.

62. "Blinded War Hero Marries Teacher," *Baltimore Bulletin,* October 28, 1919.

63. Beckley, "'Blink' Makes Good Husband."

64. Memories: Robert E. Wegner, http://robertwegner.net/default.asp, accessed April 30, 2021.

65. Helen Hoffman, "Love's Supreme Sacrifice," *Boston Herald,* May 19, 1918, War Blind Bound Collection, 1918, SPH, https://archive.org/details/perkins schoolfor1801perk, accessed July 7, 2015; "Love Is Blind," *The Sketch,* June 7, 1916, 220.

66. Bristow, *Making Men Moral,* xviii.

67. Bristow, *Making Men Moral,* xvii–xviii.

68. Bristow, *Making Men Moral,* 2.

69. Bristow, *Making Men Moral,* 6.

70. John M. Kinder, *Paying with Their Bodies: American War and the Problem of the Disabled Veteran* (Chicago: University of Chicago Press, 2015), 86 and 100.

71. Alan Johnstone Jr., "Report on Atlanta, GA.," November 1917, RG 112, Series UD-8, Box 902, Folder: Morals and Conduct, National Archives.

72. Commanding Officer of General Hospital No. 3 to the Surgeon General, November 30, 1918, RG 112, Series UD-8, Box 859, Folder: Historical Data, National Archives.

73. "Are You an 'Honor Card' Man?" *The Trouble Buster* 2, no. 45 (November 15, 1919): 1, RG 112, Series UD-8, Box 852, Folder: Publications, US National Archives; Commanding Officer of the Provost Guard to Commanding Officer of General Hospital No. 3, February 27, 1919, RG 112, Series UD-8, Box 862, Folder: Military Prisoners, National Archives.

74. "Questions for the Commanding Officer, U.S.A. General Hospital No. 7, Roland Park, Baltimore, Md.," RG 112, Series UD 8, Box 916, unnamed folder, National Archives.

75. J. T. Boyd, "General Order No. 26," October 29, 1918, RG 112, Series UD 8, Box 914, Folder: "General Orders," National Archives.

76. J. T. Boyd Jr., Medical Corps, "Memo for the Commanding Officer," March 13, 1919, RG 112, Series UD 8, Box 916, Folder: 250—Morals & Conduct, National Archives.

77. Commanding Officer, Newark, New Jersey, to Commanding Officer of General Hospital No. 3, "Arrests," March 30, 1919, RG 112, Series UD-8, Box 862, Folder: Military Prisoners, National Archives.

78. P. J. Brogan, Captain of Police of Elizabeth, New Jersey, to Commanding Officer of General Hospital No. 3, August 31, 1919, RG 112, Series UD-8, Box 862, Folder: Military Prisoners, National Archives.

79. Frank M. Mitchell, Disciplinary Officer to the Commanding Officer of U.S. General Hospital No. 2, "Report of Disturbance between Soldiers of This Post and Civilians," May 24, 1920, RG 112, Series UD-8, Box 851, Folder: Morals and Conduct, National Archives.

80. Boyd, "Memo for the Commanding Officer."

81. Captain W. B. Bradley, Quartermaster Corps, "Memo to the Adjutant," May 1, 1919, RG 112, Series UD 8, Box 916, Folder: 250—Morals & Conduct, National Archives.

82. "Statement Made by Lieutenant James M. Bryant, Medical Corps," n.d., RG 112, Series UD 8, Box 916, Folder: 250—Morals & Conduct, National Archives; "Statement Made by Corporal of Guard Ernest William Benoit about Private George Graves," May 16, 1919, RG 112, Series UD 8, Box 916, Folder: 250—Morals & Conduct, National Archives; "Statement Made by Corporal of Guard Ernest William Benoit about Private Andrew Knebel," May 16, 1919, RG 112, Series UD 8, Box 916, Folder: 250—Morals & Conduct, National Archives; "Statements Made by Pvt. lcl Joseph S. Novinski, Med. Dept.," n.d., RG 112, Series UD 8, Box 916, Folder: 250—Morals & Conduct, National Archives; "Statement Made by Prisoner Andrew Knebel," n.d., RG 112, Series UD 8, Box 916, Folder: 250—Morals & Conduct, National Archives.

83. Kinder, *Paying with Their Bodies,* 9.

84. "Blind British Soldier Comes to Help Sightless Comrades," *New York Tribune,* May 13, 1916; "Two Famous Blind Folks Share Joys in Braille: Helen Keller Writes to Blinded British Soldier That Life Is Rich, Though Dark—What Sergeant Major Robert Middlemiss Is Doing," *Hartford (CT) Courant,* July 30, 1916, War Blind 1916, Volume II, SPH.

85. Telegram, September 20, 1918. RG 112, Series UD 8, Box 914, Folder: "Telegrams," National Archives; Telegram, September 23, 1918. RG 112, Series UD 8, Box 914, Folder: "Telegrams," National Archives.

86. Paul R. D. Lawrie, "'Salvaging the Negro': Race, Rehabilitation, and the Body Politic in World War I America, 1917–1924," in *Disability Histories,* ed. Susan Burch and Michael Rembis (Chicago: University of Illinois Press, 2014), 323–24.

87. See Adriane Lentz-Smith, *Freedom Struggles: African Americans and World War I* (Cambridge, MA: Harvard University Press, 2009).

88. Lawrie, "'Salvaging the Negro,'" 328; Linker, *War's Waste,* 138.

89. Lawrie, "'Salvaging the Negro,'" 323.

90. Kinder, *Paying with Their Bodies,* 9; Linker, *War's Waste,* 135.

91. For a discussion of racism in rehabilitation, see Jessica L. Adler, *Burdens of War: Creating the United States Veterans Health System* (Baltimore: Johns Hopkins University Press, 2017), 62–67; Kinder, *Paying with Their Bodies,* 132–36; Linker, *War's Waste,* 135–39.

92. "13 Blind Soldiers Most Cheerful In Shipload of 1,172," *New York Herald,* February 8, 1919, United States War Blind, 1919–1923, SPH.

93. "Questions for the Commanding Officer, U.S.A. General Hospital No. 7, Roland Park, Baltimore, Md.," RG 112, Series UD 8, Box 916, unnamed folder, National Archives.

94. W. V. Thomas, "Schedule for Colored Soldiers on Post, as Requested by 'The Major,'" n.d., RG 112, Series UD 8, Box 916, Folder 353.8—Athletics & Amusements, National Archives.

95. "In the Social Whirl," *Baltimore Afro-American,* February 28, 1919, A5.

96. Adler, *Burdens of War,* 66–67.

97. Thomas, "Schedule for Colored Soldiers on Post."

98. *Evergreen Review* 1, no. 4 (April 1920): 40. This trend is explored in more depth by Beth Linker in *War's Waste*, 135.

99. *Evergreen Review* 1, no. 5 (May 1920): 42.

100. Jessica Adler has shown that Red Cross facilities also practiced racist segregation at the US Army General Hospital at Fort McHenry, where Black veterans could only use the Red Cross reading room when white patients were eating dinner. Adler, *Burdens of War,* 110.

101. "Sightless Eyes Awaken No Sympathy in Hearts of Evergreen Management: Red Cross Blamed," *Baltimore Afro-American*, October 24, 1919, 1.

102. "Sightless Eyes Awaken No Sympathy."

103. "Blind Hero Will Study Typewriting: Will Also Learn to Use Dictaphone at Association for Improving Poor's Rooms," *Brooklyn Daily Eagle*, January 18, 1920, 13.

104. "Blind Hero Will Study Typewriting," 13.

105. "Nothing for the Red Cross," *Baltimore Afro-American*, December 12, 1919, 4.

106. "Blind Hero Will Study Typewriting," 13.

Chapter 4. The Disability Politics of Blind Veteran Organizations in the United States

1. "Enthusiasm Marks Final Sessions of Blind Veterans," *Baltimore Evening Sun*, November 10, 1922, 48.

2. "Blind Vets Enjoy Convention Dance: Sightless, But Vigorous, Delegates Call for a 'He-Man's' Organization," *Baltimore Sun*, November 8, 1922, 7.

3. "Blind Veterans Elect Day as National Commander: 'Sightless, Not Crippled,' They Will March in Today's Parade," *Baltimore Sun*, November 11, 1922, 3.

4. "Blind Representative Pays High Tribute to Sightless Service Men," *Providence Journal,* June 8, 1922, United States War Blind, 1919–1923, Samuel P. Hayes Research Library, Perkins School for the Blind, Watertown, MA (hereafter SPH).

5. "Blind Ex-Soldier Fears Being Sent Out as Beggar," *Baltimore Sun,* November 5, 1923, United States War Blind, 1919–1923, SPH.

6. "Action Pledged Blind Veteran at Washington," *Baltimore Evening Sun,* November 3, 1923, 1.

7. "20 Blind Vets in City Denied Federal Help," *Baltimore Sun,* November 3, 1923, United States War Blind, 1919–1923, SPH.

8. K. Walter Hickel, "Medicine, Bureaucracy, and Social Welfare: The Politics of Disability Compensation for American Veterans of World War I," in *The New Disability History: American Perspectives,* ed. Paul K. Longmore and Lauri Umansky (New York: New York University Press, 2001), 239–44.

9. Hickel, "Medicine, Bureaucracy, and Social Welfare," 248.

10. Hickel, "Medicine, Bureaucracy, and Social Welfare," 248.

11. Hickel, "Medicine, Bureaucracy, and Social Welfare," 255.

12. Hickel, "Medicine, Bureaucracy, and Social Welfare," 244.

13. Jason W. A. Bertsch, "Government's First Watchdog," *Policy Review* 86 (November/December 1997): 64.

14. J. R. McCarl, *Decisions of the Comptroller General of the United States,* Volume 5: *July 1, 1925 to June 30, 1926* (Washington, DC: Government Printing Office, 1926), 7.

15. J. R. McCarl, *Decisions of the Comptroller General of the United States,* Volume 3: *July 1, 1923 to June 30, 1924* (Washington, DC: Government Printing Office, 1924), 175.

16. K. Walter Hickel writes that, because physicians were intent on maintaining control over the benefits schedule, they resisted making it available to the public. As a result, disability ratings schedules were not published until the Veterans Administration made them public in 1933. Hickel, "Medicine, Bureaucracy, and Social Welfare," 245–46.

17. House of Representatives Committee on Veterans Affairs, *The Veterans Administration Disability Rating Schedule: Historical Development and Medical Appraisal* (Washington, DC: Government Printing Office, 1956), 261.

18. United States Congress, *Hearings before the Joint Congressional Committee on Veterans' Affairs,* Volume 3 (Washington, DC: US Government Printing Office, 1933), 1268–69.

19. American Red Cross, *Handbook of Information and Instructions for Home Service Workers* (Washington, DC: National Capital Press, Inc., 1921), 239.

20. American Red Cross, *Handbook of Information and Instructions,* 235.

21. American Red Cross, *Handbook of Information and Instructions,* 237.

22. American Red Cross, *Handbook of Information and Instructions,* 243–45.

23. American Red Cross, *Handbook of Information and Instructions,* 238.

24. American Red Cross, *Handbook of Information and Instructions,* 235.

25. Alan C. Woods, "The Story of the Red Cross Institute for the Blind (1918–1925) in Relation to the Present Problem of the War Blinded," *American Journal of Ophthalmology* 26, no. 10 (October 1943): 1013–22.

26. Woods, "The Story of the Red Cross Institute for the Blind," 1022.

27. Stephen R. Ortiz, *Beyond the Bonus March and GI Bill: How Veteran Politics Shaped the New Deal Era* (New York: New York University Press, 2009), 16.

28. Ortiz, *Beyond the Bonus March,* 20–22.

29. John M. Kinder, *Paying with Their Bodies: American War and the Problem of the Disabled Veteran* (Chicago: University of Chicago Press, 2015), 154.

30. Kinder, *Paying with Their Bodies,* 154.

31. David A. Gerber, "Disabled Veterans, the State, and the Experience of Disability in Western Societies, 1914–1950," *Journal of Social History* (2003): 902; also explained in Kinder, *Paying with Their Bodies,* 154.

32. Gerber, "Disabled Veterans, the State, and the Experience of Disability in Western Societies," 902; also explained in Kinder, *Paying with Their Bodies,* 154.

33. Gerber, "Disabled Veterans, the State, and the Experience of Disability in Western Societies," 904–5.

34. "Attacks Ruling on Compensation: R. E. Day, National Commander of Blind Veterans, Declares They Mislead Many," *Baltimore Sun,* November 7, 1923, United States War Blind, 1919–1923, SPH.

35. "Blind Veterans Glad to Live at Evergreen," *Baltimore Sun,* October 17, 1924, 37.

36. "Blind Veterans Glad to Live at Evergreen."

37. "Few Blind Veterans Seem Discouraged," *Baltimore Evening Sun,* November 8, 1922, 19.

38. "Blinded War Veteran, Nerves Gone Can't Help Hungry Family," *Boston Telegram,* September 9, 1922, United States War Blind, 1919–1923, SPH.

39. "Enthusiasm Marks Final Sessions of Blind Veterans," *Baltimore Evening Sun,* November 10, 1922, 48.

40. "Attacks Ruling on Compensation."

41. "Blind Veterans to Meet at St. Louis," *Chillicothe (MO) Constitution-Tribune,* October 16, 1923, 6.

42. "'Blind Soldiers' Week' Plans Near Completion," *Baltimore Sun,* October 17, 1924, 3; "Blind Vets' Week Gets Start Today," *Baltimore Sun,* October 19, 1924, 4; "Observance of Week for Blind Veterans Is Urged by Mayor," *Los Angeles Evening Express,* October 18, 1924, 23; "Appeal for Blind Vets' Home Opens," *Baltimore Sun,* October 20, 1924, 4.

43. "Blind 'Vets' Soon to Pick Home Site," *Baltimore Sun,* August 12, 1924, 3; "Explain Purpose of 'Vets' Campaign," *Baltimore Sun,* November 16, 1924, 3.

44. "Blinded, Gassed Veterans Illustrate Need of Home: Many Find It Impossible to Earn Living and Are Glad to Stay at Evergreen—Volunteers Needed for $1,000,000 Campaign," *Baltimore Evening Sun,* October 17, 1924, 46.

45. "Blind Veterans Glad to Live at Evergreen," 37.

46. Frances A. Koestler, *The Unseen Minority: A Social History of Blindness in the United States* (New York: American Foundation for the Blind Press, 1976), 209–10.

47. "Blinded, Gassed Veterans Illustrate Need of Home," 46.

48. "Blind Veterans Glad to Live at Evergreen," 37.

49. "Continued Support to Blind Pledged," *Baltimore Sun,* October 31, 1924, 3.

50. "Blind Veterans Glad to Live at Evergreen," 37.

51. "Appeal for Blind Vets' Home Opens," *Baltimore Sun,* October 20, 1924, 4.

52. "Appeal for Blind Vets' Home Opens," 4; "Blind Veterans' Campaign Lagging: Must Raise $150,000 by End of December in Order to Get Home," *Baltimore Evening Sun,* October 29, 1924, 17.

53. "Blind Veterans Acquire Home and Clubhouse Here," *Baltimore Sun,* December 13, 1925, 4.

54. A Well-Wisher, "Letter to the Editor of *The Sun*," *Baltimore Sun,* November 17, 1924, 6.

55. C.S.B., A Gold Star Mother, "Letter to the Editor of *The Sun*," *Baltimore Sun,* November 25, 1924, 23.

56. "Blind Veteran Tells of Needs: Service Star Legion Thanked for Its Endeavors," *Ogden (UT) Standard-Examiner,* June 6, 1927, 2. David Gerber shows that this impulse to control their own organization, and the sense that they wanted to prove that their disability would not prevent them from governing their own affairs, contributed to the creation of the autonomous Blinded Veterans Association during World War II. In this sense, the USBVWW harbored similar politics. David A. Gerber, "Blind and Enlightened: The Contested Origins of the Egalitarian Politics of the Blinded Veterans Association," in *The New Disability: American Perspectives,* ed. Paul K. Longmore and Lauri Umansky (New York: New York University Press, 2001), 320.

57. Elizabeth Purdy, "Letter to the Editor of *The Sun*," *Baltimore Sun*, November 20, 1925, 12.

58. "Blinded in the War: Pvt. George M. Calvert of Syracuse, Once of Cortland," *Cortland (NY) Democrat,* September 13, 1918; "Brief History, Neurological Diagnosis and Prognosis in the Permanent Patients, U.S.A. General Hospital No. 7," RG 112, Series NM 31 (K), Box 206, Folder 314.7–2 (G.H. #7) K, National Archives, College Park, MD (hereafter National Archives).

59. "Two Blind Veterans Sightless Witnesses When Bill Is Signed," *Buffalo Commercial,* April 19, 1923, 1.

60. "Two Blind Veterans Sightless Witnesses When Bill Is Signed," 1.

61. George M. Calvert, "Letter to the Editor of *The Sun*," *Baltimore Sun,* December 14, 1925, 8.

62. "Blind Hero Wins Bride: Michael Inselbuch Met Wealthy Widow, a Red Cross Worker," *Abilene (KS) Daily Reflector,* January 31, 1920, 1; "For Remembrance," *Greensboro (AL) Watchman,* November 26, 1925, 8; "Blind Adjutant

Helps Buddies," *El Paso Herald*, June 20, 1927, 1; Vivian Shirley, "Death Recalls Active Life of 'Blind Soldiers' Mother,' Mourned Throughout U.S.: Louise Hamilton Inselbuch Was Known to Every Sightless Veteran in Every Federal Hospital as a Friend and Helper," *Pawnee (OK) Courier-Dispatch*, September 29, 1932, 4.

63. "We Don't Want Shop, Blind Vets Declare," *Baltimore Evening Sun*, January 20, 1926, 13.

64. "Says Blind 'Vets' Do Not Want Home," *Baltimore Sun*, January 22, 1926, 3.

65. "A Blind Veteran Objects," *Baltimore Sun*, March 3, 1926, 10.

66. There were at least twenty-nine blind men from New York State who trained at Evergreen. Of the twenty-nine, I have found information about the causes of blindness for nineteen. At least four were *not* battle casualties. Thomas Sullivan, for example, was a civilian. Walter Mau went blind from meningitis. Louis Sugar was blind because of a cataract. Bernard Ward's blindness was related to optic atrophy. "Brief History, Neurological Diagnosis and Prognosis in the Permanent Patients, U.S.A. General Hospital No. 7."

67. "Legislature's 'Vets' to Aid Service Men: Thirty-six Members Will Meet To-morrow to Plan Action for Financial Relief," *Brooklyn Standard Union*, January 21, 1923, 6.

68. "Legislature's 'Vets' to Aid Service Men," 6.

69. Adriane Lentz-Smith, *Freedom Struggles: African Americans and World War I* (Cambridge, MA: Harvard University Press, 2009), 9.

70. Hickel, "Medicine, Bureaucracy, and Social Welfare," 255–56.

71. Gerber, "Blind and Enlightened," 314.

72. "Another Brooklyn Soldier Awarded 'Purple Heart,'" *New York Age*, October 15, 1932, 3.

73. For a discussion on Black veterans and their struggle for recognition, as well as the context within which Charles Braithwaite served, see Jeffrey T. Sammons and John H. Morrow Jr., *Harlem's Rattlers and the Great War: The Undaunted 369th Regiment and the African American Quest for Equality* (Lawrence: University Press of Kansas, 2014).

74. "Blind Veterans Give Pledge to Flag They Are Not Able to See," *San Bernardino County (CA) Sun*, June 26, 1925, 9; "Big Parade Planned by Disabled Vets," *York (NE) Daily News-Times*, May 25, 1925, 3; "Wounded Vets Meet in Omaha," *Kearney (NE) Daily Hub*, May 28, 1925, 3. Jessica Adler briefly discusses Michael Aaronsohn in her book *Burdens of War: Creating the United States Veterans Health System* (Baltimore: Johns Hopkins University Press, 2017).

75. Michael Aaronsohn, "Resurrection: A Blind Veteran Tells His Story," *American Legion Weekly* 6, no. 22 (May 30, 1924): 16; Gene Cohn, "Blind Chaplain Is Given New Honor," *Ironwood (MI) Daily Globe*, July 6, 1922, 8.

76. "Brief History: Neurological Diagnosis and Prognosis in the Permanent Patients, U.S.A. General Hospital No. 7."

77. Cohn, "Blind Chaplain Is Given New Honor," 8.

78. For a similar dynamic, consult Kim E. Nielsen, *The Radical Lives of Helen Keller* (New York: New York University Press, 2004).

79. Cohn, "Blind Chaplain Is Given New Honor," 8; Aaronsohn, "Resurrection," 16.

80. Aaronsohn, "Resurrection," 16.

81. Dana Herman, "'A Lamp unto My Feet and a Light unto My Path': NFTS and the Jewish Blind, 1927–1952," in *Sisterhood: A Centennial History of Women of Reform Judaism*, ed. Carole B. Balin, Dana Herman, Jonathan D. Sarna, and Gary P. Zola (Cincinnati: Hebrew Union College Press, 2013), 289.

82. Bureau of War Risk Insurance, *Annual Report of the Director of the Bureau of War Risk Insurance for the Fiscal Year Ended June 30, 1920* (Washington, DC: Government Printing Office, 1920), 50.

83. Michael Aaronsohn, *Broken Lights* (Cincinnati: Johnson & Hardin Company, 1946); Michael Aaronsohn, *Red Pottage* (Cincinnati: Johnson & Hardin Company, 1956); Michael Aaronsohn, *That the Living May Know* (Self-published, 1973).

84. Herman, "NFTS and the Jewish Blind, 1927–1952," 289.

85. Nielsen, *The Radical Lives of Helen Keller*, 12.

Epilogue

1. "S.S. Leviathan Sails With 1610 Paris Voyagers," *Arizona Republican* (Phoenix), September 11, 1927, 32.

2. "Frank Schoble, Blind Soldier, Captures College Prize: Former Framingham Man Praised by Marshal Foch and General Pershing for Plucky Fight," *Framingham (MA) News,* March 10, 1923.

3. Frederick C. Painton, "An Embassy of Goodwill," *American Legion Weekly* 4, no. 1 (January 1928): 34–35; 78–79; "Pope Welcomes Legion Visitors: Lays Hands upon Head of Blind Veteran and Blesses Him," *Omaha Morning Bee,* September 29, 1927, 6.

4. M. Leona Godin, *There Plant Eyes: A Personal and Cultural History of Blindness* (New York: Pantheon, 2021), 27.

5. Godin, *There Plant Eyes,* 36.

6. Godin, *There Plant Eyes,* 81; 257–58.

7. "Pleads for the Blind: Lieutenant Who Lost Sight in War Appeals to Rotarians," *Philadelphia Ledger,* September 29, 1920.

8. "Frank Schoble, Blind Soldier, Captures College Prize."

9. "New Era for Blind Is Seen by Veteran" *Philadelphia Inquirer,* December 31, 1920.

10. "Frank Schoble, Blind Soldier, Captures College Prize."

11. David A. Gerber, "Disabled Veterans and the Wounds of War," in *The Oxford Handbook of Disability History,* ed. Michael Rembis, Catherine Kudlick, and Kim E. Nielsen (New York: Oxford University Press, 2018), 480.

Index

Note: Page numbers in *italics* denote figures.

EVAN P. SULLIVAN is an assistant professor of history at SUNY Adirondack.

The University of Illinois Press
is a founding member of the
Association of University Presses.

Composed in 11.5/13 Adobe Garamond Pro
with Gotham display
by Lisa Connery
at the University of Illinois Press

University of Illinois Press
1325 South Oak Street
Champaign, IL 61820-6903
www.press.uillinois.edu

FSC
www.fsc.org
MIX
Papier | Fördert
gute Waldnutzung
FSC® C083411

Zeitfracht Medien GmbH
Ferdinand-Jühlke-Straße 7
99095 Erfurt, Deutschland
produktsicherheit@kolibri360.de